HARLEM IS
NOWHERE

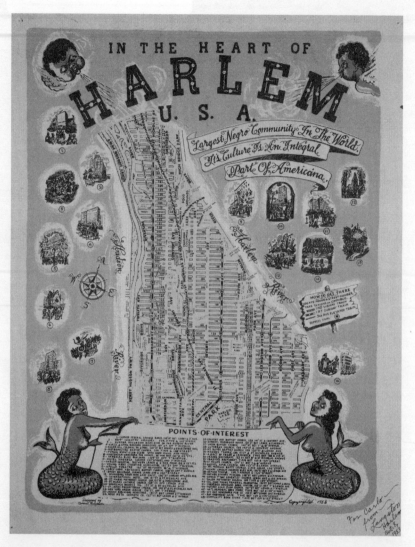

"In the Heart of Harlem" by Bernie Robynson, 1953. From the collection of Langston Hughes. (Courtesy of the Langston Hughes Papers. James Weldon Johnson Collection in the Yale Collection of American Literature, Beinecke Rare Book and Manuscript Library)

HARLEM IS NOWHERE

A JOURNEY TO THE MECCA
OF BLACK AMERICA

SHARIFA RHODES-PITTS

GRANTA

Granta Publications, 12 Addison Avenue, London W11 4QR

First published in Great Britain by Granta Books, 2011
First published in the United States in 2011 by Little, Brown and Company,
a division of Hachette Book Group, Inc.

Poems by Langston Hughes – "The Weary Blues," "Lament over Love,"
"Harlem Night Song," "Juke Box Love Song," "Harlem (2) ['What happens
to a dream deferred...'] and "Theme for English B" – are from *The Collected
Poems of Langston Hughes*, edited by Arnold Rampersad with David Roessel,
Associate Editor, copyright © 1994 by the Estate of Langston Hughes.
Used by permission of Alfred A. Knopf,
a division of Random House, Inc.

A CIP catalogue record for this book is available from the British Library.

1 3 5 7 9 10 8 6 4 2

ISBN 978 1 84708 457 6

Printed and bound in the UK by CPI William Clowes, Beccles NR34 7TL

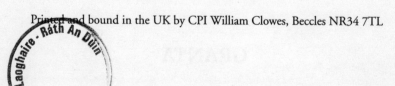

Dedicated to the memory of Minnie Davis (1923–2008),
who told me to *stop and stare,* and to all the neighbors
who looked after me on Lenox Avenue

"The writer operates at a peculiar crossroads where time and place and eternity somehow meet. His problem is to find that location."

—Flannery O'Connor, "The Regional Writer"

Contents

1. A Colony of Their Own   3
2. Into the City of Refuge   21
3. Searching for the Underground City   49
4. Harlem Dream Books   85
5. Messages   140
6. Land Is the Basis of All Independence   162
7. Back to Carolina   213
8. We March Because...   244
   Acknowledgments   263
   Notes   269
   Index   287

HARLEM IS
NOWHERE

A Colony of Their Own

I HAD ALREADY put the key into the door of my building on Lenox Avenue when the question came at my back. In one movement I withdrew the key and turned to face my inquisitor. He stood waiting for my reply and then asked again: *Do you think you'll ever go home?*

It was one of the neighborhood men who stand outside the front door during the day, sentinels keeping a vigilant watch. When I first moved here they were almost invisible to me; we did not speak and exchanged only the occasional nod. Neither I nor the men were being standoffish. There seemed to be an unspoken rule—perhaps a universal prudence for any strange girl arriving in any strange place—that I should come to know the women first. After I had been accepted by the women, the men began to make themselves known. By that point, the women had warned me about which men to avoid, I'd learned to discriminate between geezer flirtation and jive, and I could hold my own with the biggest jive talkers. Soon, I was drawn into a form of protection. My new friends declared this adoption at unexpected moments—one or another of the neighbors would introduce me as their daughter. If I was stranded in the midst of an unwanted conversation with a persistent sidewalk suitor, one of the sentinels would swoop in to see him off. But if I came home accompanied by a man of my own choosing, I was later expected to give an account of his intentions, employment, and character.

Home, he said again to my puzzled stare. *Down South. Do you think you'll ever go back home?*

It was a time when I was often in and out of the city. During phone conversations with friends, if I said I was *at home* they'd always ask, *Where?* But on this day, the man's question came out of nowhere. As I'd approached the stoop he'd remarked, *Cold enough for you?* on what was a relatively warm day a few weeks before the start of spring. I'd responded, *Not bad, not bad at all,* noting how easily that banality passed my lips—approximating the tones of a northerner, feigning comprehension of their seasons. Maybe he sensed the falseness of my reply. Maybe that's why he asked that question, presuming a desire I was not in contact with on that particular morning.

I answered cheerfully. *Home to Texas? But I go back all the time...* This sent him scattering into an apologetic retreat, as if he suddenly had a sense of invading my privacy. *Oh,* he said, and *Oh,* he repeated, as if the problem of my dislocation had suddenly been made right.

I did not ask him if he ever went home. I did not think of it until I was already in the narrow corridor that leads to the staircase that leads to my apartment, and now, in the act of recording it, this passing forgetfulness that he was also far from home strikes me as a failure of empathy. The yearning may have been more his than my own.

It was odd that he should think of me, even as I crossed my own threshold, as a stranger—someone on the verge of departure, highly susceptible to the mere mention of flight. (I might at that moment have turned around and gone; I might just then have been thinking of it.) But it says much about the impermanent status of my residence here. My neighbors were accustomed to seeing me leave with luggage in the earliest part of the morning. I had maintained an innocence of city politics and refused certain hallmarks of the committed citizen of New York, like a red or black wire rolling cart for groceries, or a tabloid newspaper selected on the basis of the best horoscopes. I should not have been surprised that some of my neighbors on Lenox Avenue were still trying to understand my presence in their midst. On a different occasion, a different man from outside my door had asked where I was from. He was surprised—pleased, even—to hear I was from Texas. *Oh,* he'd said. *I thought you were a foreigner.*

One restless, idle hour, I sat at the library on 135th Street and consulted *The Columbia-Lippincott Gazetteer of the World,* copying out the following entry, as if to gain my bearings:

> Harlem: A residential and business district of N Manhattan
> borough of New York City, SE N.Y., bounded approximately
> by Central Park and 110th St. (S), East R. (E), Harlem R.
> (NE), 168th St (W). Largest Negro community (pop. More
> than 400,000) in U.S. grew up here after 1910; one of the
> most congested districts in U.S., Harlem also has large colonies of Puerto Rican, Italian, and Latin American background. The Du. Settlement of Nieuw Haarlem was est.
> here 1658 by Peter Stuyvesant; in the Revolution, Continental forces stopped the British advance up Manhattan in battle (Sept., 1776) of Harlem Heights. Area remained virtually
> rural until improvement in 19th cent. of transportation

links with lower Manhattan. Public-housing projects (begun in 1930s) and other attempts to relieve unfavorable conditions there have been made.

At first it seems to give an all-encompassing view—complete with official borders, colonial heroics, and important urban planning highlights. Yet it manages to say nothing at all. In search of further detail I seized upon another definition, from the pages of *The Handbook of Geographical Nicknames.* This volume reveals that a city called Hankow is "The Pittsburgh of China"; that "The Happy Valley" refers to war-torn Kashmir and to the riverine gorge cut by the Tennessee; and that the Harz Mountains of Germany, the location of the silver mines where Leibniz once toiled, is now or once was "The Stronghold of Paganism." Situated near these is Harlem, whose nickname, "The Capital of the Negro Population of the United States," was not nearly as catchy or evocative as I'd expected. Though the phrase lacks poetry, it retains an accidental precision: the outdated term "Negro" (already antique when the book was published, in 1980) fixes our attention on the past.

At the library I found another source of coordinates. *Harlem is blocked in by the high ridges of Morningside Heights and St. Nicholas Terrace, by the East and Harlem rivers, and by Central Park.* Those declared boundaries did not tell me anything new. More important was the action of those physical frontiers: *Harlem is blocked in.* Geography is destiny. *The WPA Guide to New York City,* first published in 1939, goes on to describe who and what is blocked in by those ridges, those rivers, and that pastoral fiction of a park:

Negro Harlem, into which are crowded more than a quarter of a million Negroes from southern states, the West Indies, and Africa, has many different aspects. To whites seeking amusement, it is an exuberant, original, and unconventional entertainment center; to Negro college graduates it is an opportunity to practice a profession among their own people; to those aspiring to racial leadership it is a domain where they may advocate their theories unmolested; to artists, writers, and sociologists it is a mine of rich material; to the mass of Negro people it is the spiritual capital of Black America.

I went on a tour of Harlem, thinking it would be useful to know what the packs of visitors were being told. We met at the corner of 135th Street and Lenox, in front of the Schomburg Center for Research in Black Culture, just two blocks from my building. The tour guide, a young white woman, began by asking the group to shout out whatever came to mind when they heard the word Harlem. Some said *music,* others said *riots.* Those who didn't say *music* or *riots* said *Bill Clinton* and *soul food.*

After that exercise in free association, the guide led us on a brief circuit covering a radius no larger than five blocks. As we began, she gave a condensed history of what happened when blacks first moved into Harlem. With a call-and-response style reminiscent of kindergarten, she asked what happened next. The chorus of mostly white tourists shouted out: *The white people leave!*

The guide had a habit of calling Lenox Avenue, Fifth Avenue. As we passed through one block of brownstone houses, I overheard a couple marveling at the architecture, noting the *little pointy tops* of a cluster of homes. The man asked his wife, had they seen them before? Like the mansard roofs in France? Did she remember they were named after a guy called Mansard? A woman

West 133rd Street, ca. 1877. (Photo by Silas A. Holmes / Courtesy of New-York Historical Society, Department of Prints, Photographs, and Architectural Collections)

came out of one house and asked if anyone in the group knew someone to rent her top two floors. When one tourist asked the price of brownstones these days, the guide, a young graduate student in history, asserted somewhat huffily that she was not a real estate broker. One woman repeatedly interrupted the tour to ask how far away the famous Sylvia's soul-food restaurant was.

Often, I fell away from the group, trailing behind. I was familiar with most of the history being discussed. For me, the biggest revelation had come at the beginning of the tour. As we stood at the meeting point, the corner of 135th and Lenox, in the shadow of the Schomburg Center, the guide had passed around a photo. It was a picture of the street that crosses my corner of Lenox Avenue. The caption on the back read *West 133rd Street between 5th and 6th Ave-*

nues. 1880–1881. Today, standing at the corner of 133rd Street looking east across Lenox Avenue (formerly Sixth Avenue), one sees the six towers of the Lenox Terrace apartment complex. The picture showed that same area, but in 1880 it resembled a moonscape. The terrain is utterly flat and is covered by a rough sod. In the foreground stands a group of three attached brick town houses. Their windows form an orderly grid, and the steps leading up to each building look bright white, untrodden. Most important, these three houses don't connect to any others. They stand isolated, with empty space on each side. After about twenty yards, a second cluster of three attached houses is seen to the right of the first group. They are also flanked by open space. Beyond that group, after another twenty yards or so, are yet another bank of houses. Across the gaps they seem to reach toward each other. The groups of houses are built parallel to each other, in a line, respecting the logic of an invisible map. But the houses do not quite form a street. They form the beginning of a street, the intention of a street, the merest suggestion of a street.

In the far distance, visible through the gap between the first two sets of homes, there is a fourth detached set of buildings. It is the dream of another street. Toward the vanishing point, flanked by nothing at all, is a solitary tree, a remnant of what was there before this idea of a neighborhood was imposed on the landscape. The picture preserves a moment when the idea was not yet accomplished, it hangs between dream and reality. This is a prehistoric Harlem—nothing that counts for History has happened there yet. There is sky, open space, and very little shelter. Without the caption, it would be hard to know if this was the beginning or end of a civilization—a place just being built, or recently destroyed.

This is Harlem, barely inhabited—at the very beginning of its settlement in the 1880s. The buildings are only a few years old, the vast blank spaces between them are evidence of how this land—a farming suburb—was haphazardly annexed by the metropolis. The houses were built as speculative enterprises, each group of three representing a gamble by some intrepid pioneer. The bourgeois commuter society that grew up here is not yet established, nor are the other houses that would eventually complete this and other streets.

The houses in the picture all face south, toward settled Manhattan, expectantly oriented toward the people who would arrive from downtown. But there are no people in the photograph. And though the buildings themselves suggest the presence of people, the arrangement of those structures in that space and the utter quietude of the landscape collide with the clamor we know should accompany buildings like those. Curtains hang in a few windows of the first group of buildings. One window, on the top floor of the middle house, is slightly ajar. Someone is there. Or, someone has been there and just left. Or, someone is about to arrive.

Here, blank spaces—possibilities—prevail. This picture shows what is about to be built, and also what is now already gone. In the 1950s the houses and tenements and even the very streets from 132nd to 135th between Lenox and Fifth Avenues were razed in a slum-clearance program, to build the high-rise middle-class housing complex of Lenox Terrace. A single row house remains, hidden in the midst of the towers. Nuns live in that house. There is some empty space on either side, and it no longer lines any street.

I used to stare into similar wide, open spaces as a child. I grew up in a city where the combined meaning of the words *urban* and *planning* was imprecise. To reach the side of town where we lived, you took a highway from the city center that crossed vast stretches of undeveloped land. From the window of our car, I stared into these spaces. I sought evidence of activity in the deep distance—

perhaps a figure dashing across the field—from which I could invent a story. Typically, the only figures in those fields were small herds of undernourished horses or cattle. This brittle land was used as a makeshift pasture—livestock foraged for nourishment among the dry brush between oil pumps and electric towers. I looked out the windows of our car to see how far into the horizon my eyes could carry me, watching for something I hadn't noticed before. But that landscape never changed. It was twenty years before new housing was built along that highway. When I was a child, those fields were always marked with faded billboards offering the acreage for development, perpetually in search of a willing taker.

When I came to live in Harlem, the fenced-off, overgrown empty lots here also attracted my eye. At first, they were evidence: I had indeed arrived in the place I'd heard of. The empty lots held some significance; it was similar to the feeling I'd had when, riding from the airport in New Delhi, I first saw cows in the road. Yes, this is the place I have heard about, I'd thought. There are cows all over the road exactly as they were in the guidebook pictures. The empty lots in Harlem had the same verifying quality. Later, those empty lots provided something beyond veracity. They were a place for the eyes to rest. This was not some romance for ruins. These blank, disavowed spaces had been labeled as blight, but they provided a visual and mental break from the clamor of the buildings and people. There was a hint of the horizon.

Here was solace from the crowded landscape—both the physical crowdedness of buildings and people and the crowd of stories and histories. A friend of mine describes certain cities as being *full*—too much has happened there, you cannot move. Paris, he says, is the quintessentially *full* city. I suspect he'd say Harlem is another place that is too full—though its crowdedness and overpopulation have been discussed in other terms. In the empty lots, my mind escaped history.

Later I understood that these empty fields were indeed the setting of a history, the loathsome history of neglect and destruction stretching back to the beginning of black settlement in Harlem and its corollary, white flight. But at first, as in Texas, those spaces where my thoughts played were just settings for scenes and fancies whose significance was fleeting. I admired the wild patches of Queen Anne's lace that grew up in summer. Independent businessmen used some lots as locations for unofficial open-air markets, selling used furniture or vintage clothes.

Many of these places are now occupied by new condominiums. One is now a Mormon church. As the empty lots disappeared, I became more interested in what was there before. In some places it is possible to see what was there: the foundation of a building remains; a front stoop rises up from the sidewalk but leads to nothing. Such things recede into the background, part of the natural history of this place, as if they had always been like that. But this is the evidence of an unnatural history—it was not always this way, it came to be that way for a reason.

There are new empty lots different from those I noticed upon first arriving. Returning after a year's absence, I found an empty lot at the southwestern corner of Lenox Avenue and 125th Street. It was covered with fresh gravel, to stop its reversion to a wild field. When I first saw the lot something sank inside of me—the sensation mocked the feeling of a demolition, a building brought to its knees. This new empty lot opened a new horizon: from 125th Street you could see clear through the block to 124th Street. But the view was not one that gave rest or inspired the eye and mind. There was only the instantaneous, frantic search for something that once was there and was there no longer.

It was a grand old apartment house whose facade hugged the corner, making the intersection look like a stately plaza. It might have been a candidate for landmark status, but its windows were sealed up with cement bricks. Soon after I arrived in Harlem, the few tenants remaining in the building's storefronts—a decrepit Chinese restaurant, a flamboyant haberdashery, a store specializing in women's undergarments, and a shoe shine and repair service—had all closed up shop.

The building stayed in place long after those stores had gone. For a few years it brought revenue as the background for various athletic-wear billboards; for several seasons a heroic image of Muhammad Ali, having just knocked out an opponent, loomed over Lenox Avenue. I heard a rumor that the building had not been demolished because a family lived inside and that they'd defiantly refused to leave when the other tenants cleared out. This seemed impossible with all of the windows bricked over, and I never saw anyone enter or exit the building. But I did always see—through a small window in a battered door on Lenox Avenue—a light illuminating the vestibule.

There used to be an empty lot near my house, on Seventh Avenue just south of 133rd Street. One day in summer, I saw through its chain-link fence a pile of watermelon rinds at the rear of the lot. There was an open pit in the ground nearby, where someone was burying the waste. Later, the pile disappeared and the open pit was covered by recently turned earth. Soon, construction began on that site. It was only a matter of weeks before the frame of a new building rose up on the lot. A security guard was now stationed there each night to guard the property. He didn't wear a uniform, and like many of the men (and sometimes women) who work security jobs at construction sites in Harlem, he was an immigrant from West Africa.

Later, when construction was nearly completed but the premises were not yet occupied, I passed again one night and saw through the building's glass doors the outline of a man sitting in the condominium entry. He kept watch in near darkness, visible only by the light of a nearby street lamp. Whenever I passed the spot, I looked to see if anyone was inside. Sometimes the guard was there, slumped in his seat, sleeping through his shift out of exhaustion or boredom. Other times, there was only an empty chair. A few times, the watchman waved hello. Once, the figure beckoned me inside.

I didn't accept the invitation. The building still looked unoccupied, but a large sign now hung from its facade. The building is called the Ellison. To advertise the property, the sign shows a photograph of a handsome, clean-cut young black man in a suit. He is shown in regal profile, his eyes are closed, his chin is lifted toward the sky. *Change your state of mind,* begins the sales pitch for the new condominiums. The man on the sign looks lost in contemplation, on the brink of transcendence, about to receive some celestial enlightenment. Or maybe he has just thrown back his head and is about to unleash a howling laugh.

That picture from 1880 shows the beginning of what was, essentially, a failed settlement. More buildings were constructed so the isolated housing blocks eventually formed complete streets. As people moved in, Harlem became, according to one observer in 1905, *a haven for the clerks and small merchants, the family man and the newly married couple and the young professional man, who all flocked thither.* But the real estate speculation behind the Harlem housing boom had not anticipated the city's delay in extending transportation to the area. Many town houses and apartment buildings were empty or partially empty. Around 1900 the situation attracted the interest of African American businessman Philip A. Payton Jr., an associate of Booker T. Washington. Payton proposed to several landlords that he act as a broker, renting their vacant properties to black tenants. He began quietly, with a few houses on 134th Street east of Lenox Avenue (the same area shown in that photo of prehistoric Harlem). According to James Weldon Johnson,

> The whites paid little attention to the movement until it began to spread west of Lenox Avenue; they then took steps to check it. They proposed through a financial organization, the Hudson Realty Company, to buy in all properties occupied by colored people and evict the tenants.

Another group, Shaw & Company, pursued the same tactics, as did the Harlem Property Owners' Improvement Association. But Payton was equal to the challenge. When the Hudson Realty Company started buying property and evicting blacks, Payton combined with other black businessmen to launch the Afro-American Realty Company, which bought property and evicted whites. A December 17, 1905, article from the *New York Times* reported the furor with the tone of an urgent telegram: *Real Estate Race War Is Started in Harlem; Dispossessed White Men Ask Negroes to be Allowed to Stay; Colored Folks Retaliated; They Were Dispossessed First—Then Formed a Real Estate Company to Buy Tenements.* Payton and the Afro-American Realty Company are accurately credited with the invention of black Harlem. The strategy was not merely to secure rental housing or buy individual property, but to harness the collective economic power of well-to-do blacks, toward the general empowerment of the race.

The *New York Herald* described the unfolding controversy on December 24, 1905, under the headline *Negroes Move into Harlem.*

> An untoward circumstance has been injected into the private-dwelling market in the vicinity of 133rd and 134th Streets.

During the last three years the flats in 134th between Lenox and Seventh Avenues, that were occupied entirely by white folks, have been captured for occupation by a Negro population. Its presence there has tended also to lend much color to conditions in 133rd and 135th Streets between Lenox and Seventh Avenues.

One Hundred and Thirty-third Street still shows some signs of resistance to the blending of colors in that street, but between Lenox and Seventh Avenues has practically succumbed to the ingress of colored tenants. Nearly all the old dwellings in 134th Street to midway in the block west from Seventh Avenue are occupied by colored tenants and real estate brokers predict that it is only a matter of time when the entire block, to Eighth Avenue, will be a stronghold of the Negro population.

As a result of the extension of this African colony, dwellings in 133rd Street between Seventh and Eighth Avenues, and in 132nd Street from Lenox to Eighth Avenue have depreciated from fifteen to twenty per cent in value, especially in the sides of those streets nearest to 134th Street. The cause of the colored influx is inexplicable.

After a few years of this *untoward circumstance,* the good citizens of Harlem resolved to erect a twenty-four-foot fence on 136th Street, a battlement to defend their besieged city. The *New York Indicator,* a real estate publication, summarized popular opinion:

Their presence is undesirable among us...they should not only be disenfranchised, but also segregated in some colony in the outskirts of the city, where their transportation and other problems will not inflict injustice and disgust on worthy citizens.

As white Harlem gathered its forces, a spokesperson for a group of outraged citizens offered a self-serving prophecy, masked as philanthropy: *We believe... that real friends of Negroes will eventually convince them that they should buy large tracts of unimproved land near the city and there build up colonies of their own.*

Only two decades had passed when the prophecy was borne out under slightly altered circumstances. A Negro colony spread from the concentrated area around Philip Payton's original buildings on 134th Street, until it became an onslaught no wall could contain. White New Yorkers quit Harlem. Some sold their property at a loss, others abandoned houses and apartment buildings, preferring to board them up rather than rent or sell to black people. Eventually, the move of blacks into Harlem reached the physical limits of the ridges, the rivers, and 110th Street. Alain Locke, writing in the introduction to his 1925 anthology *The New Negro,* found that the concentration of black New Yorkers crowding into that physical space mirrored a metaphysical force then gaining strength.

In Harlem, Negro life is seizing upon its first chances for group expression and self-determination. That is why our comparison is taken with those nascent centers of folk-expression and self-determination which are playing a creative part in the world today. Without pretense to their political significance, Harlem has the same role to play for the New Negro as Dublin has had for the New Ireland or Prague for the New Czechoslovakia.

Locke was among the first to define Harlem as *a race capital,* a physical center that *focuses a people.* It was *the stage of the pageant of contemporary Negro life* on which would unfold *the resurgence of a race.* Locke invokes two young European republics whose people had rejected imperialism through nationalism. But he did not aspire to self-determination by means of actual political sovereignty or a separate nation for blacks. Locke believed that Harlem would be a place of cultural and social uplift. This, in time, would lead to equality for blacks within the wider American scene. In 1925, Locke asserted that *Harlem represents the Negro's latest thrust towards Democracy.*

Others tried to add their own pronouncements to Locke's prophecy. *The New Negro* anthology includes Charles S. Johnson reaching for Locke's gravitas, while waxing nostalgic about events still in progress: *And there was New York City with its polite personal service and its Harlem—the Mecca of the Negroes the country over. Delightful Harlem of the effete East! Old families, brownstone mansions, a step from wonderful Broadway, the end of the rainbow.*

In 1928, Wallace Thurman's *Negro Life in New York's Harlem* noted that the neighborhood—known as *The Mecca of the New Negro, the center of black America's cultural renaissance, Nigger Heaven, Pickaninny Paradise, Capital of Black America,* among other monikers—had been *surveyed and interpreted, explored and exploited.* But Thurman launches his own survey and interpretation, producing *a lively picture of a popular and interesting section* that reads like a travel guide, with chapters on social life, night life, amusement, house rent parties, the numbers, the church, and newspapers. The resulting vision of Harlem is a great deal less than the sum of its parts.

Langston Hughes riffs on Harlem in his contribution to a 1963 special Harlem issue of *Freedomways* magazine. Hughes mixes sentimentality with a dose of his typically biting wit, in the following incantation:

Harlem, like a Picasso painting in his cubistic period. Harlem—Southern Harlem—the Carolinas, Georgia, Florida—looking for the Promised Land—dressed in rhythmic words, painted in bright pictures, dancing to jazz—and ending up in the subway at morning rush time—headed downtown. West Indian Harlem—warm rambunctious sassy remembering Marcus Garvey, Haitian Harlem, Cuban Harlem, little pockets of tropical dreams in alien tongues. Magnet Harlem, pulling an Arthur Schomburg from Puerto Rico, pulling an Arna Bontemps all the way from California, a Nora Holt from way out West, an E. Simms Campbell from St. Louis, likewise a Josephine Baker, a Charles S. Johnson from Virginia, an A. Phillip Randolph from Florida, a Roy Wilkins from Minnesota, an Alta Douglas from Kansas. Melting pot Harlem—Harlem of honey and chocolate and caramel and rum and vinegar and lemon and lime and gall. Dusky dream Harlem rumbling into a nightmare tunnel where the subway from the Bronx keeps right on downtown, where the jazz is drained to Broadway whence Josephine [Baker] goes to Paris, Robeson to London, Jean Toomer to a Quaker Meeting House, Garvey to Atlanta Federal Penitentiary, and Wallace Thurman to his grave; but Duke Ellington to fame and fortune, Lena Horne to Broadway, and Buck Clayton to China.

The business of defining Harlem has already been perfected. You have heard them all before: Harlem is *a ruin,* it is *the home of the Negro's Zionism*; it is *a third world country;* an *East Berlin whose Wall is 110th Street.* This is hyperbolic Harlem, *the cultural capital of black America* or its *epicenter* (likening the place to a natural disaster). There is Harlem as Mecca—a city of sanctuary, a place that merges devotion and duty.

In *The New Negro* Alain Locke declared: *Harlem, I grant you, isn't typical—but it is significant, it is prophetic. No sane observer, however sympathetic to the new trend, would contend that the great masses are articulate as yet, but they stir, they move, they are more than physically restless.*

But in another essay included in the 1925 anthology, James Weldon Johnson offered a different kind of prophecy. In the tradition of the best oracles, it comes in the form of a riddle:

> The question naturally arises, "Are the Negroes going to be able to hold Harlem?" If they have been steadily driven northward for the past hundred years and out of less desirable sections, can they hold this choice bit of Manhattan Island? It is hardly probable that Negroes will hold Harlem indefinitely, but when they are forced out it will not be for the same reasons that forced them out of former quarters in New York City. The situation is entirely different and without precedent. When colored people do leave Harlem, their homes, their churches, their investments and their businesses, it will be because the land has become so valuable they can no longer afford to live on it. But the date of another move northward is very far in the future.

Johnson suspected that Locke's restless masses would be forced—as before in New York, but compelled by a different propulsion—to move yet again. But he did not dwell much on the possibility, or divulge a spell to stop events from coming to pass.

Into the City of Refuge

EMMA LOU MORGAN arrives in Harlem with the turn of a page. She has come far. How was the journey, Emma Lou? She keeps the details close to her chest, hidden away in the space between the end of one chapter and the beginning of the next. We are not told what she saw crossing the country from Los Angeles, or how long it took; whether sleep on the journey was fitful, or if there were moments on the way when she felt like getting off that train and making her way back home to Boise, Idaho, which she had fled looking for education and enlightenment in the California sun.

That didn't last long. Soon she was filled with *more determination than ever to escape should the chance present itself.* Emma Lou took her chance when it came, with little thought given to the vehicle of her flight. *Once more, Emma Lou fled into an unknown town to escape the haunting chimera of intra-racial color prejudice.*

Emma Lou Morgan is running from her black skin. Wallace Thurman tells us as much in the epigraph to his novel *The Blacker the Berry...: My color shrouds me in,* goes the selection from poet

Countee Cullen. Where better to send his heroine than Harlem, and how better for her to arrive there than not to arrive at all — the emphasis is placed on what she left behind. Leaving is the main thing. *She would have gone any place to escape*, and so she is soon in Harlem. She can hardly believe it herself: *It did seem strange, this being in Harlem when only a few weeks before she had been over three thousand miles away.* Emma Lou is philosophical: she is thinking about time, and she is thinking about distance and about the immutability of the two. Soon enough, she glimpses her own folly. *What was that line in Cullen's verse, "I run, but Time's abreast with me"? She had only traversed space and defied distance.*

Helga Crane had just as far to come. Like Emma Lou, her journey was not direct. Last it was Chicago, and before that, Naxos, the little southern town, with its stultifying black-college propriety. She leaves, and she leaves, and she leaves. But when she arrives in Harlem, *again she had that strange transforming experience* — the watchword here is "again" — *this time not so fleetingly, the magic sense of having come home.* What does Helga Crane know of home? Both black and Danish, like Nella Larsen who made her, Helga has been yanked through the pages of *Quicksand* from one home to another and then yet another. But homeless Helga sings that *Harlem, teeming black Harlem, had welcomed her and lulled her into something that was, she was certain, peace and contentment.*

Oh, to be in Harlem again after two years away. This is Jake laying first sights on Harlem, arriving home from Europe after the Great War. His ecstasy can hardly be contained; it can hardly be believed. The *deep-dyed color* and the *thickness* and the *closeness* and the *noises* and the *sugared laughter* and the *honey-talk* and *ragtime* and *blues*. Never mind that Jake sounds more like a tourist than a joyous returnee. He does not return to the bosom of a woe-begotten mother, but to *Good old Harlem! Chocolate Harlem!*

Sweet Harlem! This is the Harlem to which downtown revelers (and downtown readers of Claude McKay's *Home to Harlem*) flocked: *Oh, the contagious fever of Harlem. Burning everywhere in the dark-eyed Harlem.... Burning now in Jake's sweet blood.*

He stood up and his feet burned. Then he remembered. He remembered walking until his feet were blistered where the soles had worn bare on his shoes. He remembered walking, but he didn't know why he kept on walking. Wretched Jule wakes up after his first night in Harlem, a rainy night spent on a bench in St. Nicholas Park. He is numb and hungry, his meager belongings in a small bundle — the luggage of swift departure. He is dazed by the streetlights reflected in the wet pavement. The tall buildings of City College — up the hill from the park — remind him (or his creator, George Wylie Henderson, in *Jule*) of the walls of Babylon. Where is good old Harlem, chocolate Harlem, sweet Harlem? Nowhere. *A sign on a lamppost said W. 135th St., but it didn't mean anything to him.*

King Solomon Gillis arrives in the same spot as Jule, under the same circumstances. (They have both murdered men.) But when he emerges from the train at 135th Street and Lenox he meets *clean air, blue sky, bright sunlight. Then slowly, spreadingly, he grinned at what he saw.* Maybe he saw Emma Lou and Helga and Jule, new arrivals like himself, still staggered by the pace of life in Harlem. But perhaps he also saw, and was impressed by, the already acclimated, debonair, and citified habitués of the black metropolis. What is certain: He saw

Negroes at every turn; up and down Lenox Avenue, up and down One Hundred and Thirty-fifth Street; big, lanky Negroes, short, squat Negroes; black ones, brown ones, yellow ones; men standing idle on the curb, women, bundle-laden, trudging reluctantly homeward, children rattle trapping about the sidewalks; here and there a white face drifting along, but Negroes predominantly, overwhelmingly everywhere. There was assuredly no doubt of his whereabouts. This was Negro Harlem.

For King Solomon Gillis, escaping the South in the pages of Rudolph Fisher's short story "The City of Refuge," Harlem offered freedoms that were not merely existential. *In Harlem, black was white. You had rights that could not be denied you; you had privileges, protected by law. And you had money. Everybody in Harlem had money. It was a land of plenty.... The land of plenty was more than that now; it was also a city of refuge.*

"Who you say sentcher heah, dearie?" Zora Neale Hurston's Pinkie is full of doubts. *"Uh-a-a man down at the boat landing where I got off—North River. I just come in on the boat."* But the rooming house where she has landed is full of unsavory characters. *She wished herself back home again even with the ill treatment and squalor.* Faced with the city's unyielding harshness, she has nothing to fall back on. She has three dollars, and they are stuffed in her shoe to guard against thieves. She thinks of *flight—but where? Nowhere. For there was no home to which she could return, nor any place she knew.*

Lutie Johnson scorns 116th Street, the street where she has landed, working as a maid to make a living for her son. She hates the street, it is the source of all her misfortunes, and they are many, but yet—when she comes home from cleaning houses there is a small dose of relief.

She got off the train, thinking that she never felt really human until she reached Harlem and thus got away from the hostility in the eyes of the white women who stared at her on the downtown streets and in the subway. Escaped from the openly appraising looks of the white men whose eyes seemed to go through her clothing to her long brown legs.

In Harlem Lutie is human, and she is not alone. Ascending the subway into Harlem after a day's work in her domestic job downtown, at the very moment she enters the throng she achieves individuality.

Up here they are no longer creatures labeled simply colored and therefore all alike...in Harlem you are bigger than yourself...you take up space different. The same people who had made themselves small on the train, even on the platform, suddenly grew so large they could hardly get up the stairs to the street together. She reached the street at the very end of the crowd and stood watching them as they scattered in all directions, laughing and talking to each other.

Many of these books were among those on a reading list I made for myself around age fourteen. On the first page of a composition book I wrote the heading "Books written during the Harlem Renaissance" and plotted an itinerary through my library's shelves, searching for this El Dorado of black literature. Besides these, there was Jean Toomer's *Cane* and novels by Jessie Fauset. I read Federico García Lorca's Harlem poems from *El Poeta en Nueva York*, in which he sets an unforgettable scene. *Ay, Harlem! Ay, Harlem! Ay, Harlem!* I didn't need the facing page of my bilingual edition to translate what he saw: *Negros! Negros! Negros! Negros!* Thus goes the attempt of *el poeta* to come to terms with Harlem. *Palabras* fail. Those are the barest facts of the situation: he escapes the realm of the poetic, and tumbles toward the sociological. To understand the problems presented by this bustling horde, one need only juxtapose García Lorca's frenetic naming of things (*blacks blacks blacks blacks*) with Lutie's idea, on the pages of Ann Petry's novel *The Street:* finally she was in a place where she was not merely black.

I like to think of Emma Lou and Helga and Lutie and Jule and King Solomon brushing shoulders with García Lorca, who is unable to grasp the various paths they followed as refugees and fugitives in that black city where he was a tourist. There are many paths, but how many destinations for this journey? Some, like Helga Crane, are immediately taken in, content to live within the boundary. Some, like, Emma Lou, long to see 135th Street and then find it does not merit their expectation. Surely there must have been many like Jule, for whom the destination itself did not conjure any particular magic. Or others like Pinkie, who would like to be anywhere, not there—thinking of flight but with no place to go. There is no going home, and the place where you have arrived offers no substantial shelter.

Emma Lou and Helga Crane both leave Harlem. Lutie is driven to commit a gruesome murder, and then flees, too. Reading their stories as a teenager in Texas, I only cared about the first part of their irresistible trajectory—an outward, upward momentum.

Of my own arrival, I can say that it is difficult to tell the beginning without any inkling of the end, to show you the light of enchantment without any shadow of disenchantment. I no longer find anything remarkable about my own arrival here. It was not the arrival of a fugitive or a refugee. That feeling—of running from something or running to something—only came later, in the very streets where I was living, and often simultaneously.

I cannot fit my entry into Harlem into a neat narrative arc, like those of Emma Lou and Helga, or Lutie and Pinkie. I had come to New York for a visit, with the faintest unresolved notion of making a move. I bought the *Amsterdam News* on a Thursday, when the apartment listings would be new, and called up the cheapest spots. I saved the paper, so I can tell you that the listing described as *Harlem 1 bedroom / Renovated, locked doors / No fee. By Owner,* for $775 with a minimum income of $40,000 that I did not have, was already taken when I called. The *one bedroom for $775 with hardwood floors and new appliances in an elevator bldg and quiet neighborhood* must also have gone quickly. That would have left the studio apartment on Edgecombe Avenue for $675, which was not actually an option. A previous bad experience of cramped studio living had taught me the true nature of my Texan sense of space.

At the top of the page I found the ad for *3 Rms. Floor-thru apt. No Kit. Clean, Non-smoker. Ref's req'd, $750/mo.* When I called the number the owner said the apartment wasn't taken. In the margin of the now-creased and aged newsprint are the directions I quickly scrawled. I went uptown at once.

The apartment was located in the very last house on the block of 120th Street between Lenox and Seventh Avenues. I met the landlady on the garden level and followed her up three flights of decrepit stairs. We entered the available apartment on the top floor. Its green-painted hallways and matching green carpet were hideous, but there was light streaming in from the front and back windows and a skylight presiding over the entryway and landing. To cross from the front to back required a short stroll. It was, even without a kitchen, the very definition of happiness. I wrote a check for the first and last months' rent, then went downtown to collect my things.

At the time, the miraculous location of a floor-through brownstone apartment—even a floor-through brownstone apartment without a kitchen and with a lamentable green hallway complemented by ugly green wall-to-wall carpeting—held a certain sense of destiny. It was somehow meant to be. The notion that an apartment without a kitchen was ever anyone's destiny has to do with the general desperation of real estate in New York City, but it is a good indicator of how I saw the world then. I needed providence as an escort on my own ascent from the subway station into Harlem. I, too, was going to meet a place I had already filled with so many expectations. I, too, would have to match the pictures in my mind—the ones I'd invented and the ones I'd seen in books—with the world that was now my own.

But I did not immediately rush out to follow the trails of my favorite Harlem characters; I did not rush to stand before the hallowed sites where history had been made. I did not rush at all. I moved slowly, keeping a deliberately languid pace, because some part of me needed to pretend that my body was still in Texas. And my eyes were still in Texas, too, because I could not give up the habit (and did not lose it until much later) of meeting the eyes of everyone I passed. I didn't know (or did know and didn't mind) that it was through the eyes I would be dragged into stories.

I met eyes with the older ladies who gathered in front of buildings and with the elderly men who sat on park benches in the median, as the traffic rushed north and south around them. When crossing paths with young men who seemed about to make an unwanted advance, I smiled brightly and shouted *Hi!* like an overexcited flight attendant, and then kept walking while they were too stunned to reply. But often I did not refuse when a man offered to walk with me some part of the way down Lenox Avenue, always ending such promenades at the corner of my block. Once, I saw an old lady struggling with her groceries and offered my hands. We walked together for a while, but when she, too, stopped at the corner where her street met Lenox Avenue I was puzzled—alarmed that my assistance could be confused for predation.

I did not make a pilgrimage to the home of Langston Hughes. Instead I met—probably in the street—a young man who lived in Hughes's old house and who made certain everyone knew this fact within minutes of making his acquaintance. I did not immediately go up to the Schomburg Center. Instead I spent hours at a branch library, reading the newspaper and waiting to use the public computers in order to look for a job. Eventually I started going out to dances and art openings, but many more nights I stayed inside, listening to the radio and to the sounds of traffic on Seventh Avenue.

I furnished my apartment with discoveries from junk shops and neighborhood antique dealers whose premises were filled to the rafters with half-upholstered sofas and repaired lamps that would likely never again give light. I purchased a barely functional but finely crafted chair that was sold to me on assurance that I was "handy." I pined after an Art Deco bedroom set that had supposedly belonged to Billie Holiday. It would have cost more than a month's rent, which I could not spare, and my mother warned me by phone from Texas not to trust the pedigree. I picked up tables from the sidewalk, bought cut-glass goblets from the Salvation Army on 125th Street, and purchased knickknacks from elderly ladies having tag sales to raise money for their church. I spent the money for two weeks' worth of groceries on an exotic folding table with a copper-tray tabletop. The seller said it was Persian; his final, successful sales ploy was that although it was his sincere desire to give me a bargain price, he could easily get more money from buyers of *the other persuasion*—by which he meant white shoppers at flea markets in suburban Connecticut. And though I could not remove the sickly green carpet, my landlady relented to my capricious wish to paint the walls of my study an overheated red. (It was the presence of that extra room, just for my work, that had caused me to accept the kitchenless dwelling.)

I had the sense, when putting together these implements for life in my first apartment, that I was bringing in castaways, remnants of other lives that had been lived here. During those early days in Harlem, I also saw great piles of furniture and clothes on sidewalks, of greater quantity and less organization than one would see in an average trash disposal. These piles confused me, until I realized they were the aftermath of evictions.

Even though it was just a few short years ago, nearly all of the stores where I bought the items for my first apartment are gone — there is no room for the junk of old Harlem. But then, the junk prevailed, in shops and on piles in the street. Though I didn't know who lived in my rooms before me, I was already aware of the furor in Harlem about gentrification. I arrived the very week a long, hand-wringing article on the subject had appeared in *The New Yorker*. More recently a plaintive piece in the *New York Times* sought to find common ground between Harlem old and new, but instead skillfully illustrated the distance between them. In an interview, one new resident described parties featuring a parlor game in which she and other recent arrivals joked about what amenities the neighborhood needed most. The answer agreed upon at the latest gathering was that Harlem was in dire need of a Thai restaurant. At the time, Harlem was also experiencing a housing deficit, lacking over 38,000 units of housing needed by its poorest residents.

When I was new to Harlem and experiencing my own pangs of complicity on the issue, I asked a politically minded friend if I was a gentrifier. He firmly answered no — because I was black and poor. I was not convinced. Another friend laughed at the archetypal narrative of my move north and dubbed me Miss Great Migration 2002.

If I was part of the new Harlem, that meant the new café at the end of my block, opened only a few months before I moved to town, should have been my natural habitat. It was lauded as a marvel of civilization and progress—one *New York Times* reporter theorized that the availability of a quality latte in Harlem was a symbol of the neighborhood's imminent conversion. Yet I couldn't help but wince when noticing my elderly neighbor Mr. Edward standing outside the door of that new café, but never going in. He hovered next to the entrance, drinking a seventy-five-cent cup of bodega coffee.

Once, while sitting inside the café, I happened to overhear a conversation between two white men seated nearby. One seemed to be a stay-at-home dad who worked in marketing; he talked business while nursing a toddler in a stroller. I gathered from eavesdropping that the other man was visiting his friend's new neighborhood for the first time. *This is fabulous*, he exclaimed. Then, noting the first man's skills in marketing, he added: *Really, you have to do something to get the word out. There need to be more* people *up here!*

I later read an article in the *New York Sun* that joyously reported that developers had purchased several high-rise rental buildings in Harlem and would be turning them into expensive condominiums. The buildings, long a stronghold of Harlem's middle class, were originally built as a consolation prize because blacks were barred from living in similar developments in lower Manhattan. The article ended by celebrating the return of *people* to Harlem, which used to be a place *people* only visited, during Prohibition, for booze and big bands.

The visitor I overheard and the journalist I read were afflicted by that exuberant myopia common to colonists of varied epochs and ambitions: thus did the explorers conquering Africa for God, king, country, and commerce, declare with the endorsement of the Vatican that any land where the native people were not Christians was officially a *terra nullius*, a no-man's-land. (*There need to be more people up here!*) Thus did the nineteenth-century British architects of the plan to restore Europe's Jews to Israel as a refuge against pogroms (a plan conceived mostly from British theological and political self-interest) examine the map of the ancient homeland and declare that it was an empty territory, *a land without a people for a people without a land. (There need to be more people up here!*)

I should not have been shocked by those careless quips, but it was the sort of thing that made me especially tight-lipped when I happened to run into a white acquaintance downtown who, upon hearing I had moved to Harlem, and perhaps having read that recent *New Yorker* article, was pressingly curious to know about *interesting things going on up there* ....

During those first months in New York, I was busy with an assignment at my new job with a Harlem-based publisher: to pore through the archives of photographer James VanDerZee in order to make a new book of his images. VanDerZee's photo studio operated during the height of the Harlem Renaissance, capturing Harlemites in elegant portraits, wearing their finest threads. His were the kind of pictures that would have pride of place on a mantel or be tucked into an envelope along with a letter sent back home, a tableau of the good life available up north. When VanDerZee's work was rediscovered in the late 1960s by curators of the controversial "Harlem on My Mind" exhibition at the Metropolitan Museum of Art, his photographs of cosmopolitan Harlem provided an antidote to the destitute, shell-shocked image then attached to the neighborhood and formed a new iconography of its best days.

VanDerZee's Harlem is a province of extravagance, culture, and high society. We meet the delicate young students of a dancing school, adorable in a hundred different ways, and the dandified members of all-male social clubs. In individual portraits of cultured ladies and fine gentlemen, unidentified Harlemites whose personal histories are not preserved display the glamour and bearing of celebrities and aristocrats. A couple poses in front of an exquisite convertible sedan clad in matching full-length raccoon fur coats. A group portrait shows a vast wedding party, the bridesmaids wearing matching taffeta headgear and the men dressed in white tie, all attended by a retinue of flower girls and ring-bearers. Improbably, VanDerZee's signature—etched into the negative of these photos—shows that both pictures were taken in 1932, during the depths of the Great Depression.

Outside the archive, I compared the buildings and the faces I saw in the street to the buildings and faces in the photographs. It was easy to establish which intersection was the setting of a certain parade and easy to note how soot and grime had attached to the facade of a certain church. But it was not possible, just by looking, to establish a direct connection between the people I saw motionless in the photographs and coursing through the streets. One could assume a trajectory, the continuity of families across eight or nine decades. *Here we have arrived*, the photographs whispered. *And here we remain*, came the answer from the streets. But I noticed in the contemporary faces some alteration, the consequence of a force not visible within the frame.

Then, I was always looking for approval, seeking it out in a returned smile—I was looking for mutuality. I was not known by anyone; they could not verify my background. I was unable, therefore, to truly lay claim to this place where I'd landed. My relationship to it was, for some time, like the effect of a picturesque landscape that hangs as a backdrop in a portrait studio, with the sitter arranged statically in the foreground.

It was a setting. It was not, exactly, History.

VanDerZee's portraits escort the viewer halfway into the interior life of Harlem, but anonymity brusquely slams the door. It is not possible to learn about the journey each person made to this place, or how that congregation managed to acquire its fine premises, or just what those all-male social clubs were getting up to in their smartly matched gear. The piles of VanDerZee photos in the archive and that frantic line from García Lorca (*Blacks! Blacks! Blacks! Blacks!*) speak a common tongue. It is the noise of the crowd.

The faces in the archive and the ones in the street were equally out of reach. We shared color and we shared location. At the moment when those two elements had just begun to collide in black Harlem, the combination produced a shared aspiration and a shared riddle. On the one hand, to cross the physical boundary was to overthrow the color line. But the forces of color and culture could be harnessed and endowed with a liberating power. Alain Locke, serving in his role as chief interpreter and philosopher of the New Negro movement, explained it as a question of velocity:

A railroad ticket and a suitcase, like a Bagdad carpet, transport the Negro peasant from the cotton-field and farm to the heart of the most complex urban civilization. Here in the mass, he must and does survive a jump of two generations in social economy and of a century and more in civilisation. Meanwhile the Negro poet, student, artist, thinker, by the very move that normally would take him off at a tangent from the masses, finds himself in their midst, in a situation concentrating the racial side of his experience and heightening his race-consciousness.

Locke speaks of the *Negro peasant* and his educated counterpart; both are transformed by their new surroundings. Both are subject to the original conundrum of the place: it is the result of bigotry and exclusion. It is also a proving ground for aspirations. It is a place that contracts one's possibilities, and a place where all things are possible.

In *Invisible Man,* Ralph Ellison joins Locke's two Harlem archetypes in one body. His narrator's entry into Harlem was much like the others I'd read about, but with an added dose of poetry: *When I came out of the subway, Lenox Avenue seemed to careen away from me at a drunken angle, and I focused upon the teetering scene with wild, infant's eyes, my head throbbing.* Ellison's Invisible Man is intoxicated by what he sees:

> This really was Harlem, and now all the stories which I had heard of the city-within-a-city leaped alive in my mind.... This was not a city of realities but of dreams; perhaps because I had always thought of my life as being confined to the South. And now as I struggled through the lines of people a new world of possibility suggested itself to me faintly like a small voice that was barely audible in the roar of city sounds.

This was not a city of realities but of dreams. This is a curious and perhaps dangerous proposition, one we might fly over if riding Locke's enchanted carpet. What does a preference for dreams over realities portend for life in this *new world of possibility*?

One of those Negro poets, students, artists, and thinkers streaming into Harlem was Langston Hughes, in the thrall of dreams that preexisted his arrival:

> I spent as much time as I could in Harlem, and this I have done ever since. I was in love with Harlem long before I ever

got there, and I am still in love with it. Everybody seemed to
make me welcome. The sheer dark size of Harlem intrigued
me. The fact that at that time poets and writers like James
Weldon Johnson and Jessie Fauset lived there, and Bert
Williams, Duke Ellington, Ethel Waters, and Walter White,
too, fascinated me.

Despite his enduring love for the place, Hughes admitted that
this *youthful illusion that Harlem was a world unto itself did not last
very long.* There was the city of dreams and the city of realities.
White downtown pull[ed] all the strings in Harlem.

Many years later, in 1965, another poet arrived uptown; this
was Amiri Baraka. He was then still known as LeRoi Jones, but
he was already storming the gates of Harlem in order to found the
Black Arts movement, having abandoned his interracial life downtown after the assassination of Malcolm X. Baraka seems to have
paid close attention to Locke. His memory of that entry to Harlem preserves the fevered expectation of the New Negro movement, tempered by equal parts jive and hindsight:

The arrival uptown, Harlem, can only be summed up by the
feelings jumping out of Césaire's *Return to My Native Land*
and Fanon's *Wretched of the Earth*, or Cabral's *Return to the
Source.* The middle-class native intellectual, having out-
integrated the most integrated, now plunges headlong back
into what he perceives as blackest, native-est. Having dug,
finally, how white he has become, now, *classically,* comes
back to his countrymen charged up with the desire to be
black, uphold black, etc.... a fanatical patriot!

When we came up out of the subway, March 1965, cold
and clear, Harlem all around staring us down, we felt like
pioneers of the new order. Back in the homeland to help

raise the race. Youth in their fervor know no limitations, except they are celebrations of them. Narrow because they lack experience, yet fervent, super-energetic, super-optimistic. If we had known what faced us, some would've copped out, some would've probably got down to study, as we should've, instead of the nowhere shit so many of us were involved with.

From Locke to Baraka and beyond, a single dream persisted, even in the face of reality. But the persistence of such a dream is not only a testament of endurance. It is also a testament of unfulfilled dreams. The wished-for thing had not been attained. Harlem was in the eternal process of becoming—in 1925 and 1965 and now—that place which, according to Locke, represented *the Negro's latest thrust towards Democracy*. The original reasons why the place existed (white supremacy, segregation) endured. The place endured. The fact that, like many of the by-products of American oppression, from chitlins to Christianity, black folk recuperated a dire situation, causing Harlem to be extolled, celebrated, and converted into a proud symbol, does not undo the original circumstance. It does help explain the persistence of this city of dreams: a kind of utopia to which dreamers continue to flock, bringing that quality of aspiration that Baraka characterized as *nowhere shit*. It is also, often, known as hope.

Upon arriving in Harlem, the narrator of Ellison's *Invisible Man* is initiated into that lineage of hope, and admonished about how easily it could slip away:

"It's you young folks what's going to make the changes," she said. "Y'all's the ones. You got to lead and you got to fight and move us all on up a little higher. And I tell you something's else, it's the ones from the South that's got to do it, them what knows the fire and ain't forgot how it burns. Up here too many forgits. They finds a place for theyselves and forgits the ones on the bottom. Oh, heap of them *talks* about doing things, but they done really forgot. No, it's you young ones what has to remember and take the lead."

———

I had only been in Harlem for about six months when my land-lady announced I had to leave the apartment; she wanted the top floor of the brownstone for her own family's use. I later heard a rumor that she'd rented it to a number of undocumented workers. If this is true, they probably ended up paying more money than I did, while living in far greater density.

That winter I looked for a new place, sometimes taking to the street with no guiding principle except the fever brought on by every FOR RENT sign in sight. I called the numbers from apart-ment listings in the *Amsterdam News*. When I didn't receive an answer, I would go directly to the addresses in the paper, hoping for some improbable sidewalk meeting with a landlord. If I liked a house because of its stained-glass fanlight transom or because of the tower window of its top floor, I'd send a letter to that address, telling the owner how I hoped there might be a vacancy because I had always wanted to live in a house with a window like that.

These methods did not yield any results. By then, in despera-tion, I began to consider the brokers who showed me tiny, over-priced studio apartments and also the listings in the *Amsterdam News* for rooms rented by the week. I knew these were single-room–occupancy (SRO) brownstones, mansions whose grand quarters had been carved into rooming houses. They are identifi-able by a board, usually nailed to the side of the doorjamb, bear-ing an incredible number of jerry-rigged doorbells, one for each resident of the house. On the brink of their apotheosis/restoration from being SROs to their original bourgeois destiny as single-family homes, these brownstones eventually feature in a different class of real estate listing, where they are presented with an ominous sales pitch: *Can be delivered vacant.*

I answered an ad for one of the weekly rentals. That particular SRO building had no doorbells at all—and no doorknob. There was a hole in the door where the knob should have been. The entry was unsecured, which should have sent me away immediately. Instead I went inside and called up the stairs to see if anyone was home. When no one answered, I waited in the vestibule for the owner to appear for our appointment—prepared to explain my presence if someone emerged from within. Eventually the owner did come—she was a Caribbean woman and she had a sweet-faced daughter with her. Both of them were wearing knitted skullcaps drawn tight around the head without an inch of hairline showing. In my short time in New York I had already identified this as a style particular to immigrants from the islands, abandoning all vanity in desperate protection against unfathomable cold.

I remember very little about the house. I remember going up the stairs and seeing the many doors that led to the various lodgers' rooms. I don't remember the bathroom, or whether the bathroom was within the quarters or down the hall. I don't remember the kitchen, or whether there was a kitchen. I do remember that once we were inside the available room, I could scarcely stretch out my arms. On its shortest side it was as wide as I was tall.

I remember the ornate mantel of an inoperative fireplace. It had details of turned wood spiraling toward the ceiling; white paint obscured what was probably the rich natural tone of a fine wood. The mantelpiece was a thing to be appreciated from a distance, from the comfort of a grand armchair placed across the room where one could catch a view of the fire and the woodwork. There could be no fire in this small space; to light a fire in such a space would produce an infernal heat, and you would be sitting so close you could scarcely focus on the woodwork.

Though the asking price for that tiny hovel was more than I was willing to pay per week, for one moment I was foolish enough to think that my search had come to an end, that my days would be improved by glancing at that mantel upon waking, that to be in the presence of this fireplace would effect a change in me, even if I could not light a fire to be appreciated from a safe distance.

I have caught myself indulging this same tendency when marveling at old architecture in cities like Havana or Cochin — places described in guidebooks as possessing "faded grandeur," which means the buildings left behind by colonizers are now blistered by saltwater and underdevelopment. In that SRO apartment, I chastised myself for swooning with architectural necrophilia in a place where aesthetics were probably of little concern. But my inclinations were not so far off. Many have noted that in the age of the New Negro the quality of the housing stock had been one of the delights of Harlem, where former sharecroppers sometimes found themselves in distinguished houses originally intended for various levels of suburban bourgeoisie. Later, speaking to a man outside my doorstep after I'd moved to Lenox Avenue, I asked how he'd felt upon arriving in Harlem from down south. With the astonishment of his initial impression still intact, he said that he *could not believe people lived like that.*

Nella Larsen, in *Quicksand*, foreshadows the eventual tragedy of her heroine's inflated outlook when Helga Crane searches for her first domicile in Harlem: *She eschewed the "Y" as too bare, impersonal and restrictive. Nor did furnished rooms or the idea of a solitary or a shared apartment appeal to her.* When Helga has the good fortune to be taken in as the houseguest of a Harlem society maven, Larsen devotes lavish detail on *the furnishings which so admirably graced the big cream-colored rooms.*

Beds with long, tapering posts to which tremendous age lent dignity and interest, bonneted old highboys, tables that might be by Duncan Phyfe, rare spindle-legged chairs, and others whose ladder backs gracefully climbed the delicate wall panels. These historic things mingled harmoniously and comfortably with brass-bound Chinese tea-chests, luxurious deep chairs and davenports, tiny tables of gay color, a lacquered jade-green settee with gleaming black satin cushions, lustrous Eastern rugs, ancient copper, Japanese prints, some fine etchings, a profusion of precious bric-a-brac, and endless shelves filled with books.

Despite such refined surroundings, Helga slips into a malaise that erodes her belief that she had found, in Harlem, a haven of peace and contentment.

Little by little the signs of spring appeared, but strangely the enchantment of the season, so enthusiastically, so lavishly greeted by the gay dwellers of Harlem, filled her only with restlessness. Somewhere within her, in a deep recess, crouched discontent. She began to lose confidence in the fullness of her life, the glow began to fade from her conception of it. As the days multiplied, her need of something, something vaguely familiar, but which she could not put a name to and hold for definite examination, became almost intolerable. She went through moments of overwhelming anguish. She felt shut in, trapped.

Helga Crane, and Lutie Johnson, of Ann Petry's *The Street*, are separated by nearly two decades, about twenty blocks, the strictures of intraracial social caste, several shades of skin color, and perhaps as many degrees in expectations. When Lutie searches for a place to live and raise her son, she does not consider existential disenchantment. She is already resigned to her limited options when being shown, by a lecherous building superintendent under the beam of a flashlight, *the dark, dirty, three rooms called an apartment.* The wretchedness is evident even as she climbs the staircase, littered with trash. Before she has even reached the rooms, which are, predictably, *barely large enough to walk around in,* Petry's scene of Lutie's ascent illustrates the same sense of enclosure that Helga found in Harlem's streets:

> The farther up they went, the colder it got. And in the summer she supposed it would get hotter and hotter as you went up until when you reached the top floor your breath would be cut off completely.... The halls were so narrow that she could reach out and touch them on either side without having to stretch her arms any distance. When they reached the fourth floor, she thought, instead of her reaching out for the walls, the walls were reaching out for her—bending and swaying toward her in an effort to envelop her.

Now when I think of the room I did not rent, I think of the wall that made it so narrow. It must have been a false wall, a partition to divide a formerly grand parlor into two small units. I had read of the warm-bed system by which, during the height of the Great Migration, lodgers doubled up in rented rooms all over Harlem, sharing sleeping arrangements according to whether they worked day or night shifts. I had read also of the time-honored practice in Harlem of charging too much for quarters too cramped for a peaceful existence. Despite having read all that, my astonishment was opposite to that of recent arrivals in decades past: I could not believe people lived like that. On the other side of the wall in that SRO, there might have been someone sitting in another room. It, too, was too narrow, and too short. There was no original fireplace—and, perhaps, also no dream of fire.

———————

When I lived in the house on 120th Street, sometimes I did not leave Harlem for weeks at a stretch. I didn't need to: my new job was only three blocks from my home. I would walk back to my apartment for lunch, and I didn't have much money to spend exploring the rest of the city. When I was in need of entertainment I found plenty to do above 110th Street. Sometimes this felt like a comfort—I was cosseted by those streets. By restricting my own movements I avoided the complication that a life lived in the whole of the city would later bring. But for me this was a choice. One of my new acquaintances around the corner was a teenage girl who went to school in deepest Brooklyn and made an epic underground journey there and back each school day, but had never in her brief life been to Greenwich Village.

I was always in the streets in those days, and they were usually filled with lively and amusing scenes. But once, walking down Lenox, I passed a large family group sitting outside their building to escape the summer's heat. There were people of all ages, from toddlers to grandparents. I noticed in particular a tiny girl entertaining herself in an inspired moment of make-believe; she was chattering with great animation into a pay phone. No sooner had I noticed her at play, than a man in the group, perhaps her father, had noticed her, too, and he rushed up behind the child to punish her, shocking her out of that mime with severe blows about the back of her legs. It all happened so quickly, her face contorted with terrible shrieks, the receiver dangled as she was reprimanded. I do not record this so that it should stand in for all little girls in Harlem or all fathers in Harlem, but because, as that scene played out before my eyes, those substitutions *were* made, all at once.

Only one thing crossed my mind, and it arrived without the intervention of any rational thought: *Burn it down.* At that moment, I wanted any place in any corner of the universe that could contain what I'd just seen to no longer exist.

Sometimes I remembered a line from Ntozake Shange's play *for colored girls who have considered suicide when the rainbow is enuf.* The words had puzzled me when I read them as a teenager in Texas. A character remarks: *I usedta live in the world, but then I moved to Harlem, and my universe is now six blocks.*

And elsewhere, the poet Melvin Tolson mused: *Black boy / O black boy, / Was the port worth the cruise?*

During the years when New York was swelling with newcomers from Europe's shores, Victoria Earle Matthews established a refuge specializing in the welfare of those not included among Lady Liberty's huddled masses. Mrs. Matthews—prominent in New York's black society and the daughter of a Georgia slave—founded the White Rose Home in 1897, providing classes in cooking and sewing to black women along with meals and education to children of the black poor. The White Rose was similar to the mission societies and settlement houses then opening in New York for the uplift and assimilation of immigrants from southern and eastern Europe. It filled a need those other charities did not address, for at the White Rose, *sometimes a few little Italians and Jewish children come in with the others and they are never turned away. But the settlement is there for the dark-skinned little Americans who are not very welcome elsewhere.*

Mrs. Matthews expanded this program of good works when she was called upon by a friend to give hospitality to a young girl from Jacksonville, Florida, arriving in New York to seek employment. Victoria Matthews arranged to meet the girl at the dock;

the young traveler would wear a red ribbon drawn through a buttonhole in her coat. According to the memoir of a White Rose Home associate writing in 1925:

> Although Mrs. Matthews was at the dock promptly, one of those unprincipled men who haunted the wharves in those days (and to some extent do so still), managed to seize upon the girl and lure her away from the wharf. To the most earnest inquiries only one answer was received—yes, such a girl was aboard but nothing had been seen of her since the boat landed. A general alarm was sent out but nothing was heard of the girl until she wandered back to the wharf after three days. She could not locate the place to which she had been taken, but her experience was sad and bitter. She was sent back home and Mrs. Matthews resolved that she would use all her energies in seeking to prevent another such disastrous occurrence.

Thus, the White Rose Industrial Association took up its new mission, to be a *friend of the strange girl in New York*, a sanctuary for the migrant. *Let us call it White Rose*, Mrs. Matthews declared. *I shall always feel that the girls will think of the meaning—purity, goodness and virtue and strive to live up to our beautiful name.* Acting as an unauthorized society for the aid of travelers, Mrs. Matthews and her collaborators took turns at the pier in order to meet every steamer of the Old Dominion line arriving from the principal southern port of Norfolk, Virginia. They delivered the witless and lonely travelers out of the hands of job sharks and into a setting where they would find *pleasant lodgings for girls with privilege of music and reading rooms, dining room, kitchen and laundry* offered at reasonable rates. In some cases, the neediest wayfarers were housed for free. By 1925, more than 30,000 girls and young women had passed through the doors of the White Rose Home. *Some were well educated, earnest, of sterling worth, capable and willing to take care of themselves, needing only the advice and encouragement of a good woman. Others were in need of help in many ways. They had no money, no knowledge of the ways of a great city, no friends.* They were *sheltered, guided, fed, clothed when necessary, many taught to work acceptably in the homes of the Metropolis and many others saved from lives of shame.*

The original White Rose Home was located on the Upper East Side. By 1918, when the black population of New York was in the midst of its move to Harlem, the White Rose Home followed, leasing and then purchasing a brownstone on West 136th Street. When young women like Emma Lou, Lutie, Helga Crane, and Pinkie arrived in Harlem, they could find a warm bed and companionship in its elegant rooms. But the White Rose was more than an employment agency or a rooming house; it also provided moral guidance. How the custodians of the home kept their charges away from the nearby speakeasies, taverns, and ballrooms is unrecorded.

The young women received assistance in job placement and classes in "Race History." Whereas the domestic training was necessary for the new arrivals to make a living in the very limited field of work available to black women, the classes in literature and "Race History" were a particular passion of Mrs. Matthews. She was a writer and an intellectual; her own development had been encouraged by an employer who interrupted her in reverie while she was supposed to be dusting books in his library. In 1905, the original White Rose Home was said to possess *one of the most unique special libraries in New York.* It included works by Booker T. Washington, Charles Chestnutt, and Paul Laurence Dunbar; rare volumes like a 1773 second edition of Phillis Wheatley's poetry; a bound edition of the 1859 *Anglo-African Magazine*, which gave an account of John Brown's raid on Harper's Ferry and his subsequent trial and execution; and several narratives of escaped slaves.

If Matthews provided the tools of domesticity, including *a good stock of aprons, dust caps, dusters etc always on hand,* her library and classes held their own utility. *Our history and individuality as a people not only provide material for masterly treatment, but would seem to make a Race Literature a necessity as an outlet for unnaturally suppressed inner lives which our people have been compelled to lead.*

The library of the White Rose Home provided a shelter for souls, based on the conviction that racial uplift could be accomplished by young women whose only value in the white world was as maids.

Thus she hoped to inspire in them confidence in their group and in themselves — confidence and a hope that she believed would incite them to noble thoughts and great ideas and deeds. Who dares to estimate to what extent her dream was realized?

The seventieth anniversary of the White Rose Home was celebrated in 1967 on the society pages of the *Amsterdam News,* in an article that bordered notices about a Mardi Gras ball, the installation of new officers at the Imperial Elks Home, marriage announcements, and the Founder's Day festivities for a sorority. In addition to its purpose to avert the perdition of innocents, the White Rose had also become something of a society enterprise. The archives of the White Rose held at the Schomburg Center preserve the records of regular garden parties, annual linen showers, "gypsy teas" featuring performances of operettas, and a "tea bag festival" that raised money for roof repair by imploring invited guests to "drop herein three pennies for every year old."

Upon its 1967 anniversary, the house on 136th Street still received lodgers in its dormitory rooms, which could be *decorated to the taste of the occupant*. The whole house had been recently renovated, reported the *Amsterdam News*.

> The rooms retain their soft, nostalgic glow with its home-like atmosphere. Pale yellow walls in the first floor meeting room provide a cheerful background for the mahogany paneling and treasured antiques, one a chair from the home of the founder is one of the most revered pieces...

The article is illustrated by a picture of three members of the White Rose Home and Industrial Association and a clergyman attending the anniversary occasion. They flank the empty chair of Victoria Earle Matthews—one woman lays a hand upon its seat, as if in supplication to a holy relic.

One day I went to find the White Rose Home. It had been operational—in name, at least—into the early 1980s. I found it on a street of brownstones that were plain and modest in comparison with the distinctive manses of nearby Striver's Row. Arrangement of silk flowers adorned the exterior window boxes. The building was well kept, and the address was fixed to the front in oversized gilt numbers. I thought of knocking on the door to gain entry. Instead I stood across the street to have a better view. Soon, a man came to the house, walked up the stairs, and went in. I tried to look as though I was not paying unusual attention to his home, while half wishing it had been open to receive me upon arriving in Harlem with a suitcase full of tales.

Searching for the Underground City

I FOUND A PICTURE in the digital archive of the library. The circumstances were not extraordinary; I was not looking for anything in particular. I had merely typed the word "Harlem" into the image archive to see what it would yield.

The picture shows an intersection, but nothing about the juncture is immediately recognizable. A large apartment building sits in the background, and in the foreground stand a man and a boy. The back of the man is turned against the camera, the boy is in partial profile; they are watching the scene coming toward them and toward me.

The scene is only people walking; it is not remarkable. The men all wear dark suits with waistcoats, and fedoras or newsboy caps. There is a woman in the group wearing a skirt of black organdy that shines against the dominating flatness in view. Another group stands under the awning of a storefront, their backs also turned against the camera. The store's sign — w. a. HOLLEY PHARMACIST — is crowded alongside advertisements for Coca-Cola and other billboards. One promotes a new comedy

A street scene close to the 135th Street Branch of the New York Public Library, 1920. (Courtesy of Schomburg Center for Research in Black Culture / Photographs and Prints Division, The New York Public Library, Astor, Lenox, and Tilden Foundations)

called *39 East*. At ground level is a sign for STRAW HATS, a partially obscured sign for a cigar shop, and another sign, DRUGS. At the left edge of the frame is the slightest suggestion of street furniture: a lamppost or subway entrance. There is an unidentifiable piece of debris on the pavement. Most people in the picture walk determinedly, in the typical city-dweller's trance, but one walker—forever caught in the middle distance—is worth noting. His hands are in his pockets, his upper body torques as if he is turning, midstep, to greet a friend. There is something familiar in his stance. It is the strut of a Harlem dandy, and his descendants can still be seen on the streets. Although the quality of the photo is poor and the camera is too far away to capture any defining features, there is the faintest flash of white where his mouth would be. He is in the middle of a shout or a smile.

An apartment building occupies the background on the far side of the intersection. Just visible in a few of the upper-story windows are figures looking out from their apartments—people surveying the happenings on the street, keeping watch from within. No one looks at the camera. I can tell from the clothing of the walkers that the picture dates to the 1910s. The shadows should tell me the time of day, but I can't decipher the angle at which they fall.

It is a Harlem street scene. It is another Harlem street scene. It is not an especially crowded scene, so it does not tell the story of Harlem's legendary crowdedness. The people are elegantly dressed, so it does not tell the story of Harlem's legendary destitution. The comedy advertised on the billboard is the movie adaptation of a 1919 stage play of no great distinction—the story of a minister's daughter who comes to New York, lives in a boarding house, winds up a chorus girl, and then falls in love—so it does not tell the story of Harlem's legendary artistic outpouring of racial consciousness.

In fact, the story that captured my attention was not told by the photograph itself but by its caption. The picture is titled *Within Thirty Seconds Walk of the 135th Street Branch*. Nothing indicates whether these words were fixed to this image by its maker or by its cataloguer. It gives information not contained within the frame: there is no street sign in view alerting us that this corner is the intersection of 135th Street and Lenox Avenue. For the caption's author, the crucial thing was not the exact location—we do not learn whether you could reach this scene by walking north, south, east, or west. Essentially, the caption does not describe what the photo shows. Instead, it offers a lesson about perspective that has nothing to do with the position of the photographer's camera. According to the caption, the people we are looking at, and their various activities, are not of primary importance. The scene is important only in relation to what is nearby. For the author of the caption, defining this image for the official record, the crucial thing was time: thirty seconds was all it took to go out and meet this scene. Its significance is in its distance from the library; all things in the street refer back to the library, just as the hour of the day around the world is determined by one's distance from Greenwich. I scan the image looking for some other sign and wonder how many times I have hurried over that very spot.

It has the character of a clue from a treasure hunt: *Within thirty seconds' walk of the 135th Street Branch you will find....* But there is a tear in the parchment. It is not possible to hunt treasure with such incomplete instructions. Within thirty seconds' walk of the library you find a Halal grill cart manned by Egyptians, and West African women standing at the subway entrance selling the *Daily News* and *New York Post*. Walk in another direction and you find the Yemeni bodega where I go for tea and junk food while working at the library. At the intersection of 135th and Lenox, within thirty seconds' walk of the library, I once found a man toting a portable xylophone who offered to play me a song. He walked with me in the direction of my building, chiming his keys, but he would not tell me, when I asked, the name of the tune he played. He acted as though it were an insult to ask and a blasphemy to answer.

Within thirty seconds' walk of the library, just near the corner of 136th Street, a handsome and serious-looking African man sells incense, perfume oils, and shea butter. Watching him during my breaks from the library, I notice that usually he is not minding his wares, but sits planted beneath a sidewalk tree reading the Koran, making notes, and manipulating a length of prayer beads. I imagine him to be a diligent scholar of Islamic law and wonder how he came to be a street merchant outside the library. One day, taking my break under a nearby tree, I saw that he'd been joined at his station and in his activity by two attentive students. I could not hear his voice, but the tender incantations of his young charges, timidly repeating their lessons for review, carried over the sound of traffic from that makeshift classroom beneath a shade tree. First they answered in concert, then each child spoke alone. The smaller of the two boys struggled to stay focused. He scribbled hurriedly in his composition book when his eyes were not darting up and into the crowd, as if searching for clues in the faces of the people streaming by.

Before moving to Harlem, I often visited the library as a college student, during trips to New York. At the time I didn't think of this as "going to Harlem," because I was "going to the library." Technically, when setting out on such journeys I was already in Harlem, because I always stayed with a boyfriend who lived just north of Columbia University. If I'd been more enterprising, I could have walked to the library or taken a series of buses, but instead I'd take the local 1 or 9 line from its elevated tracks at 125th Street and Broadway downtown to 96th Street. From there, I would then take the express train back uptown to 135th Street and Lenox, via the 2 or 3 line, which deposited me directly at the library door.

When I came up from the station, it was necessary to get my bearings. This was not difficult—on one side of the intersection at 135th and Lenox was the hospital, on the other side was the library. I could invent for you the street scene of a decade past, some loud summer noise or curious encounter, but they would be just that, inventions, because I don't remember a thing. I don't remember a thrill that was specific to being in Harlem. The thrill was in the library. Harlem was the place I rushed past to meet it. The library was my true destination.

Once inside, I settled into my work. My research at the time was scattered but intense. I went to the library armed with a list of topics, usually for some writing project that was never accomplished. The library was where I read the history of the Scottsboro trial. I read about the cult of the Black Madonna shrines scattered throughout Europe, deciphering the controversy about whether the faces of the Madonna statues had been black intentionally, perhaps hearkening back to dark-goddess worship beginning with Isis, or whether the images had become blackened through the operation of time and the residue of smoke from candles burned by her devotees. I studied minstrel shows. I read about the Great Migration and about the public execution of a twelve-year-old slave girl in 1786. All of these subjects consumed me at the time, the answers to a series of questions whose urgency I have since forgotten. Even though the hours spent at the library in those years did not produce any tangible achievement, my pilgrimages were carried out with a great sense of purpose: I was in the place I needed to be in order to know all things. But my visits to the city were brief. I would leave the library and dash out past Harlem, back to New York.

Looking through my own old photographs I found a strange souvenir of those days, a picture I do not remember making of a vista I don't recall having admired. It is a street scene, a Harlem street scene. It shows the intersection of 135th and Lenox Avenue—looking south down Lenox and taken from a slightly elevated view. When I first discovered the picture, it took some moments to understand how I could have achieved such an angle. Looking closer, a slight glare revealed that it was taken through a window. I soon realized only one place could have offered this particular vantage point: the library. Perhaps I'd abandoned my research that day and had been staring out the window. But I was looking out at nothing in particular, it seems. I did not train my lens on an event taking place in the distance or on any specific person. The clothes of the people in the street reveal that it was winter. There are no shadows by which to tell the time of day.

———

Another picture in the library shows the point of departure for that thirty-second journey. It is the reading room of the 135th Street Branch, in 1935. A group of fashionable aesthetes are gathered for a portrait. They sit in a formal semicircle, with some in chairs and others standing behind in a second row.

The static composure of these figures suggests none of the clamor that could be found in the intersection just a few yards away. The *Staff and friends of the Negro Division of the 135th Street Library* occupy a distant realm. The gentlemen sit with legs placidly crossed and arms folded in their laps, the women tuck their ankles in quiet propriety. One man wears white spats over his shoes; some of the women hold pocketbooks. The ladies are coiffed with hairstyles plastered into finely marcelled curls. One woman's dress fastens with a multitude of buttons, another woman wears a corsage. In the center of the room is an Italian marble sculpture of the great nineteenth-century actor Ira Aldridge as Othello at the moment when he mournfully clutches Desdemona's handkerchief. Around the room, framed pictures hang salon-style, and bronze busts decorate the tops of bookshelves. In the background, African masks jut out from the wall. Standing in the back row, unassuming, is Arthur Schomburg, the man whose collection was housed in that library, the man whose search for origins made the place a destination.

What became the Schomburg Center for Research in Black Culture began as the 135th Street Branch of the New York Public Library. Indeed, the now world-renowned special collection was, at first, just a few files of newspaper clippings on black history, curated by a white librarian, Ernestine Rose, and her black assistant, Catherine Latimer. Upon arriving at that post in 1920, at the moment when the slowly accumulating mass of blacks was beginning to assert its permanence and purpose in Harlem, Ernestine Rose devoted herself to creating a facility that might answer the question posed by the crowd in the streets outside. As she saw it, *Instead of considering the Negro problem shall we not treat the Negroes as individuals, with the opportunities and restrictions only which surround all individuals?*

If the street was the place where black Harlem constituted "the Negro problem," where people were only of sociological interest, then the library would be a temple of the individual, worshipping the personal aspirations and collective triumphs of black people and their culture. The purpose of the 135th Street Branch, articulated early on by Rose, was *to preserve the historical records of the race; to arouse the race consciousness and race pride; to inspire art students [and] to give information to everyone about the Negro.*

Rose and Latimer set up a program of poetry readings and book discussions, and, most important, they began to build a small collection of books, periodicals, and clippings related to the history of black people in Africa and America. The novelist Nella Larsen worked there as a librarian. The young poets Countee Cullen and Langston Hughes were regular patrons. Of course, a great many other seekers whose purposes and accomplishments will never be known also came to the library. The black history collection soon became so popular that the librarians, after consulting with a committee of local intellectuals, removed the items from general circulation in the lending library, keeping them on the upper floor of the branch, where they could only be retrieved for reference on the premises. The few books available on black history were so frequently used and so much in demand that many hard-to-find and irreplaceable books were read until they fell apart.

Readers at work in the Schomburg Room of the 135th Street branch library, ca. 1926. (Courtesy of New York Public Library Archives, The New York Public Library, Astor, Lenox, and Tilden Foundations)

By the time this mania for the black past was unfolding at the 135th Street Branch library, Arthur Schomburg was already a noted bibliophile, well known for the breadth and value of his collection and the ardor with which he pursued it. Schomburg belonged to a circle of "race men" who were also book fiends, sharing and trading recent acquisitions. Before there was such a thing as the New Negro movement, he had cofounded the Negro Society for Historical Research, was a member of the Negro Book Collectors Exchange, and had served as president of the American Negro Academy. These organizations were all ambitious in their aims, and they were all short-lived, but their existence tells us much about the spirit of their age. The desire of these men to uncover the forgotten history of black people was matched by a desire to protect and steward that knowledge.

The books and documents Schomburg and his colleagues hunted were precious, and they had to compete with better-funded white collectors. According to one account, Schomburg once refused to sell his collection to a wealthy white man because the prospective buyer wouldn't reveal his plans for the materials. Upon learning that many white institutions had impressive collections of historic black books, Schomburg wrote to a friend, *You would be surprised to know that libraries in the South who bar the Negro's admittance have a large amount of his literature.*

Arturo Alfonso Schomburg was a native of Puerto Rico, born to a German father and a black mother. His interest in black history was sparked when a teacher told him that black people had no history. By the time he was living in Brooklyn and making a respectable, middle-class living as a mail clerk at a bank, he was still passionately attempting to refute that charge. Schomburg was said to have a magic sense that guided his quest for new material, spending his lunch hours and weekends digging through New York's antiquarian bookstores. In his search for treasures, Schomburg corresponded with other collectors around the country and abroad, including Haiti and Liberia. He drafted friends into his research, sending requests to travelers like James Weldon Johnson, Langston Hughes, and Alain Locke when they were just about to depart for sojourns in Europe. He also traveled around the country, partly because of his duties as a Freemason.

In addition to collecting, Schomburg produced monographs and papers on neglected black figures from world history. His pamphlet *Is Hayti Decadent?* investigated the political situation of that country leading up to and in the midst of the American occupation. He researched and wrote of notable men of African descent who made important but sometimes forgotten contributions to world history, including the Chevalier de Saint-Georges, the Guadeloupe-born composer and courtier; Antonio Maceo, a black officer in the struggle for Cuban independence from Spain; Alessandro, the Florentine duke who was known as "the Negro Medici"; and Leo Africanus, the Moorish geographer from Granada, a place Schomburg visited during his only journey to Europe.

In 1925, the 135th Street Branch library hosted an exhibition featuring a small assortment of Schomburg's collection. *There is a Negro exhibit at the New York Public Library*, one report began. *Within a dozen cases there lies the story of a race. A dozen cases, narrow, shallow, compressed and yet through their clear glass tops there shines that which arrests, challenges, commands attention.*

Writing of that same exhibition, without mentioning that the collection on display was his own, Schomburg issued what may have been a challenge to that old schoolteacher who had robbed him of his claim to history:

> Not long ago, the Public Library of Harlem housed a special exhibition of books, pamphlets, prints and old engravings, that simply said, to skeptic and believer alike, to scholar and schoolchild, to proud black and astonished white, "Here is the evidence."

The exhibit was so well received that in 1926 the New York Public Library, with a grant from the Carnegie Corporation, purchased the entire collection for $10,000. The Schomburg accession included more than 5,000 books, 3,000 rare manuscripts, 2,000 etchings and portraits, clippings albums, and several thousand pamphlets. Among the treasures were original manuscripts of poems by Paul Laurence Dunbar; an original, signed edition of Phillis Wheatley's poems; and an original proclamation of Haitian independence, signed by Toussaint L'Ouverture.

Schomburg's collection was added to the existing holdings at the 135th Street Branch, forming the New York Public Library's Division of Negro History, Literature, and Prints. Though he relinquished ownership of his collection, Schomburg did not give up its stewardship or his quest. He continued to acquire items and in 1932 was appointed curator of the Negro Division, overseeing the fulfillment of his vision until his death in 1938.

The original 135th Street Branch building still stands. It is one of several libraries in Harlem dating back to the philanthropic atonements of the Gilded Age, all funded by Andrew Carnegie and all featuring facades in the Palladian style. The Schomburg Center was enlarged in 1977. The new addition was made to connect to the old building via an atrium, though its style does not at all communicate with the old one—one is a civilizing fantasy of the European Renaissance, the other a purifying fantasy of Afrocentric brutalism. After the library closes in the evening, the upper rooms of the old library remain lit. Walking across 135th Street at night, I am often startled by shadows that can be seen through the ivy-covered windows. They are only busts and statues in a windowsill—their silhouettes throw outlines against the drawn blinds. But at first they look like moving figures, busy in the library after dark.

Long before Arthur Schomburg dreamed of his library, a retail space of the St. Phillips Apartments, just a few doors away at 135 West 135th Street, housed the first black bookstore in Harlem. George Young's Book Exchange came to be known as the "Mecca of Literature Pertaining to Colored People." A pilgrim there would find nothing less than the holy books of the New Negro—not only histories written by blacks, but also any book the proprietor could find with enlightening references to Africa, which were often written by abolitionists and explorers. *Revealing volumes expressed the consciousness of Africa and marshaled evidence of early African culture and its significant contribution to Europe and the world in crushing refutation of the racist theories of inequality.* Typical of the bookstore's offerings were universal histories of black people documented by Joel Augustus Rogers in *From Superman to Man* and by W. E. B. DuBois in *The Negro*. Both titles can still be purchased from Young's heirs, the West African book vendors who operate from folding tables all along 125th Street. Young was also a publisher, and among the works bearing his imprint was an edition of the inaugural address given by Edwin Wilmot Blyden on January 5, 1881, at his swearing-in as president of Liberia College; William Lloyd Garrison's treatise on *The loyalty and devotion of colored Americans in the revolution and war of 1812;* and *The mote and the beam: an epic on sex-relationship 'twixt white and Black in British South Africa.*

A few decades later, Lewis Michaux opened his National Memorial African Bookstore at the corner of 125th Street and Seventh Avenue. Signs above its storefront, captured in many photographs, blared its significance as the "House of Common Sense," the "Home of Proper Propaganda," and the "World History Book Outlet on 2,000,000,000 (Two Billion) Africans and Non-White Peoples." An American flag was placed out front, and so was a sign urging passersby to "Register Here," for it was also the "Repatriation Headquarters for the Back to Africa Movement." The area in front of Michaux's bookstore was called Harlem Square; it was the starting point or endpoint of many street marches and a place where rallies convened and impromptu street speakers held court.

Michaux's iconic bookstore is gone, but when I arrived in Harlem another famous destination for black thought was still in existence. Liberation Bookstore, at the corner of 131st and Lenox, dates back to the late 1960s. Its proprietor, Una Mulzac, recalled to a journalist the trouble brought on by her store's name. *When I first thought of opening a bookstore and calling it "Liberation" I met with a lot of comments and discouragement from certain people about the name. They said I shouldn't call it liberation. I would be inviting trouble, I should name it after myself or my father or just call it "Bookstore."*

My father remembers making special trips to New York to visit the shop during his college days. I passed it many times before I ever went in — often the door was locked, and it seemed to operate on an irregular schedule. When I finally did visit, I found the elderly Ms. Mulzac minding the store alone. She was happy to have a visitor and make conversation, and she was still fiercely dedicated to propagating the knowledge whose importance blared on several posters decorating the store windows and facade. By the time I returned there, the irregular business hours of the bookstore had apparently ceased altogether. I heard that Ms. Mulzac was ill and noticed piles of mail accumulating in a heap inside the door. I copied down the words from signs in the windows and the titles of books that could be seen through the glass. Later I passed and saw a small hole in the window, surrounded by the spiderweb pattern of shattered glass. I heard a rumor that all the books inside were going to be sold off. Soon the old, faded sign was whitewashed, and someone made a half-hearted attempt to cover the windows with newspaper. But the books remained inside, untouched, for a long while to come.

Now, when I go to the library, I do not make such a tortuous journey. I live just minutes away, and it is not even necessary to turn a corner. One of the security guards, Mr. Kingston, always greets me with kind words and a smile. When I leave, he bids me good-bye with a wish for safe travels. Once I told him it would only be two blocks before I reached my door, and he said he wished me safety all the same.

Some time passed before I knew Julius Bobby Nelson by name. This is because when I first arrived on Lenox Avenue, I did not know anyone and was not known by anyone. When I passed into and out of my front door, the people standing at my stoop would part to let me enter and part to let me leave. For a long time, little was exchanged between us except *excuse me* and *thank you*. I didn't know who they were or where they lived, these older people who stood facing Lenox Avenue during the day, or the younger ones who came at night to guard the same spots. But they seemed to belong there more than I did, provoking in me the impulse to apologize for my presence at my own front door. I was not used to living in the middle of it all, right there on the avenue with only the thinnest of veils to pass through before meeting the world.

Eventually I did begin to know my neighbors and be known by them, but this process happened by degrees. I came to know Ms. Bessie and some of the others, even those who eyed me with suspicion at first and did not speak unless I insisted on it. Sometimes I would pause when going out or pause before going in; this became my habit, so I was often late to wherever I was going on account of having paused at my door to chat.

I don't remember if I was going out or coming in the day I met Julius Bobby Nelson. I don't even remember for certain if what I am about to tell you happened on the day we formally met, or if it is simply a day I remember with some clarity because what he said compelled me to write it down. I would have already known his face by then, and he would have known mine. It was spring. I had probably stopped under the tree to speak with Ms. Bessie or Ms. Minnie when Julius Bobby Nelson got my attention and beckoned me to him with a pull of his eyes and his hand and a flick of his chin. I knew he wanted me to come closer and listen.

To listen well one must come close indeed, for his speech is somewhat impeded. I am not sure of the reason, but the longer I listened, the clearer he became and the more I understood. Sometimes I heard him with a tantalizing clarity, but then a crucial word would disappear into the back of his mouth, never reaching my ear. Before I knew him by name, I knew him by this manner of speaking; in my head I thought of him as the Mumbler. He did not seem bothered by or necessarily aware of my difficulty in understanding him. I never noticed anyone else having this difficulty. When I still knew him as the Mumbler, we had at least one exchange: he told me that he was *a champ,* that he'd been *almost pro.* I never did ask what he was a champion of. I assumed it was boxing, and I assumed that was why he spoke the way he did.

On the day I learned his name, Julius Bobby Nelson beckoned to me and said, *I live here...I grew up here,* and I knew immediately he did not mean the city or even our neighborhood, but the block in which we stood. He is a tall man, and as he stood there, it was like he stood on the whole block all at once. He waved his large hand in a gesture only slightly more dramatic than the one that drew me into his audience. He took the whole block into view, indicating the breadth of his knowledge and the passage of time. He told me that his mother and father had lived in No. 469 — the building adjacent to mine — his sister had lived in No. 471, and his school had been P.S. 89, the Douglass School. He pointed out the Douglass School, which was no longer there. We both faced the direction of where it was not, on the southwest corner of 135th Street and Lenox Avenue, directly across from the library, where a tall apartment building now stood.

He mentioned names and characters and happenings without any explicit suggestion of their significance. It was in this way I learned about the *gypsies,* about the *guinea Italian* in the cigar shop who wouldn't sell him a hot dog, about *Dick's liquor,* and about *Chicken*

Joe and *the butcher*. It was in this way I learned that *they didn't kill the white lady at the school*. At the time, these facts hung together in a manner that fails in the retelling, and you will understand that I did not stop him to ask who were *they* or who was *the white lady* or under what circumstances did they not kill her at the school.

To point in a different direction was to land upon another set of disjointed facts. He pointed across the street where Lenox Terrace is now, and he said *I built it* and he said *bricks* and he said *twenty-year lease* and he said *horse and carriage*. As before, I did not stop him to beg for clarification. He told me that his nine brothers had lived across the street, he said something about the *all-boys school* on 119th (he said *'19th*) while looking down the avenue in that direction. When his eyes came back to rest on me he said, *I live here. I grew up here. I know all of it.*

Julius Bobby Nelson told me more of what he knew, and I continued not to understand all of what he told me. He said he was born in Charleston, South Carolina, and later, when I went inside and wrote this part down, I noted that *he repeated it with a certain glint in his eye*. He told me about a river, but I did not understand the name of it, and his repetitions did not help. Ms. Barbara was sitting there under the tree with us, and she understood what I did not. He was talking about the Cooper River, she said, and she asked *What about that river?* Whether he answered or what was the meaning, I did not record. *Some importance was attached it,* I noted, *or merely my own curiosity.* He returned to more immediate geography. First he pointed northeast to the Franklin Theatre on 135th Street just off Lenox, which is now a church, then to another theater, the Lincoln, on 132nd Street behind McDonald's, which is now an empty shell.

He pointed behind me, and for a moment I did not turn in that direction. I knew he was pointing at the funeral home on the next block. He said he was friends with *the man*—I don't know if he meant the proprietor or the man being buried that day. It was then he began to present riddles even stranger than before. *Watch the walking, not the dead,* he told me, and I had to have him repeat it. *The ones who are walking, not the ones lying down,* he said. I asked him to run it by me one more time, and then he said something about having *laid a body out.*

I am what I am, he told me. *I am the law.*

That was it. Was there anything more to say? Thus did God rebuke the impudence of Moses, when he dared to ask the unspeakable name. I went inside. Later that afternoon I left the house again and I saw Julius again, and he began again: *I am what I am who I am.*

Now Ms. Bessie was sitting under the tree. He pointed to her and said he knew her son, her daughter, her daughter-in-law, and a long list of other relatives. Ms. Bessie nodded to affirm his knowledge of her whole family. I did not doubt he could tell me the name of every person who had ever lived on the block. *I know everybody,* he said, and pointed again in the direction of the funeral home, as if to continue the point he had begun earlier. Clearer than anything else he said that day, he asked, *See that hearse over there?*

My notes drop off here. I didn't write down what he told me about the hearse or who was in it. I did write down that Julius Bobby Nelson mumbled something more about the South and about Mississippi, but those were the only words I made out. I did not speculate as to what he meant to tell me, *but I was sure it was something pertinent.* Once, he pointed toward the library but he made sure to indicate that he meant *the old library.*

I went through all the books, he told me. *I've read every book that you've read.*

After that day, we seemed to understand each other. Our conversations take the pattern of a strange dance: he leans in too close and I step back, trying to look as though I am not in retreat; I step in, and his attention is carried off by someone else passing by or by some drama unfolding down the block. Often, Julius Bobby Nelson says something that makes me throw my head back in laughter, only just now I cannot remember any details to pass on the jokes. When I came back after a year's absence, I saw Julius Bobby Nelson and we picked up precisely where we had left off: *the gypsies, I built this, I know everybody.*

Julius Bobby Nelson is not the only one with stories to tell. When I meet Ms. Minnie at the door of our building, she is often alone. She goes out early in the morning to get fresh air. As soon as winter comes, she scolds me for not having enough clothing on. She does not want to see even a triangle of skin between the top button of my coat and the scarf wound about my neck, because she says the tiniest gap is enough space for a cold to get in. If I am bundled up when we meet, she takes equal note—I have heeded her suggestions.

Often our conversations veer back toward her home. Without any specific motivation, she will tell me how they used to make soap out of lye and lard in a cauldron in the backyard and how she used to pile into cars with her girlfriends and drive from South Carolina to Georgia to go to dances. Mostly our conversation happens out of doors, though once—when I passed her standing at her threshold on my way upstairs to my apartment—we spoke and exchanged our usual greetings, and she brought me inside her place. She showed me her collection of precious objects that included delicate Chinese pieces and carved wooden sculptures and heavy antique irons, the kind you'd heat on a wood-burning stove. As she showed me each item and explained its provenance, I was in awe of this unexpected intimacy that rarely accompanies alliances made on the street.

Often Ms. Minnie's stories have the quality of a sudden revelation: we are talking about something that happened yesterday and end up a few decades in the past, back in South Carolina; we are exchanging polite greetings and I end up in her apartment looking at some of her most treasured possessions. Once when I passed her and she asked me about my day, I produced my own unprompted intimacy. It was the birthday of my dead grandmother, Cora. Ms. Minnie, noting the date, March 17, said it was a good number. I was headed inside, but I told her I wanted to show her a picture of my grandmother, so I dashed upstairs, collected it, and then came back down. Someone else was there, so I explained again that it was my grandmother's birthday, though my grandmother was dead. Ms. Minnie looked at the picture and said, *Still, we celebrate.*

She warns me of certain unsavory characters on the block. She says that to get this information you must sit and watch, stop and stare. When she declared that she was street smart, I asked her if she'd always been that way, even when she was new in New York. She said that she had been. Often now, when stopped on the street writing down some detail in fear that it will not be there when I return, I think of Ms. Minnie gathering her information and telling me to stop and stare.

Then there is Monroe. For a long time I did not know his name, so in my head I called him Mr. Mississippi, because he is always asking me, *When are we going to Mississippi?* He asks this because I am always saying I want to go there, and he is always telling me about his home. He is from a place called Yazoo City, near the Mississippi River. Although I have been on that river in New Orleans (staggered by its breadth, its murk, its riverboats advertising a journey back to that more graceful time *when Cotton was King, Sugar was Queen, and Rice was the Lady in Waiting*), in my imagination I've always pictured that when the Mississippi rolls through Yazoo City it is a mere creek, a bit of water trickling through. This might be because Monroe once told me that to get to the house where he grew up you have to cross the river. Something about the way he told it made me think that this was a crossing made as easily as I sometimes jump over puddles by the curb. I later learned that even in Yazoo City, the Mississippi River is still mighty. One day I intend to see that place. Monroe told me that after the river you have to cross railroad tracks. It is a white house on the hill, impossible to miss, and there is a great plum tree there. I like to think that by these particulars I could find my way through Yazoo City to the setting of Monroe's stories, like the time he was trapped in an empty country church as a boy; how he'd gone and sat at the mourner's bench where sinners are supposed to confess and disbelievers are encouraged to abandon the fate of certain damnation. There, he told me, he was attacked by a horde of wasps that descended from the rafters, and he said they'd never before made a sound during Sunday services, when the church was full. As he told it, the story seemed to deliver a great unspoken parable, whose lesson I could not determine. He tells me he knew Emmett Till, and that he used to ride the rails, never venturing too far from home. He left for New York on a truck heading for the strawberry fields upstate, but eventually he made his way to Harlem and did not go back to picking.

One day I ran into him and my simple question of how he was doing was met with a dark glower. It was a bright morning in late summer, but he said he was *in the middle of a storm,* and that *it don't feel good,* and that he was *trying to push it back.*

He was all alone, he said, and it had something to do with people in North Carolina. I didn't understand the reference to North Carolina, since he was from Mississippi, but as soon as I expressed my confusion, he changed the subject.

I dreamed of my home, he said. *My home must have been a devil's town.*

He'd seen a field of cotton, and the cotton heads, the bolls, looked like the heads of snakes. *Then,* he said, *the plane came and killed the cotton.* I did not know what he meant. It killed the cotton?

Don't you know about the boll weevil? he asked. *Do I have to tell you the boll weevil story?* He did not seem to want to tell the boll weevil story, but I knew that the boll weevil had its part in the history of Harlem, because when southern cotton crops were overrun by this scourge that had come from Mexico, many sharecroppers gave up and came north. I didn't mention this, I simply asked with some enthusiasm for him to tell me the boll weevil story.

It's too long, he said. *That's a long story.* He gave me the short version. The boll weevil eats the cotton. The plane comes to kill the cotton. Without any further explanation, he returned to the scene of his dream. The cotton was lying down. *Miles and miles and miles,* he said, *of cotton laying down.* He was in the back seat of a car with two people. *They must have been the devil's disciples,* he said.

That was the end of his dream, or the end of his telling it. He said it made him worried—maybe there would be a hurricane. I told him I wanted to go Yazoo City. He misunderstood me. *You been?*

I told him I hadn't been, yet. He said, *You better go before it's gone. The river is right there! The Mississippi River is* right *there.* This shadow of destruction was overtaken by another. *It's thick with white people. You got to go to a certain part to see black people.* I asked him if it had always been that way, and he said it had been, as long as he'd known. He said the black part was full of black people *shoulder to shoulder, like blackbirds flocking. You ain't seen the blackbirds flocking,* he said. *They fly in and take over the whole space. I would like to see it again.*

That's a long story. Once, my neighbor Ms. Barbara was telling me about growing up in South Carolina on land owned and farmed by her grandparents. She was on her way there to attend the annual family reunion and said the best thing about going back was that all the family still lived on the land, in different parcels nearby, so she didn't even have to get in a car during her whole trip, they just walked back and forth visiting with each other. Ms. Barbara told me I should join her at the reunion one year, and I said I would very much like to. She told me how her grandfather used to own a lot more land and that they'd never had to work for white people, but he had sold it off for $150 per acre. Because she used to help him with his business by doing the receipts, she had suggested he sell for $500 per acre. He had not taken her advice, but he had only sold to blacks.

During the course of her telling me all this, and about which cousins would try to flirt with me at the family reunion and about all the things they used to grow on the land, Ms. Barbara mentioned in passing that she had been born in Harlem but taken back to South Carolina as an infant to be raised by her grandparents, and that she'd come back here as a young woman. It was related as a minor detail, but the thought of Ms. Barbara being born in one place, carried away as a tiny baby, and then returning sounded like an epic.

There are other stories I have forgotten because I didn't write them down, and if I lived on a different block I would be told different stories. This fact strikes me when passing a corner that is not my own, where, in front of the liquor store or the bodega there stand arrayed a group of men — strangers to me, but familiar in disposition. They warily eye my advance until I broach a hello, inviting a chorus of returned salutations. If I tarried a bit longer or invented a reason to pass those other spots with regularity, I might gain a new set of friends and a new set of stories. Another writer might have done just that, trawling each gathering of streetcorner men as doggedly as Arthur Schomburg once searched dusty bookshelves. But I say hello and continue, thinking to mind my own business, thinking I should not turn my daily life into a hunt for "material," and knowing that I could never linger long enough on enough different corners to hear all that everyone had to say.

Once, I was far from my usual circuit — "far" being 127th

Street near 8th Avenue as opposed to 133rd and Lenox. I was not walking slowly; I was not looking for a story. Despite carrying on at a normal pace—with a normal attention to my own business—I heard an old man tell a short yet complete, and completely staggering, tale: *He kicked me in the head and I stabbed that cracker in the heart and he died. My daddy brought me here in the back of a truck.*

It's a long story, indeed.

At times I go to the library on a daily basis, so that when I pass the neighbors on the way—calling out *Good morning* or *Good afternoon*—certain ones of them ask, *Going to the library?* and most of the time I am. My researches there have grown only slightly more focused, so that when I am on assignment and need to learn everything about the history of Liberia in a week's time, or all there is to know about the Haitian Revolution, I spend some days at the library.

When I am bored with my own efforts there is much else of interest. High above the main reading room are the four mural-sized paintings by Aaron Douglas. They portray various stages in "the black experience." The figures are all in silhouette; they don't have faces, and their bodies are dark and angular. But this characteristically modern lack of expressive features does not detract from the anguish of the scene of Africans being kidnapped into bondage, the scene in the cotton fields, or the muscular striving in the scene of blacks moving into the industrialized cities. In the painting depicting slavery, a figure stands apart from the rest. He reaches out with his arm and points into the distance. There are no cardinal directions in a painting, but it is safe to assume that he is pointing north—he is indicating: *Onward!* He leads the way to freedom, and also progress. So when I am discouraged by my own progress, I am reminded to take some of his initiative, look back down at my work, and carry on.

Once, I was looking for information about the numbers game because I never understood my neighbors' attempts to educate me about Harlem's clandestine lottery. On finding me a hopeless pupil, one neighbor abandoned the effort, adding that I didn't need to know about the numbers anyway. This is why I was at the library with Rufus Schatzberg's *Black Organized Crime in Harlem: 1920–1930* open on my desk. Schatzberg, a former New York City police detective who in his retirement acquired a PhD in criminal history, gives an account of petty crime in Harlem as

> a three-way standoff in which the white policeman, racketeer and politician standing on Harlem street corners find themselves at the very center of a silently contemptuous world. There was no way for them not to know it: few things are more unnerving than unspoken hatred and hostility. Thus exposed, they retreat from their uneasiness in only one direction: into callousness and violence that become second nature.

My study effort about the numbers racket was accompanied by other research fulfilling a separate line of inquiry, an article I was writing about the national movement seeking reparations for slavery. So, aside from my extracurricular investigation, among the books which I'd called down that afternoon was *We Charge Genocide*. The book compiles the effort, led by Harlem-based Communist Party leaders William Patterson and Henry Haywood and endorsed by Paul Robeson and W. E. B. DuBois, among many others, to enumerate the crimes committed against black people in America, from lynching and other forms of mob violence to police harassment and brutality. The 1951 document of grievances was presented to the United Nations to lodge a case on human rights violations in the United States.

I must have been moving from one train of thought to the other when a name in the litany of abuses and abusers jumped out at me. One episode mentioned in *We Charge Genocide* was the May 4, 1950, case of a *Mrs. Charles Turner of New York City, prominent proprietor of "Mom's" restaurant.* Mrs. Turner *was beaten by officer Rufus Schatzberg and other unidentified police when she and a very fair-complected Negro man companion, Melvin Barker, were leaving her place of business after closing time. Schatzberg was suspended.* The information stunned me. I could not make any sense of it. There was not any sense to be made. Yet it seemed to suggest an order within the library. Its design was unfathomable and inaccessible from any catalog system—a great labyrinth whose center could only be reached by walking steadily, blindly, with one foot placed in front of the other. One book held the key to another, though it solved a riddle I had not been trying to answer and provided information I did not know how to use. What other mysteries might be unraveled the more often I came and the longer I stayed?

I heard a man ask the librarian for a map of Africa *with the whole thing on it: Tanzania . . . and Khemet.* I heard a different man ask the librarian for a book that would show him a secret underground city in Egypt. The librarian did not know the place and probably suspected, as I did while listening to their exchange, that this secret underground city did not exist. When he insisted, she tried to direct him to the well-known subterranean carved churches of Ethiopia. A library patron who was also a Rastafarian once filled the reference section with his booming lilt. He complained that he shouldn't have to speak softly, or not speak at all, in a library devoted to the culture of black people, because we were originally an oral people whose histories and stories were preserved by speaking. At the microfilm machines I looked over the shoulder of a man who had a fist pick stuck in the back of his Afro: he was looking through reels of old issues of the Black Panther newspaper. I noticed that he paused at certain articles, including "In Defense of Self-Defense," "Breakfast Programs," and "Eldridge on Black Capitalism." The man must have been observing me as closely as I observed him, because later he approached and invited me to attend the weekly meeting of the New Black Panther Party. He said that in preparation I would need to visit www.newblackpanther.com, study the Ten Point Platform, the Nine Objectives, and consult a list of study guides. Because I didn't want to engage him in a long discussion, I accepted his card and nodded when he told me a name I would need to mention at the door, like a password, which I have since forgotten.

It was also at the library that I made the acquaintance of a man who said he was a member of the original Black Panthers, which means, for clarification, more original than the ones from Oakland, and certainly more original than the ones who meet these days in Harlem, under cover of secret codes. As a token, he gave me a copy of the item he had come to the library to find. It was an article in the *New York Times,* in which he himself was quoted. He had marked the quotation with blue asterisks in the margin. The headline said *City Proposal to Rebuild Harlem Gets Stony Community Response.* The dateline was February 3, 1983. *One speaker, David White of United Harlem Growth, described the proposal as "another game trying to get us out."*

He also gave me a photocopied poem called "The Protector (about David White)." The author of that poem was not credited on the page, but a footnote mentioned that

David White was a founding member of the original Black Panther Party started in Harlem, N.Y. Summer, 1966, which had spun from the Loundes [*sic*] County Freedom Organization in Alabama.... This was pre–Huey Newton whose California group had received its orientation from the NYBPP, then developed its own separate agenda.

One section of the poem was pertinent to the newspaper article, describing the forces against which protection was needed:

Flashing through the streets
covering kickbacks
documenting the process of deals made
to demonize the rightful rulers who seek
to grow the community
documenting the process of deals
dealing away what we want and never get

Rape of our village
Rape of our landmarks
Rape of our future
the minds of the children
of all things near and dear
to the underpinning of what sustains
a people filled with hope

I am sometimes distracted by what goes on at the library, but Arthur Schomburg anticipated all this activity in his contribution to Alain Locke's *New Negro* anthology, "The Negro Digs Up His Past." It is worth quoting at length.

The American Negro must remake his past in order to make his future. Though it is orthodox to think of America as the one country where it is unnecessary to have a past, what is a luxury for the nation as a whole becomes a prime social necessity for the Negro. For him, a group tradition must supply compensation for persecution, and pride of race the antidote for prejudice. History must restore what slavery took away, for it is the social damage of slavery that the present generations must repair and offset. So among the rising democratic millions we find the Negro thinking more collectively, more retrospectively than the rest, and apt out of the very pressure of the present to become the most enthusiastic antiquarian of them all. . . .

But they do so not merely that we may not wrongfully be deprived of the spiritual nourishment of our cultural past, but also that the full story of human collaboration and interdependence may be told and realized. Especially is this likely to be the effect of the latest and most fascinating of all of the attempts to open up the closed Negro past, namely the important study of African cultural origins and sources. The bigotry of civilization which is the taproot of intellectual prejudice begins far back and must be corrected at its source. Fundamentally it has come about from that depreciation of Africa which has sprung up from ignorance of her true role and position in human history and the early development of culture. The Negro has been a man without a history because he has been considered a man without a worthy culture. But a new notion of the cultural attainment and potentialities of the African stocks has recently come about.

History must restore what slavery took away. The imperative of these words has chased me since the first time I met them on the page. I was not the only person thus affected: in the copy of *The New Negro* at the library, some other reader, perhaps decades ago, had underlined those very same words. Schomburg proposes a daunting task for the student of history, one that may be beyond satisfaction. Yet when I look up at the various students, scholars, hobbyists, and crusaders working at Mr. Schomburg's library, I know he was accurate in describing the melancholy that compels us all: a yearning for the past from which our ancestors were irrevocably torn. Thus, Rufus Schatzberg, thus Khemet. We are all looking for the underground city. Sometimes it seems the library *is* that city, and we at the library wander its unnamed streets—alone yet in a crowd—walking with our heads down to solve mysteries written on the pavement.

The emblem on the *ex libris* of the older books in the library—the bookplate that labels them as property of the Schomburg Collection—is a new interpretation of the Egyptian winged orb, adapted for some personal myth. The original symbol once guarded the entrances to all the temples in Egypt, thresholds to the underground domain of pharaohs and gods. The symbol celebrates the victory of Horus over Set, the victory of light and goodness over darkness and evil. In the version depicted on the Schomburg bookplate, the traditional orb at the center of the symbol is replaced by a simple drawing of an opened book, with the typically Egyptian wings unfurling from its pages. The Egyptian symbol is also associated with Freemasonry; the bearer of this sign has attained the highest degree of knowledge.

When we consider the facts, certain chapters of American history will have to be reopened. Schomburg had an unyielding faith in the facts, a faith in some latent power to be unleashed once all the facts have finally recovered from oblivion. And now? The facts are there at the library, open for consideration. I have only scratched the surface, stumbling through Mr. Schomburg's labyrinth. I have not even ventured to touch the audio recordings of oral histories and photo collections, the complete correspondences and the boxes archiving the exhaustive research of various long-ago scholars for books that were never written. Schomburg was delighted by what he called *the dust of digging*. But I confess to sometimes feeling buried by it. *So the Negro historian today digs under the spot where his predecessor stood and argued.*

But I remember what Julius Bobby Nelson told me: *Watch the walking, not the dead.* Langston Hughes's ashes are interred under the lobby of the Schomburg Center. Often, the poet's remains are mentioned along with other notable items in the library's holdings, as if they are merely another item on the miles of bookshelves. I am not sure if it was the poet's own desire for his earthly remains to spend eternity beneath the feet of library patrons. I walk gingerly across the expanse of tile beneath which his ashes are sealed, observing as much decorum as possible, when taking a break from various labors in the underground reading room. Fragments of Hughes's poem "The Negro Speaks of Rivers" ring the cosmogram on the floor created in his honor. It is a map of the world, but not an easy one to read. Blue streaks flow from the center. In the poem, the rivers tell time: the Euphrates, the Congo, the Nile, the Mississippi.

The Langston Hughes Atrium is available as a rental facility, so that Hughes's resting place is also the location for receptions, conferences, and cocktail parties. Once I came up from the reading room to find a reception and conference taking place there. It was attended exclusively by Senegalese and was being conducted in French and Wolof. It seemed to be a conference focusing on business and real estate development in Senegal. I would have ignored it, but one of the many displays crowded into the space caught my eye. It showed the map of a vast city. I recognized its name, Touba. Along the stretch of West 116th Street called Little Senegal there is a shop called Touba Wholesale, whose business involves shipping goods to Africa. It is adjacent to a restaurant that advertises its dual specialties in "Jamaican and Southern Style Cuisine." Several other African stores on 116th share the name Touba; it is also a brand of coffee sold in those same shops. The store windows are filled with shelves bearing cans of Touba coffee stacked in alluring displays, among other dry goods imported to supply homesick West Africans. The picture decorating the package shows a tall minaret rising from the mosque at the city's center.

Touba is the holy city of the Mourides, a sect of Sufis in West Africa. There is a concentration of Mouride faithful in Harlem's Little Senegal. Touba means "bliss," referring to the eternal life afforded the pious. The city's mosque holds the shrine and burial place of the Mouride saint Cheikh Amadou Bamba. It is now the destination of a pilgrimage so grand that detractors charge it as blasphemous for attempting to compete with Mecca. During the life of the Cheikh the same land was a vast wilderness; it was the place where he launched his teachings on how seekers could keep to the spiritual path by emphasizing work and generosity, along with other teachings that made him an enemy of French imperialism. According to the conference brochures, a massive suburb was being developed in the neighborhood of Touba — *un projet de réalisation de 12,000 logements à Touba* — presumably allowing those Mourides who are both faithful and well heeled to dwell as near as possible to the resting place of their ascended master.

On another occasion, I visited the library and found that a large gathering was taking place in the auditorium just beyond the Hughes memorial. It was a public hearing convened by the United Nations special rapporteur on racism, who was then traveling the country to take testimony that he would present in a report to the international body. The hearing went on for hours, with hundreds of people signing up to bear witness to historic and contemporary experiences of injustice, violence, and indignity.

These ranged from the treatment of Haitians seeking asylum to inequalities in education and housing, and from the plight of mothers whose children had been taken by a sometimes draconian child welfare system to the difficulties faced by ex-convicts who wished to find work. Some speakers presented their testimony with the cool detachment of academics. Others, relating the more immediate horrors of their daily lives, approached the rapporteur as if he were endowed with the power of direct intervention. The rapporteur listened to them all, and when the hearing was done, he thanked everyone profusely but took great care to mention that his only power was to listen and then to submit a written report to the larger body. He said he hoped the facts would be taken into consideration.

Around the same time, the library hosted an exhibition in its gallery on the art of that Senegalese mystic sect whose saint's shrine is found at Touba. Their holy men minister with words. If you are in need of guidance or are in ill health, the priest will write out a prayer that is also a prescription. The ink is washed from the wooden board where he writes; you are cured by drinking the water that washed away the words. In other instances, he might write out the remedy on a cloth. You make a shirt from it and wear it till it falls apart, or wrap yourself in it and, while covered in this shroud, are healed as you sleep.

There are many things you will not find at the library. I am thinking of my friend Ms. Bessie. At some point early in our friendship, she told me that she used to write home every week in the days after her arrival in New York, at nineteen, from a town called Scotland Neck in North Carolina. I have often wondered what she said in her letters home. She did not elaborate; she probably mentioned those letters in a sharp-eyed aside between asking after the health of my mother back in Texas and lamenting the unfortunate constellation of the number that had just hit.

Dear Family, all is well here, I imagine they began. *Do not worry, the winter is not so tough. I am putting away money for a new coat and here is a bit for you.* She told me she lived on Lenox Avenue when she first came here, around 126th Street, and at some point I walked past that location and it looked as though a very long time had passed since anyone had called it home. *The apartment is nice, sister is here, on Thursday nights we go dancing, the lady at the job is not so mean.*

The lady at the job would make her clean a spot and then clean it again and stand over her watching as she worked. This lady was a *Russian Jew,* Ms. Bessie told me without malice. *That lady is long gone,* she said.

The boss lady is long gone, and so is young Ms. Bessie, on her knees scrubbing a floor somewhere on the Upper East Side during the middle 1950s. Also gone are Ms. Bessie's letters home not describing that scene as it was happening—this perhaps, was not the kind of news you sent home in the weekly letter. *Dear Family, New York City is full of charms and I miss you.*

Ms. Bessie once said that there wasn't anyone left, that she would like to go home but there wasn't anyone at home. If there isn't anyone there any longer, there is almost no question that her letters weren't preserved. They are all scattered; they are all gone. If she hadn't mentioned them to me, I would not have thought to ask. Ms. Bessie's letters are not at all the kind of thing you can expect to find in Mr. Schomburg's library, because they are not, in his sense, evidence of anything of much importance. They would give evidence of a girl going from a small place to a much larger place; evidence of the people she left behind and those she came to know; of the places that gave her shelter that are no longer there; of the cruelties she suffered at the hands of people who are *long gone.* But not evidence that could be lodged in an argument about a people's humanity or claim to civilization, or a refutation of the charge that black people have no history. The letters of Ms. Bessie and the other dutiful daughters writing home to North Carolina and South Carolina on a weekly basis would be summed up as a footnote in a story about migration and boll weevils and the war-driven manufacturing boom.

The letters are gone, and so is the building across the street where Ms. Bessie once lived. She points to the towers of Lenox Terrace. They were erected where tenements and brownstones once stood, razed during the hyperactive slum-clearance programs of the 1950s. Ms. Bessie remembers all of the addresses of all of the buildings where she's ever lived in Harlem. She sometimes plays their digits in combination for the daily number, along with the addresses of the buildings where her sisters lived, and the birthdays of her sisters, and the birthdays of her dead husband and dead children.

My neighbor Bing always asks me how this book is going. *How was your day? How is the library? How is the writing?* Once, after many months of asking those questions, Bing greeted me as I came out of my building on the way to the library. He took my shoulders firmly in his hands, sent me off with a kiss on the cheek, and said he hoped I'd finish the book soon. On another occasion, when I arrived home in the evening, I found him at the stoop, and he asked me how the day had gone. A younger man, whom I did not know, was standing nearby. He was interested in the book, too, and upon hearing I was writing about Harlem, he began to be excited. *Everything you need to know you can just ask him,* said the younger man, indicating Bing, somehow acting as a broker for all that Bing knew. I agreed, saying there was a great deal I would like to learn. But Bing protested that everything I possibly needed to know was in the library. The younger man didn't listen to me or to Bing. He eagerly began to list what Bing could tell me about Harlem, about all the famous writers and artists and musicians and athletes that had lived here, about the riots and the hustlers and much more, but I had stopped listening to him and Bing was staring across the avenue into the dark.

Eventually the younger man left. Bing sat down next to the door in one of the discarded dinette chairs that serve as sidewalk furniture. There was a second empty chair, so I sat down, too. I told him I would like very much to hear about his youth. He told me he had grown up on 135th Street, where the hospital is now, where his tenement building stands no longer. He said I'd find in the library a picture of the building the way it used to look. (I did not realize it then, but I had already found such a picture; that apartment building looms in the background of the photo labeled *Within Thirty Seconds Walk of the 135th Street Branch*). I told Bing I'd look it up next time, and that he would have to tell me more about it. Though he nodded at the suggestion, Bing resumed staring. After a few moments during which neither of us said a word, he declared it was time for dinner and that he would be going in. I went inside, too. I did not return to the library the next day, or for many days thereafter.

Harlem Dream Books

The instructor said,
   Go home and write
   a page tonight.
   And let that page come out of you—
   Then, it will be true.

The opening lines of the poem contained the homework assignment. The poem was "Theme for English B" by Langston Hughes. The class was English II, sophomore English. I am in Texas, age fifteen.

I already knew the name Langston Hughes; my mother's bookshelves held a copy of his biography along with a thick volume of his correspondence with Arna Bontemps. These I used to comb selectively, looking for bits of juicy Harlem Renaissance gossip. Also, there was a volume called *The Best of Simple,* which I had never read. By the time we studied him in my high school class, I must have heard at least one poem, probably the one about the

Negro whose soul has grown deep like the rivers, or the poem in which a mother admonishes her child that *life for me ain't been no crystal stair.* Both were popular selections for Black History Month assemblies and talent shows.

I dutifully followed the instruction for the homework assignment: we were to write a poem in the style of Hughes's "Theme." My imitation did not improve upon the original. Like that poem's protagonist, I was also *the only colored student in my class.* I was too young to properly consider the riddle that distinction provoked for Hughes's student and for me: *So will my page be colored that I write?*

I remember reading the lines in which the protagonist described himself as *twenty-two, colored, born in Winston-Salem* and recently displaced to *this college on the hill above Harlem.* I assumed Hughes was writing of Columbia University, where he'd briefly been a student. My knowledge of Harlem geography was then nonexistent; now I know that *the steps from the hill* that lead *through a park* and across *St. Nicholas, Eighth Avenue, Seventh,* to the protagonist's lodgings at the YMCA on 135th Street, describe a descent I have made many times, from the Gothic spires of City College, through St. Nicholas Park, and into the neighborhood's heart.

Back then, in Texas, I relied on an imaginary map of upper Manhattan. The directions it gave suited me, for I could think of no gap greater than between what I knew of Columbia University and what I believed I knew of Harlem. It was a gap that corresponded precisely with the distance between my private Episcopalian high school and the house where I'd write my own theme. *I guess I'm what I feel and see and hear, Harlem, I hear you...* wrote Hughes. I pictured the poet looking down from his perch onto the streets of Harlem below. Finding the sounds of Hughes's Harlem more intriguing than the noise in my own neighborhood, I tried to hear Harlem, too.

And what did I hear of Harlem? It is difficult to reach across time toward the echoes of that earlier perception. What I find there is another Langston Hughes poem, and another homework assignment. This poem was full of questions:

What happens to a dream deferred?

Does it dry up
like a raisin in the sun?
Or fester like a sore—
And then run?
Does it stink like rotten meat?
Or crust and sugar over—
like a syrupy sweet?

Maybe it just sags
like a heavy load.
Or does it explode?

We weren't required to imitate this poem, answer its successive questions, or map its rhyme scheme. The poem was an object for our study of figurative language. We were instructed to pay special attention to the similes embedded in each line: the dream that dries up, festers, stinks, crusts over, and sags. Each action was a tiny metamorphosis, in which the subject of Hughes's inquiry darts across the space of language, from the concrete and observable to the realm of imagination and emotion.

I would not have noted then, as I do now, that the final line takes a shorter path to meaning. It defies the established pattern, expanding the field of our lesson: it is not a simile. When the dream explodes, it doesn't do so after the manner of anything else. It explodes because that is the natural resolution of all unfulfilled dreams—combustion is their destiny. To deliver his message, Hughes switches from similes to the more urgent vehicle of metaphor.

I remember appreciating the simplicity of the poem's title: "Harlem." The name did not appear anywhere else in the poem, but by virtue of that title alone, the images described in Hughes's lines took on a documentary quality. Faithfully trusting the poet as a source of reportage, I thought: of course Harlem is a place where dreams are consumed by various degrees of frustration. We (my white classmates and me) did not have to know much about the place to be somehow certain of that.

Armed with a new appreciation of figurative speech, I looked for more Hughes in the school library and discovered the romance of his love poems. There was "Harlem Night Song":

Come, Let us roam the night together
Singing.
I love you.
Across
The Harlem roof-tops
Moon is shining.
Night sky is blue.
Stars are great drops
Of golden dew.
Down the street
A band is playing
I love you.
Come,
Let us roam the night together
Singing.

I memorized the poem and imagined a bard at least as handsome as Langston Hughes singing those words to me. And there was "Juke Box Love Song":

I could take the Harlem night
and wrap around you,
Take the neon lights and make a crown,
Take the Lenox Avenue busses,
Taxis, subways,
And for your love song tone their rumble down.
Take Harlem's heartbeat,
Make a drumbeat,
Put it on a record, let it whirl,
And while we listen to it play,
Dance with you till day—
Dance with you, my sweet brown Harlem girl.

Hughes had harsher songs, the tone of which would have pierced the mood and cleared the dance floor of all love-struck couples. So, until many years later I skipped over poems like "The Weary Blues." Lenox Avenue was still the bandstand, but the poet was not striking up Tin Pan Alley love songs. This was a funereal dirge, sung without accompaniment. Reading its opening lines in the midst of my Harlem rhapsodies, I moved on to another poem. Here's what I missed:

"I got the Weary Blues
And I can't be satisfied.
Got the Weary Blues
And can't be satisfied—
I ain't happy no mo'
And I wish that I had died."
And far into the night he crooned that tune.
The stars went out and so did the moon.
The singer stopped playing and went to bed

While the Weary Blues echoed through his head.
He slept like a rock or a man that's dead.

———

Also at the school library, I found pictures that I associated with Hughes's Harlem poems. They were from Aaron Siskind's *Harlem Document,* a collection of photographs made during the Great Depression. They showed families crammed into tenements and dancers at the Savoy ballroom, marchers on Seventh Avenue, and schoolchildren playing stickball. I found shots of a street vendor selling watermelons from the back of a truck, and children playing in the shell of an abandoned building whose doorway is marked KEEP OUT. Siskind ventured into private apartments to record family scenes: Here is a woman in a crowded, disheveled

Untitled [Street Facade 1], from "Harlem Document Series," ca. 1937–1940. (Photo by Aaron Siskind / Courtesy of the Aaron Siskind Foundation and George Eastman House, International Museum of Photography and Film)

Untitled [Street Facade 2], from "Harlem Document Series," ca. 1937–1940. (Photo by Aaron Siskind / Courtesy of the Aaron Siskind Foundation and George Eastman House, International Museum of Photography and Film)

kitchen. She stands before an icebox with the door open, looking in. Her face is just barely in profile; the camera seems unconcerned with her defining features. On the nearest side of that turned-away face, you can nearly glimpse a smile, or at least a hint of amusement. She wears a stylish ensemble—a fluted tea-length black skirt that falls above elegant yet sensible shoes, a blouse with draped keyhole openings at the shoulders.

The photograph could be read as "Depression-era woman looking for food," but the woman stands with the poise of a spokesmodel for a kitchen-appliance store showing off the latest modern conveniences. The picture captures her fine clothes, her grace, and that hint of a smile. But perhaps we are meant to register only her black skin, her cramped surroundings, and wonder if the icebox is empty.

Siskind was concerned with showing the destitution of Harlem

Untitled [Street Facade 3], from "Harlem Document Series," ca. 1937–1940. (Photo by Aaron Siskind / Courtesy of the Aaron Siskind Foundation and George Eastman House, International Museum of Photography and Film)

during the Depression. But among the photos I studied in *Harlem Document,* the one that occupied me most carried the fewest social signifiers—no skin, no appliances, no face denying the

Untitled [Street Facade 4], from "Harlem Document Series," ca. 1937–1940.
(Photo by Aaron Siskind / Courtesy of the Aaron Siskind Foundation and
George Eastman House, International Museum of Photography and Film)

camera's view. It showed only the front of an apartment building,
its facade staring blankly at the camera, its many windows
boarded up with horizontal slats. The repetition of the windows

and the boards created a jarring visual beat, abstracting the poverty that was figured elsewhere so explicitly.

This was a rhythm to which you could not dance. Beneath their bleak and bitter sheen, the other pictures had a bit of sepia charm from having passed into history, but this facade did not provide the comfort of the long gone. I knew—even then, growing up in Texas—that Harlem was a place where you could still find buildings boarded up like that, forsaken for more than half a century.

Hughes's love poems still floated through my mind, along with the amorous territorialism of a jazz ballad I listened to as a teenager, playing the cassette in an infinite loop: *You can have Broadway / give me Lenox Avenue.* Those lyrics and everything I had heard about the Harlem Renaissance collided with the repulsion thrown off by the boarded-up buildings. I did not understand how this place existed as both haven and ghetto. It seemed, to my teenage mind, a great paradox. It also revealed something damning about the history I had learned—a flattened version of events where a place is allowed to be only one thing or the other.

The unpublished outtakes of Siskind's Harlem project offer a submerged narrative. I was surprised to find many more disconcerting images of facades. It's as if, while trawling uptown streets to record the scenes that became *Harlem Document,* Siskind had often retreated from the easy schematics of reportage, drifting toward photography as architectural survey. Frame after frame shows abandoned buildings and brownstones, elegant and majestic if not for the bricks and boards. Here, Siskind releases Harlem from the scrutinizing grip of the social realist's eye, but the abstractions of his facade studies also tell a story.

I realized much later, that, though Siskind's photos of abandoned buildings could not be classed as street life reportage or used as evidence for social programs of the New Deal, the images still documented events in motion. Just as the natural inclination of a dream is not explosion but expression and fulfillment, the natural destiny of a building is not to be sealed off from the world around it, no longer offering shelter. The buildings had been abandoned and boarded up for a reason. There *was* human activity captured within the frame of those eerie photographs. The activity was contempt.

What you call a ghetto, I call my home. The voice of a young man who opens the introduction to Bruce Davidson's book *East 100th Street* is a challenge to that project before it has even begun—a taunt to the photographer and viewer. The voice matches the stark, frank portraits in high-contrast black-and-white. The subjects often stare directly into the camera, unlike Siskind's Harlemites—turned away or looking into the distance. I am still in the library as a teenager, but my taste for the real as defined by twentieth-century photographers has veered from nostalgic to gritty. Davidson delivered this quality in his 1960s portraits of street toughs and the tender shots of families whose lives seemed to sag along with their furniture. These images came closer to the realities I was by then reading about in Harlem coming-of-age memoirs by Claude Brown and Piri Thomas. How close? Davidson takes us into the bedroom of Harlem odalisques—one is draped naked across a bed that is itself stripped nearly to the ticking-covered mattress. Another photo shows a woman in a negligee, the heart-shaped cardboard top of an old Valentine's candy box fixed to the wall as decoration. In another, the rotting carcass of a dead horse crowns the abundant debris piled in an empty lot.

My study of Davidson's work was not limited to observation. In the pages of a commonplace book where I collected quotations from my favorite writers (at the time, Hurston and Baldwin, Ellison and Fanon, Whitman and Dickinson and Walcott), I also made sketches from the photographs of *East 100th Street.* If the poetry of Hughes was one kind of apprenticeship (*Go home and write / a page tonight...*), Davidson's pictures provoked another. But one element of the photographs could not be revealed by way of careful sketches—the white lie of the realist photographer, a sin of omission. We rarely learn under what circumstances such photographs are made. How did Davidson and Siskind gain entry? Were the reclining women in Davidson's dingy rooms aspiring models, the photographer's lovers, or whores? Who granted access? And after access, who granted permission?

These questions are necessary, because such photographs are destined to play a role, cast out of art's refuge to the harsher realm of sociology and political propaganda. These pictures make an argument about the way life is lived. The people in a photograph end up as symbols. They are both specific and generic—the photographs capture moments in time and space, but the subjects are transformed into representative specimens.

Too often in documentary photographs, the transaction is obscured and the presence of the eye is not accounted for. As a film student experimenting with photography, I could never take pictures of people on the street. In those days—visiting Harlem to use the library—I made photo expeditions halfway across 125th Street before giving up and turning back toward Broadway. My efforts resulted in a mediocre collection of photos featuring no people at all, only words on signs. My eyes were drawn to two slogans in particular, united in their ubiquity: *JESUS SAVES* and *LIQUOR*.

In *Harlem Document,* Siskind's images are paired with texts from the Works Progress Administration's Federal Writers Project. The project deployed a number of young writers, scholars, and journalists to collect oral histories from black New Yorkers, especially in Harlem. While a number of unknown writers participated as interviewers, *Harlem Document* includes the work of a few who went on to prominence, including Ralph Ellison and Dorothy West. Though not included in the Siskind volume, the wider project also gave a boost to the young Zora Neale Hurston, as well as to Margaret Walker, Arna Bontemps, and Richard Wright. They were paid twenty dollars per week for their services.

The question of access that sounds so urgently from the Harlem photographs of Siskind and Davidson also arises from the stories collected by these oral historians. FWP writer Frank Byrd answers it this way: *I was a neighborhood boy.* So Byrd could easily join games of hardball, basketball, and stickball, and then strike up conversations. *That way you got to know the people. And that was the beginning, you see.... Then you had to pass the time of day with them until you felt a warm relationship so that you could talk, so that* they *could talk.*

Ralph Ellison remembered a similar method. *I hung around playgrounds. I hung around the streets, the bars. I went into hundreds of apartment buildings and just knocked on doors. I would tell some stories to get people going and then I'd sit back and try to get it as accurately as I could.*

Both men describe a kind of stakeout, where their proximity led to friendship, which eventually led to talk. But there was also a proximity of circumstances, for *they were black and themselves "on relief."*

In some cases, the writers later converted the FWP material into their own artistic product. One encounter, transcribed by Dorothy West and included in *Harlem Document,* shows the young writer clearly trying out her powers of narrative, pathos, and poetry within the confines of her sociological mission. Ralph Ellison uses the words of one woman—whom he must have approached in one of those hundreds of apartment buildings he canvassed for the FWP—in his essay "The Way It Is." He records the suspicion with which his questions were met:

"So you want to know about how we're doing? Don't you live in Harlem?"

"Oh, yes, but I want to know what *you* think about it."

"So's you can write it up?"

"Some of it, sure. But I won't use your name."

"Oh I don't care 'bout that. I *want* them to know how I feel."

She became silent. Then, "You didn't tell me where you live, you know," she said cagily. I had to laugh and she laughed too.

"I live up near Amsterdam Avenue," I said.

"You telling me the truth?"

"Honest."

"And is your place a nice one?"

"Just average. You know how they go," I said.

"I bet you live up there on Sugar Hill."

"Not me," I said.

"And you're sure you're not one of those investigators?"

"Of course not."

"I bet you are too." She smiled.

I shook my head and she laughed.

Another example is the barstool testimony of a railroad porter interviewed by Ellison:

I'm in New York, but New York ain't in me. You understand? I'm in New York, but New York ain't in me. What do I mean? Listen. I'm from Jacksonville Florida. Been in New York twenty-five years. I'm a New Yorker! But I'm in New York and New York ain't in me. Yuh understand? Naw, naw, you don't get me. What do they do. Take Lenox Avenue. Take Seventh Avenue. Take Sugar Hill! Pimps. Numbers.

Cheating these poor people out what they got. Shooting, cutting, backbiting, all them things. Yuh see? Yuh see what I mean? *I'm* in New York, but New York ain't in me! Don't laugh, don't laugh. I'm laughing but I don't mean it; it ain't funny. Yuh see, I'm on Sugar Hill, but Sugar Hill ain't on me.

Yuh understand? Naw, naw, you don't get me. The railroad porter's existential musings later appear verbatim, from the mouth of a character in Ellison's *Invisible Man.*

"And you have to take care of yourself, son. Don't let this Harlem git you. I'm in New York, but New York ain't in me, understand what I mean? Don't git corrupted."

Ralph Ellison, Langston Hughes, and James Baldwin (left to right), ca. 1955. (Courtesy of the Langston Hughes Papers. James Weldon Johnson Collection in the Yale Collection of American Literature, Beinecke Rare Book and Manuscript Library)

Zora Neale Hurston, 1934. (Photo by Carl Van Vechten / Courtesy of the Van Vechten Trust and the Carl Van Vechten Papers. Yale Collection of American Literature, Beinecke Rare Book and Manuscript Library)

Langston Hughes was not a member of the FWP, but since the earliest days of his career, he, too, was concerned with fidelity to "the way it is." As early as 1926, he argued that *the low-down folks, the so-called common element* would be the only launching ground for a *truly great Negro artist, the one who is not afraid to be himself.* The other classes, producing greater numbers of artists of lesser quality, were too self-conscious and too concerned with European standards, he thought, to make a great achievement.

Hughes himself was from a modest background, but he was well educated and well traveled. He had his own moment of confusion about European standards when, famously, his white patroness Charlotte Osgood Mason rejected some of his writings as lacking the authentic and primitive qualities of the work that had first gained her attention and accolades from the white publishing world. This episode sent Hughes into a crisis—he broke with Mason and went on an extended trip to Haiti to recover. His crime had been attempting poetry that was, in the opinion of his patroness, inauthentic. *And let that page come out of you—/ Then, it will be true.*

Throughout the rest of his career, Hughes hewed closely to a style of poetry that could better be labeled "authentic" and pertaining to *the so-called common element*. He enjoyed wide popularity, earning the unofficial title of Harlem's poet laureate. But some of his work, including the collection *Montage of a Dream Deferred*, caused at least one reviewer to grumble about *the limitations of folk art*.

Through the 1950s and 1960s, Harlem's beloved poet wrote a popular weekly column for the *Chicago Defender* that borrowed the voice of the *low-down folks*. Like Ellison and the other WPA writers, Hughes was a denizen of Harlem barstools. From that perch he copied down as accurately as possible the humor, cadences, and quandaries of his neighbor's lives, animating them though his barfly avatar Jesse B. Semple, also known as Simple. Though Simple was a fictional creature, Hughes explained the nature of his material: *I cannot truthfully state,* confesses Hughes, *as some novelists do at the beginnings of their books, that these stories are about "nobody living or dead."*

> The facts are that these tales are about a great many people—although they are stories about no specific persons as such. But it is impossible to live in Harlem and not know at least a hundred Simples, [and, referring to other characters in the Simple tales] fifty Joyces, twenty-five Zaritas, or reasonable facsimiles thereof.

On one occasion, Hughes came face to face with a facsimile of his hero. When entering the local pub, a bartender who was an avid reader of the Simple columns introduced the writer to a patron. *Without me saying a word, a conversation began so much like the opening chapter in my book that even I was a bit amazed to see how nearly life can be like fiction or vice versa.*

Hughes opened himself as a medium for the voices of the public. I wonder what effect that had on what he could or could not say about his private life. Hughes, like many of the most prominent figures of the Harlem Renaissance, was a homosexual, although his biographer is content to class him as asexual. While Hughes's love for his people received full-throated, unequivocal expression in his writing, his love for men could not.

There was one love poem by Langston Hughes that I did not encounter back as a never-been-kissed teenage girl. It is written in the voice of the folk:

I hope my child'll
Never love a man.
I say I hope my child'll
Never love a man.
Love can hurt you
Mo'n anything else can.
....
I'm goin' up in a tower
Tall as a tree is tall,
Up in a tower
Tall as a tree is tall.
Gonna think about my man—
And let my fool self fall.

——————

Zora Neale Hurston is a writer about whom the questions of fiction, fact, and authenticity are always urgent. She is one of the most iconic writers associated with the Harlem Renaissance, yet it is rarely noted how little of her written production concerns the place itself, and how little time Hurston actually spent there. This particular trick played on literary history seems fitting for a writer who thought of New York as both *a basement to Hell* and the place where she was most free: *At certain times I have no race, I am me. When I set my hat at a certain angle and saunter down Seventh Avenue, Harlem City, feeling as snooty as the lions in front of the Forty-Second Street Library, for instance... the cosmic Zora emerges.*

The cosmic Zora was the one brought up in the protective landscape of an all-black town in Florida, with little interaction from the white world to disrupt the certainty that she and her people were the center of existence. The cosmic Zora had lied about her age in order to further her education. Cosmic Zora was the scene-stealer who made jaw-dropping entrances at parties. She spoke *carefully accented Barnardese* but abandoned that refinement when it hindered her collection of anthropological materials during trips down South.

Langston Hughes tells a hilarious but possibly apocryphal story that shows the unflappable Zora Hurston at work in the streets of her Harlem City. He describes the research she pursued for her studies at Columbia University:

> Almost nobody else could stop the average Harlemite on Lenox Avenue and measure his head with a strange-looking, anthropological device and not get bawled out for the attempt, except Zora, who used to stop anyone whose head looked interesting, and measure it.

Hurston gives a wonderful mission statement for her work: *Research is a formalized curiosity. It is poking and prying with a purpose. It is a seeking that he who wishes may know the cosmic secrets of the world and they that dwell within.*

Hurston was as resourceful in her research as she was in procuring the means to pursue it. She was a protégée of the same demanding patroness who rejected Langston Hughes. But Charlotte Mason did not cause Hurston any angst, at least none that Hurston later wrote about. Hughes only barely conceals the scorn left over from his colossal falling out with Hurston when he describes how *[to] many of her white friends, no doubt, she was a perfect "darkie," in the nice meaning they gave the term—that is a naïve, childlike, sweet, humorous, and highly colored Negro.* But Hurston also manipulated those patronage relationships to her advantage, gaining support for the research trips that took her throughout the American South, to Jamaica, and to Haiti. In some ways, her association with both the *niggerati* (as she deemed her black creative contemporaries in Harlem's artistic and literary bohemian set) and the *negrotarians* (as she called the enthusiastic white supporters) happened from a distance. Harlem was a point of access and a point of departure. Harlem was the place that launched her into the wider world. She was not blocked in.

I have always been intrigued by a particular product of Hurston's research. Her "Glossary of Harlem Slang" accompanied a short piece of fiction that was called "Story in Harlem Slang." Indeed, the story's plot is so thin that it seems her main intention was to showcase her fluency in the fast-flicking mother tongue of the street. What happens is not as important as how it's said, and the uninitiated will need Zora Neale Hurston nearby to explain.

A brief selection from the glossary shows her vivid mastery of the language. There are many variations on the provinces of Hell among other place names:

Bam, and down in Bam – down South
Beluthahatchie – next station beyond Hell
Diddy-wah-diddy – a far place, a measure of distance. (2) another
    suburb of Hell, built since way before Hell wasn't no bigger
    than Baltimore. The folks in Hell go there for a big time.
Ginny Gall – a suburb of Hell, a long way off

And then there are the many synonyms for black:

Aunt Hagar – Negro race
Conk buster – cheap liquor; also an intellectual Negro
Dark black – a casually black person, also low black, lam black,
    damn black
Eight-rock – very black person
Handkerchief-head – sycophant type of Negro; also an Uncle
    Tom

Inky dink – very black person

Jar head – Negro man

Jig – Negro, a corrupted shortening of zigaboo

My people! My people! – Sad and satiric expression in the
    Negro language: sad when a Negro comments on the back-
    wardness of some members of his race; at other times, used
    for satiric or comic effect

But for all its value as research, and its possibly diverting pleasures
for those white patrons who, according to Hughes, considered Hurston a *perfect darkie,* Hurston's Harlem dictionary defines a trou-
bling conundrum. If Hughes was the unmediated, celebratory voice
singing of the folk to the folk, Hurston acted as a filter, collecting,
preserving, and exalting the genius and artistry of black folk life
even as she acted, sometimes literally, as a tour guide and interpreter.

This complexity extends to other aspects of Hurston's thought.
On the one hand, she celebrated the all-black town that grew her
up, eventually arguing in favor of segregation on the grounds that
black people had nothing to gain from mixing with white folk.
But, just as often, she casts off the shared burden of racial experience: *Since I wash myself of race pride and repudiate race solidarity,
by the same token I turn my back upon the past. I see no reason to keep
my eyes fixed on the dark years of slavery and the Reconstruction.*

What does it mean to turn one's back on the past, as Hurston
pronounced? It means more than her experiments with personal
mythology. It is, perhaps, a stony kind of realism. From where she
stood, the past did not hold any mystical key to the present. (*My
old folks are dead. Let them wrestle all over Hell about it if they want
to.*) From where she stood, the future did not necessarily hold salvation. (*Standing on the watch-wall and looking, I no longer expect
the millennium. It would be wishful thinking to be searching for justice in the absolute.*)

In almost every essay James Baldwin wrote about Harlem, there is a moment when he commits a literary sleight-of-hand so particular that, if he'd been an athlete, sportscasters would have codified the maneuver and named it "the Jimmy." I think of it in cinematic terms, because its effect reminds me of the technique wherein camera operators pan out by starting with a tight shot and then zoom out to a wide view while the lens remains focused on a point in the distance.

Baldwin's classic Harlem essays "The Harlem Ghetto," "Notes of a Native Son," and "Fifth Avenue Uptown" all have examples of this tactic. The earliest of these, "The Harlem Ghetto," finds Baldwin pacing the streets of the neighborhood where he was born in 1924. *Harlem, physically at least, has changed very little in my parents' lifetime or mine. Now as then the buildings are old and in desperate need of repair, the streets are crowded and dirty, there are too many human beings per square block.*

Baldwin goes on to enumerate other hardships of Harlem life: rents that are higher than elsewhere in the city, food that is of lesser quality yet more expensive than elsewhere in the city, job discrimination, and low wages. Baldwin's first deployment of "the Jimmy" happens almost immediately. *All of Harlem,* he observes, *is pervaded by a sense of congestion, rather like the insistent, maddening, claustrophobic pounding in the skull that comes from trying to breathe in a very small room with all the windows shut.*

It could be another example for my high school lesson on similes, but it reveals much besides the linguistic force Baldwin perfected as a teenage holiness preacher. Baldwin's description of life in Harlem suddenly quits the specific and, through that powerful image of the stifling, sealed-off room, makes a dash for the general. It is one of those grand, poetic generalizations that are

Baldwin's great gift to literature, as well as his great rhetorical weakness. But Baldwin's trick is not just a matter of figurative language. We are so accustomed to these kinds of sweeping statements about Harlem and—as they're often called—the "Harlems of America," that it's difficult to measure the work done by that simple phrase: *All of Harlem*. With those words, Baldwin positions himself as an expert/interpreter of the place which in "Fifth Avenue, Uptown" he describes as *the turf (bounded by Lenox Avenue on the west, the Harlem River on the east, 135th Street on the north and 130th on the south. We never lived beyond these boundaries; this is where we grew up . . .*). Having transcended those boundaries to reach the pages of *Commentary* magazine, Baldwin's phrase *All of Harlem* indicates not only the place he is speaking about, but to whom he speaks. That great leap, from speaking about particular situations of particular people in a particular place to voicing the generalized conditions of Negroes, is performed for the benefit of the mostly white audience. It's possible to think of the move Baldwin makes as a kind of transcendence, insofar as he leaves behind the boundaries of Harlem itself, and the specifics of its daily, lived reality, in the process of describing it. Sometimes it seems that Baldwin's wide angle looks past what he is describing toward the people he is describing it for. The price of this particular transcendence is to become a spokesperson, a representative. But in February 1948, when the essay appeared, that conundrum was still in Baldwin's future. By the end of the year, Baldwin was living in Paris. It was the first of a series of departures, a deliberate attempt to escape that very small room of Harlem, and America, where he could no longer breathe.

In 1955, when Baldwin was already established in Paris, *Harper's* published the essay "Me and My House." It was later renamed and became the title essay for the collection *Notes of a Native Son*. The essay concerns the death and burial of Baldwin's father, which coincided with the writer's nineteenth birthday and the 1943 Harlem riot. It is more narrowly a memoir, so Baldwin is mostly limited to the landscape of his own psyche, the events of his own life, and the relationship between himself and his father, rather than to the relationship between a whole race and the rest of the world. But "Notes of a Native Son" still contains some moments of Baldwin's particular form of transcendence. In the days leading up to the riot, Baldwin remembers a peculiar silence. *All of Harlem, indeed, seemed to be infected by waiting.* Later, after the riot, Baldwin surveys its aftermath in the form of smashed plate glass all over the streets and interprets the debris pattern as if reading tea leaves.

> Harlem had needed something to smash. To smash something was the ghetto's chronic need—most of the time it is the members of the ghetto who smash each other and themselves. But as long as the ghetto walls are standing there will always come a moment when these outlets do not work. If ever, indeed, the violence which fills Harlem's churches, pool-halls, and bars erupts outward in a more direct fashion, Harlem and its citizens are likely to vanish in an apocalyptic flood.

Here, Baldwin switches into prophet mode, and the events in Harlem become a parable for the racialized soul-sickness plaguing America. Baldwin the prophet is also Baldwin the healer, so "Notes of a Native Son" ends with a prescription: *Blackness and whiteness did not matter, to believe that they did was to acquiesce to one's own destruction.* It is a message found in much of Baldwin's work, where he is so often addressing a *we* that is startlingly mobile. At times the *we* is Baldwin's family, or the people he grew up with in and around the turf. At other moments, the *we* seems to be the mostly white audience of the middlebrow magazines where Baldwin was a frequent contributor. At its most profound, Baldwin addresses a *we* that, perhaps, had not previously been taken for granted in American literature, challenging white America to align itself with the *we* of black Harlem. In "Fifth Avenue, Uptown," Baldwin challenged the readers of *Esquire* to *walk through the streets of Harlem and see what we this nation have become.*

As early as my high school lessons on Langston Hughes, I had absorbed the platitude that the task of the writer was to glean universal lessons from specific and personal experiences. But in Baldwin, I learned the particular peril of that path for a black writer. As Baldwin admits in his "Autobiographical Notes," *I have not written about being a Negro at such length because I expect that to be my only subject, but only because it is the gate I had to unlock before I could hope to write about anything else.*

After working for the Federal Writer's Project, when he was still in the midst of writing *Invisible Man,* Ralph Ellison accepted an assignment to report on a free mental health clinic in Harlem. It begins with a perspective that is the reverse of Baldwin's trademark move. Ellison makes a panoramic survey of Harlem before zooming in on his chosen topic.

> To live in Harlem is to dwell in the very bowels of the city; it is to pass a labyrinthine existence among streets that explode monotonously skyward with the spires and crosses of churches and clutter underfoot with garbage and decay. Harlem is a ruin; many of its ordinary aspects (its crimes, casual violence, crumbling buildings with littered area-ways, ill-

smelling halls and vermin-invaded rooms) are indistinguishable from the distorted images that appear in dreams, and which, like muggers haunting a lonely hall, quiver in the waking mind with hidden and threatening significance. Yet this is no dream, but the reality of well over four hundred thousand Americans, a reality which for many defines and colors the world. Overcrowded and exploited politically and economically, Harlem is the scene and symbol of the Negro's perpetual alienation in the land of his birth.

By 1948, when Ellison wrote those words, Harlem was the scene and symbol of a great deal. Alain Locke had begun with the dissection of Harlem as a representative specimen for all of black America, and photographers like Aaron Siskind used the neighborhood as a laboratory for their experiments in atomizing reality.

His masterful description takes us, as near as a realist photographer's lens, into a typically gritty Harlem scene, but Ellison keeps the shifting and fugitive quality of dreams nearby. The very circumstances make it difficult to tell one from the other, for real life is *indistinguishable from the distorted images that appear in dreams*. Ellison reverses the arrangement of dreams and realities that appears in *Invisible Man*, when his protagonist arrives in Harlem from the South and declares, *This was not a city of realities but of dreams*.

The South hovers above Ellison's landscape. That lost place and lost way of life cannot be reconciled with the present, due to

a vast process of change that has swept [the American Negro] from slavery to the condition of industrial man in a space of time so telescoped (a bare eighty-five years) that it is literally possible for them to step from feudalism into the vortex of industrialism simply by moving across the Mason-Dixon Line.

Ellison attempts to ignore sociology and economics in favor of psychology, keeping to his stated subject. But recently, a sociologist using Ellison's essay to establish the framework for her study of gentrification in Harlem in the 1990s found much that was relevant to her field—especially what she called Ellison's depiction of Harlem as a *metaphoric space.*

That description of Ellison's Harlem reminds me of something from W. E. B. DuBois. At the beginning of *The Souls of Black Folk,* DuBois describes his amused irritation with the pressing and searching inquiries from well-meaning whites about life as a Negro. *How does it feel to be a problem?* was his summary of their curiosity. Reading that sociologist, and Ellison, I wondered, How does it feel to live inside a metaphor?

Ellison is interested in a different question. How have black people who were *the grandchildren of those who possessed no written literature* come to *examine their lives through the eyes of Freud and Marx, Kierkegaard and Kafka, Malraux and Sartre?* This juxtaposition, for Ellison, results in a *world so fluid and shifting that often within the mind the real and the unreal merge, and the marvelous beckons from behind the same sordid reality that denies its existence.* And that world, as lived out on the streets of Harlem, produces *the most surreal fantasies:*

A man ducks in and out of traffic shouting and throwing imaginary grenades that actually exploded during World War I; a boy participates in the rape-robbery of his mother; a man beating his wife in a park uses boxing "science" and observes Marquis of Queensberry rules (no rabbit punching, no blows beneath the belt); two men hold a third while a lesbian slashes him to death with a razor blade; boy gangsters wielding homemade pistols (which in the South of their origin are but toy symbols of adolescent yearning for manhood) shoot down their young rivals. Life becomes a masquerade; exotic costumes are worn by day. Those who cannot afford to hire a horse wear riding habits; others who could not afford a hunting trip or who seldom attend sporting events carry shooting sticks.

Thus Ellison describes the psychic breaks and identity crises that lead to the Lafargue Psychiatric Clinic in the basement of St. Philip's Church on 134th Street, a place founded and operated by black and white psychiatrists because blacks could not receive mental health care at other hospitals.

But, inevitably, mental health cannot be divorced from sociology and economics.

Not quite citizens and yet Americans, full of the tensions of modern man but regarded as primitives, Negro Americans are in desperate search for an identity. Rejecting the second-class status assigned them, they feel alienated and their whole lives have become a search for answers to the questions: Who am I, What am I, and Where? Significantly in Harlem the reply to the greeting, "How are you?" is often, "Oh, man, I'm *nowhere*" — a phrase revealing an attitude so common that it has been reduced to a gesture, a seemingly trivial word.

Ellison's essay "Harlem Is Nowhere," written in 1948, finds that the general condition of life in Harlem is the source of the specific mental conditions of the clinic's patients, whose specific names and histories he does not explore. The *general* condition of second-class citizenship among black Americans leads to a *general* condition that is, or approaches, collective insanity. He does not remark upon whether he includes himself among the afflicted.

Within the essay, his position, to the degree he is located anywhere, is slightly outside the boundaries of the landscape under scrutiny. His function is related to the interpretive roles of Hurston or Baldwin, but he doesn't match Hurston's entertainments or Baldwin's exhortations. His beautiful, clinical descriptions emit a kind of hostility. A similar hostility is heard in "No Apologies," Ellison's 1967 contribution to a heated exchange with Norman Podhoretz, the editor of *Commentary*. Asserting that Podhoretz was *throwing his typewriter at the whole unsuspecting Negro people,* Ellison's lengthy response to Podhoretz is nothing short of an evisceration. But Ellison's gripe isn't merely a reflexive defense against injury done to himself or all black people. He takes specific issue with *how often white liberals, possessing little firsthand knowledge of any area of the society other than their own, eagerly presume to interpret Negro life while ignoring their primary obligation as intellectuals—which is to know what they are talking about.*

Likening Podhoretz and other would-be white interpreters of black life to *absentee owners of tenement buildings [who] exploit the abstract sociological "Negro" as a facile means of getting ahead in the world,* Ellison issues a decree banishing trespassers and pretenders from the realm of his culture and his thought, demanding that members of other cultural groups

> respect the sacredness and inwardness of my own, and that they recognize my right to define it, glorify it, affirm it, criticize it—even though to them it seems wrapped in the black-

est of mysteries. I must insist because such regard for others is seldom reciprocated when the Negro American's sense of his own reality is in question.

Ellison directly addresses some of the dilemmas of interpretation and orientation found in Hurston and Baldwin. In claiming the *sacredness and inwardness* of his position as a black writer concerned with black lives, Ellison rejects the position of tour guide or interpreter. His activity—defining, glorifying, affirming, criticizing—takes place behind a curtain of mystery. Crucially, in this 1967 essay Ellison raises, once again, the question of reality, that conundrum that he tracks through the Harlem streets in 1948 and runs from in the pages of his 1952 novel. For Ellison in 1967, reality is still *in question*. Perhaps even more so because this is the moment when Ellison was at his height as author of *the most distinguished American novel written since World War II*, and also was being denounced by young writers who, like Amiri Baraka, were getting up to some *nowhere shit* in the name of a programmatic, didactic notion of the role of the black artist. Additionally, as far as his sense of reality was concerned, this was also the period when Ellison was stumbling into the deferrals, excuses, and diversions that prevented his ever completing another novel.

Which brings us back to "Harlem Is Nowhere." Among his dizzying haunted-house descriptions of life in the neighborhood, one of the most intriguing pronouncements is that *this is a world in which the major energy of the imagination goes not into creating works of art, but to overcome the frustrations of social discrimination.* This causes the crises leading to that free psychiatric clinic. But, Ellison also acknowledges, that energy also led to various other forms of creative response, including the slang of his title. In the 1967 polemic where Ellison so defiantly stakes out the claim of his intellectual territory, his insistence on *sacredness and inwardness* reads like his own attempt to overcome such frustrations, groping toward that inward and sacred space where literature is possible.

"Harlem Is Nowhere" was not published by the magazine that commissioned it in 1948. It did not appear in print until 1964, when it was published in *Harper's*. As the editorial note preceding the piece observes, *how little has changed in the everyday life of the ghetto in the past sixteen years. Ellison's essay helps explain, and in hindsight justifies, the impatience of the American Negro in 1964.* The essay was published in August. Perhaps by coincidence, that issue must have hit the newsstands around the time the third major riot in Harlem occurred. It is unclear if *the impatience of the American Negro in 1964* is an oblique reference to this event or an uncanny presentiment. The explanation and justification mentioned in the editorial note are worth a mention. Interestingly, the version of the essay that appeared in *Harper's* omits the section about the Lafargue Clinic, which had been the very impetus for the piece in 1948. Possibly it was no longer in operation and the editors didn't want to include anything that wasn't, according to that maddening adjective of the magazine trade, timely.

But in the original essay (published in full in *Shadow and Act*), the clinic is the scene where the madness of white supremacy could be overcome. The clinic was a place where its clients could *explain* and *justify* to themselves the conditions inside their minds and in the world. Unmoored from the setting of the psychiatric clinic, Ellison's essay becomes another occasion to *explain* and *justify* the *whole unsuspecting Negro people* to the same readers of *Harper's* who were already used to being—variously—horrified, soothed, chastised, and exhorted by James Baldwin.

We find Ellison carefully watching the perimeter, defending his right to live and create from beyond a veil, but also oriented outward, toward maintaining his position upon the elevated dais of various panel discussions, a dignitary in the republic of letters, a spokesman even—the most exceptional Negro novelist of his generation. To the degree his call for inwardness coincided with his talent turning in on itself, Ellison occupied a negated position, a nowhere. *One "is" literally, but one is nowhere; one wanders dazed in a ghetto maze, a "displaced person" of American democracy.*

In the best of circumstances, that dazed wanderer is also the dreamer, creating a world that hasn't yet come to be. Utopia, after all, means nowhere. Ellison's biographical note in *Harper's* stated, *He is best known for "Invisible Man," a novel about "one Negro's effort to find his place in the world."*

In 1948, Ralph Ellison heard the street slang *Oh, man, I'm nowhere* and heard the identity crises, negation, and psychic despair provoked by daily life under white supremacy.

In 1961, James Baldwin, writing "Fifth Avenue, Uptown," perhaps writing from Paris, remembered a different greeting:

> "How're you making it?" one may ask, running into them along the block, or in the bar. "Oh, I'm TV-ing it" ... with the saddest, sweetest, most shame-faced of smiles, and from a great distance. This distance one is compelled to respect; anyone who has traveled so far will not easily be dragged again into the world.

Baldwin's greeting also referred to a state of negation, but now it was expressed in reference to the lives of certain young men in Harlem, who, unemployed and without prospects, were spending their lives at their mother's house, watching daytime TV.

In 1981, when Aaron Siskind's photos were published as *Harlem Document,* the writer, photographer, and director Gordon

Parks contributed a brief introduction to the volume. His piece fulfils the typical obligation of writing about Harlem — offering pronouncements that Harlem is this or Harlem is that. His reminiscence of Harlem also includes something he heard on the street.

> "Heh, baby, how you doing?" That was a familiar greeting when I was a young man up in Harlem. Today it's "What's happening, brother? What's shaking up and down the line?"
> . . . Jobless young people with anger in their eyes stand on the corners and stare into space. "Nothing's happening," they say. "Nothing's shaking *up* or *down* the line."

Perhaps it is just a coincidence that these three writers emerge from their descent into Harlem with the trophy of a greeting from which to derive a metaphor about all of black existence. I think it has more to do with the instrument of the writer's art, a blade that is sometimes destructive and reductive, though it also flashes light. Perhaps those greetings and their interpretations say more about the interpreters than about those who are purported to use them.

Don't get corrupted.

The town house at 2144 Fifth Avenue is located within the boundaries of James Baldwin's turf—near the corner of 131st Street, where Baldwin grew up. The house has a varicolored brick facade on its two lowest levels, with typical brownstone above. Someone has carefully painted the bricks in alternating shades of pastel blue, green, and pink. For years I passed that building, noting its strange decoration, noting the plate-glass window that looked out onto Fifth Avenue from the second floor, noting how the windows above never gave any indication of lives lived within. A minimum of business was transacted in the appliance, furniture, and lamp repair shop operating at street level.

Later, I found out this had once been the location of L. S. Alexander Gumby's Book Studio. Then I passed the building with more curiosity, wondering how to gain entry and what would be the proper way to approach, thinking that I should take a companion because I might disappear into one of those dark upper stories. My relationship with the building went on like this for a long while: it was the setting of my worst single-girl-doing-research fantasies. In the meantime, I collected information about the life of the man whose ambitions had reached their height inside the confines of that room with the plate-glass window looking out over upper Fifth.

Alexander Gumby came to New York from Baltimore around 1906. According to an unpublished autobiographical essay, immediately he *became a New Yorker in spirit and principle,* having discovered *more freedom of action than [he] had ever known before.* A passionate theatergoer, he collected Broadway playbills, pictures, and newspaper clippings as souvenirs. He made scrapbooks of the material, a carryover from a childhood hobby, and when he worked at Columbia waiting tables, he made scrapbooks about Columbia, too. He worked as a butler and caretaker for a banker in Riverdale. The banker was also a collector, so Gumby's responsibilities included the stewardship of *pottery, bronzes, ivories, etc.* Upon leaving that situation, he was armed with a letter of introduction recommending him highly on account of services rendered: *I have been going to Europe for a number of years,* wrote his employer, *and have left him in full charge of my house and all its contents and I have never had occasion to regret it.*

Gumby's impulse to compile, collect, and curate the detritus of his reality matured when he found himself overwhelmed by what he called his *overflowing collection of clippings*. He attacked the problem with intense seriousness, describing it in a detailed statement of purpose:

> I decided to gather them into scrapbooks. Without experience in the arranging of such a vast amount of miscellaneous material, I naturally made a botch of it in my first efforts. When I finally admitted to myself that it would all have to be done over, I decided to classify the material into groups. I soon found, however as my collections continued to grow, that even this arrangement was unsatisfactory, for it was impossible to interfile new material. It was not until I adopted the looseleaf method that I found a satisfactory answer to my problem. That, of course, meant remounting my material once more. After sorting it into master subjects, I found out that I had enough Negro items for a scrapbook on that subject alone. This Negro scrapbook I in turn divided into master subjects; and because the leaves could be shifted, I was able to break the master subjects into chapters. I arranged the clippings chronologically that were not too badly damaged by their repeated remountings in the unsuccessful scrapbooks. I soon had a bulging volume of Negro items, whereupon I broke the chapters up into separate books. Thus began my Negro Scrapbook collection.

The birth of Gumby's Negro Scrapbook, or "Negroana" as it was later called, came just before two other significant developments in his life. First, he became *acquainted with a young man who was a few years my junior*. A bawdy song by Gumby, written in 1907, using the voice of his alter ego Count DeGumphry, perhaps tells us something about their meeting:

I am a Count, —
The Count DeGumphry.
I am looking for an heir,
Of some yankie millionear
That has a income of a hundred thousand pounds a year.

In his typewritten memoirs, Gumby describes this relationship as a *staunch friendship* that lasted nearly three decades. The man, a scion of a New York business family, was Gumby's lover and patron. It was with the help of this friend, Charles W. Newman, that Gumby began to amass a collection of rare editions, manuscripts, and ephemera to complement his scrapbook productions. Hardly anything is known about their relationship—whether it was a true love that had to be suppressed because of its challenge to the racial and sexual order, or whether it was a less tender transaction. Alexander Gumby's story, when it is told at all, is usually mentioned as a minor footnote to other more celebrated queer lives of the Harlem Renaissance era. There is Richard Bruce Nugent, with his bohemian disregard for neckties and socks, throwing off his bourgeois pedigree with defiant dishevelment. There is Countee Cullen, marrying the daughter of W. E. B. DuBois in a lavish ceremony and then leaving her behind to embark on their European honeymoon in the company of his alleged lover, the Harlem man-about-town Harold Jackman. There are the rumors about A'Lelia Walker and Langston Hughes, and rumors about many others. Those rumors serve a purpose for the history of love that mirrors a similar tendency in black history to insist upon its "firsts," and to speculate about the African blood coursing through the veins of historical figures like Beethoven. But while the life of Gumby is known—and, thanks to Gumby himself, ferociously documented—it is not much celebrated. It is not necessary for rumors to swirl about Gumby's sexuality. In a letter to his friend Bruce Nugent, Gumby was frank about the many charms of Columbia University to be found outside the library. Perhaps part of the silence around Gumby is that the terms of his relationship with a white man mirrored the patronage relationship going on throughout Harlem, where art was paid for by white enthusiasts and fetish-collectors, and where black gangsters paid tribute to the white mob. Perhaps the open combination of white patronage and sex in Gumby's life accounts for the way his story has disappeared. Or maybe the silence also has to do with the fact that Gumby's story is, in part, a narrative of failure.

But now I am getting ahead of the story, because at this point, when he has just begun the passionate project of his Negroana scrapbooks, Gumby himself had no intention of disappearing. Indeed, his entire activity seemed to guard against oblivion. Gumby arrived in Harlem in the earliest days of the New Negro push into the neighborhood. He established himself (or Newman established him) at 2144 Fifth Avenue almost immediately, for that is the return address supplied in correspondence related to the second chief occupation of his early years, the Southern Utopia Fraternity.

The S.U.F. was dedicated to the support and edification of *young college men from the South for the purpose of helping themselves as well as all young men from Southern schools who come to New York seeking a larger experience.* The actual activities of the fraternity are not described in the materials Gumby pasted into a few of his scrapbook pages. It seems as though its mere existence, and the notice it garnered, were most important. Its founding was noted in local newspapers: *Young College Men from South Organize.* A subsequent mention announces the election of officers, including the election of Gumby himself to the position of treasurer. The scrapbook preserves a bank draft drawn in Gumby's name in the amount of five dollars *for S.U.F. premiere dance.* There are elegantly printed ephemera: the cover of a program to be held *Thursday evening, April the Sixth, Eight-thirty* announces that *Mr. Justice of the Fraternity will entertain Members and Friends of the Frat.* A small calling card expresses the Fraternity's mission statement: *Its purpose is to bring into closer relation for mutual cooperative help ambitious young men from the various schools who spend their time wholly or in part in New York and vicinity.*

The major document we have of the fraternal order is a letter, written by Gumby in 1917, which resembles the marching orders for a coup. In six pages of feverish prose Gumby solicits the aid of members for his faction: *It is now that your help is needed, in order that our Fraternity may be launched on the waves of life.* The source of the controversy is not clear; he proposes amendments to the constitution and doing away with lengthy debating during meetings. He mentions that the fraternity needs its own clubhouse, because members are being snatched away by other groups that boast facilities.

With a level of detail that tells us much more about the character of Gumby and the other young men who comprised the Southern Utopia Fraternity than it does about their aims, Gumby fills several pages with purple prose about the status of the organization and the problems at hand:

S.U.F. was organized in the year of 1915 by a body of very able men, and it can be truthfully said, what they did, was well done in parts. But they failed to rivet the parts together. Tis the rivteing we must now do. This Fraternity must be united in one body, its parts working in unison, if it is to fulfil the purpose it was so religiously organized to do. Today it stands in parts.

So well did those able men of uncommon ability create the parts, that its ghost has forever since walked among those that were associated with the move.

Tis the haunt of that ghost that has forced this body of men to seize all credential of the S.U.F. and attempt to place a body round its ghost by riveting the parts together with amendments to the constitution, that the ghost may cease to wander and dewing [*sic*] honor to those that created the ghost.

The document reveals Gumby to be a young man of great feeling: *May the banner, spouting greatness and glory beyond the expression of words...be carried on.* He was a young man of great feeling who could not spell: *These talks wer plain talks. We threw off all faulce forms of politenest or display of rhetorical phrases or sincear or fishy friensdhip.*

The high ambition revealed in Gumby's hopes for the Southern Utopia Fraternity matched the hopes then being harnessed on the streets, which were just beginning to fill with blacks moving to Harlem from the South and from other parts of the city. As the migration reached its peak, other organizations were formed, including the Sons of Georgia, the Sons and Daughters of North Carolina, the Virginia Society, the Georgia Circle, and the Southern Beneficial League. While Gumby's somewhat pompous document may not be an accurate reflection of the other groups, all connected the new Harlemites with their origins, while encouraging their aspirations in the North.

Before the occurrence of any of the events that historians use to fix the official beginning of the Harlem Renaissance, the Southern Utopian Fraternity was founded and failed. Or at least we can assume it failed, because there are no further notices of its activities in Gumby's scrapbook. His employment for the next period is difficult to pin down—at some point he worked for the postal service—but this is when his attentions turned even more toward scrapbook making. His brief memoirs note, rather vaguely, that *in the years from 1914 until America went into the first World War, I had the opportunity of going to several large cities in towns in this country and in Canada.* Gumby's mission, on these tours, was to visit libraries to study *various methods of compiling and mounting scrapbook material.* Also during these trips, he scoured bookshops for items to add to his collection, such that he soon *became better known for my collection of choice books than for my scrapbooks.* In 1922, Gumby was registered in the latest edition of *Who's Who in Book Collecting.*

A typewritten bibliography lists some of the items of his collection, including an 1804 copy of *The Life and Achievements of Toussaint L'Ouverture,* a signed edition of *The Life and Times of Frederick Douglass,* William Lloyd Garrison's *Thoughts on African Colonization,* and a 1900 title by W. E. B. DuBois, *College-Bred Negro.* Rare editions from the era of slavery were joined by contemporary productions that probed the history of Africa, the conditions of blacks in the South, and recent novels. When his collection began to outgrow his two and a half rooms on Fifth Avenue, Gumby took out a lease of the entire floor.

This expansion gave Gumby the opportunity to establish the Gumby Book Studio in 1925. It was intended

for my personal use, to entertain my friends, and as a place in which to master the art of making scrapbooks. It should have been called "The Gumby Scrapbook Studio" as it was intended, but at the time I thought the name a bit too long. Soon other friends formed the habit of visiting the Studio, and they in turn brought their friends who brought their friends, regardless of race or color, those who were seriously interested in arts and letters. The Studio became a rendez-vous for intellectuals, musicians, and artists. I daresay that the Gumby Book Studio was the first unpremeditated inter-racial movement in Harlem.

Nineteen twenty-five was the year that brought Alain Locke's special Harlem edition of *Survey Graphic* magazine, which became the anthology *The New Negro*. It was also the year when Gumby's fellow bibliophile Arthur Schomburg enjoyed success for the exhibit of his collection at the 135th Street Branch library. Locke's anthology solidified his role as spokesman of the new generation of black artists, scholars, and aesthetes; Schomburg's exhibit led to the acquisition of his collection by the New York Public Library. Alexander Gumby's tea parties to celebrate his scrapbooks may not seem to match the achievement of those other men. He would have read Locke's grand pronouncements and known that Schom-burg had made a small fortune. His retrospective clamoring for some distinction of his own (*the first unpremeditated interracial movement in Harlem*) may reveal some self-consciousness in com-parison to the other heady undertakings of the era. But it also shows Gumby's solid commitment to his enterprise. He was mas-ter of the very small territory that was his domain.

Gumby's scrapbooks went on view for Negro History Week exhibitions in Philadelphia, Boston, and New York City. In the course of such travels, parts of his collection inevitably went miss-ing. But mostly his activity happened outside of institutions. The production of scrapbooks is a private endeavor, rather different from the intellectual heroics of his contemporaries. It requires papers, scissors, and paste, as well as lots of time to pore over materials. It doesn't happen on street corners or on barstools or at meetings. Crucially, the art of the scrapbook is an act of preservation rather than creation. It is accomplished through juxtaposition and accretion. Within the pages of his scrapbooks, Gumby assembled a mass of information on the history and achievements of black people that was something like that mass accumulating within the boundaries of Hurston's Harlem City. He focused on the most exceptional and the most beautiful, rather than on the most wretched or the most "authentic." And Gumby completely ignored the mundane.

His perspective brings to mind the opening pronouncement in Zora Neale Hurston's *Their Eyes Were Watching God,* in which she describes the ambitions of women who *forget all those things they don't want to remember, and remember everything they don't want to forget. The dream is the truth.* Gumby's dreams, what he remembered and what he failed to remember, reached their fullest expression through his rather feminine, peculiar occupation. He was building a diorama while his contemporaries engaged in the outward, upward, excavating, campaigning activities more typically associated with the race man. The interior nature of Gumby's vocation and his private, idiosyncratic interaction with history is perhaps another reason why his memory is scarcely kept.

But at least for a while, Gumby lived a charmed existence. Pictures of him inside the book studio (preserved in one scrapbook) show the handsome Gumby flashing an inviting smile as he sits with legs crossed, taking coffee in a dressing gown. His table is covered with a crisp tea cloth, and his coffee service looks like quality china—at least one source remembers it as Spode. Other pictures show different views of his residence: a long chamber with a low ceiling seems to be the room with the plate-glass window that I had seen from the street. His walls were lined with shelves specially fitted to house his oversized scrapbooks; various pictures hang above a piano.

In April 1929, an article celebrating Gumby appeared in the

"Who Is Who" column of the *New York News*. In December 1929, the *New York Times* published an article about him, "Negro History in Scrapbooks." That same month, Gumby's lover lost a fortune in the stock market crash and was laid low by a *war ailment*, which might be a polite term for nervous breakdown. Gumby's activities would henceforth not be as well funded.

Despite this misfortune, the first part of 1930 was full of activity at Gumby Book Studio. The studio gave a Sunday afternoon tea hosted by a debutante group called the Primrose Patch, at which *Maurice Hunter, artist's model, gave some interpretive poses; O. Richard Reid gave a talk on art; Theodore Hernandez and Thomas Corbett sang*. The studio's fifth anniversary was celebrated with another tea given by a Miss Willie Branch, in which she performed "The Gypsy Maid," "The Maniac," and "Hagar." A report on the event declared, *While much cannot be said for the vehicles which Miss Branch included in her repertoire, her interpretation of them was noteworthy. One could only wish that Miss Branch had chosen lighter and more pleasing themes instead of the morbid and melodramatic ones mentioned above.*

On the occasion of his anniversary, the *New York News* heralded Gumby's efforts. *Not only does Mr. Gumby seek out the great things that has [sic] been done, but also the seeds of things that will be great in the future. Thus his studio is a laboratory for the youth of the race, struggling in art, music, poetry or other creative expression.*

In 1930, Gumby also launched a publication to serve as a printed laboratory. *Gumby's Book Studio Quarterly: A Journal of Discussion* appeared, bearing cover articles including "A Plea for Intolerance," by George S. Schuyler, and "The African Origins of the Tango," by Arthur Schomburg.

But at the end of May 1930, a small notice appeared in the *New York News*:

The Gumby Book Studio, 2144 5th Avenue, which has been the center of many brilliant musical and poetical recitals and exhibitions for the past five years has closed for the summer and alterations. It will re-open in the fall with a full line of current books, magazines, newspapers, music, rare books, pamphlets and manuscripts relating to the race. It will be the market place and barter mart of race art and letters for the literati of America.

This was a hopeful program for the future. In reality, according to his own memoirs, after his friend's illness Gumby had to sell some of his rare editions in order to keep the studio going. When he closed *for the summer and alterations,* he put his belongings in storage.

This closing of the studio began a tragic chapter. *The loss of my Studio and the fact that I was overworked combined to send me to the hospital I remained there for four years.* Near the beginning of his convalescence, in 1931, a benefit was held at the Renaissance Ballroom. The organizing committee was led by the artist Augusta Savage and included Bessye J. Bearden (mother of the artist Romare), the society columnist Geraldyn Dismond, and actress Rose McClendon, among others. An advertisement for the benefit listed a number of prominent patrons sponsoring the event, including Paul Robeson, Zora Neale Hurston, Countee Cullen, W. C. Handy, Langston Hughes, Arthur Schomburg, and Bill Robinson. Entertainment was furnished by *principals of the Cotton Club Revue and Noble Sissle* among other *Harlem Night Club Stars.* Gumby himself was not well enough to attend, but a page in his scrapbook preserves items announcing the event—including a scrawled message sent by a friend as she prepared for the party. It is full of a socialite's breathless flutter: *Dear*

Gumby, Just to say hello and that I'm thinking of you, we are expecting a great affair tonight we shall all be thinking of you—everything is working fine, hope you can read this I'm so excited. Love, Alta.

Support from the benefit and other friends provided enough money to pay for Gumby's storage expenses for a short while, but eventually he fell behind in his payments and an auction was arranged to sell his belongings. Facing this newest difficulty, Gumby was aided by a friend who offered to take care of the debt in exchange for *certain first editions* and his Americana scrapbooks. The friend, who *did not want any of the scrapbooks of Negro items,* offered to keep them in his home until Gumby could retrieve them.

But when Gumby left the hospital in 1934, he contacted his friend and found that *our gentlemen's agreement had not been strong enough to assure the collection's security.* His books were stored in a cellar without any protection. Friends and family of the steward had been allowed to take whichever of the rare books they desired. Meanwhile, Gumby's Negroana scrapbooks were languishing in more than a dozen cases in a low-lying part of the cellar. A watermark on one trunk gave the first clue of their condition. Two cases of scrapbooks were completely ruined, only *paper mud and mildew inside.* Gumby was able to save some of the items from within those books, and the rest he took to the inadequate lodgings he'd rented for six dollars per week after his release from the hospital.

On the ruins of his scrapbooks, Gumby intended to rebuild.

I decided to remove all Negro items from scrapbooks that were not essentially Negroic and to add them to the Negro collection, as that part had suffered the least damage. While I was doing the revamping, I got the idea of making this part of the collection a far-reaching historical items of Negroana, with each one of its volumes so fine and selective in its makeup that no other collector could ever hope to equal it.

Yes, things have been different since I came back from out there. A 1934 article in the *Amsterdam News* that declared Gumby's *come-back* has the collector looking *reflectively* at the walls of his new rented room on 126th Street. *Out there* is the sanitarium, and it is not far-fetched to wonder whether Gumby's assessment of things that were different included—in addition to his own circumstances—the changes that had taken place in Depression-era Harlem, at the end of the not-yet-coined Renaissance. *No, times are not what they once were.*

His cheer returns when speaking of his new plans. *I have an idea and I'm going to put it over.* The article does not mention the sorrow of the lost items, but instead describes his dream to display the 160 scrapbooks, 3,000 books, and rare prints and paintings that comprised the remains of his library. Having *no where to display them in a proper atmosphere where people genuinely interested may come and browse them,* Gumby was consumed by a vision:

Now, I believe that there should be some place in Harlem where all of this...could be made available to the people who wish to make use of them for research work. It should also be a place where the talented Negro artist, poet, author, actor, journalist and musician could gather and meet in mutual friendship and exchange of ideas with contemporaries—a place where he would not be expected solely to sing spirituals or create art and poetry of a strenuously Negroid and grotesque sort, a place free of religious bigotry, political ballyhoo, social and academic snobbery, a place where artists of all races could meet and mingle freely for art's sake, expressing their own individualities.

Gumby's art center would provide a social and research facility for artists and intellectuals of all races, including a theatre, an art studio and gallery, instruction in the arts, a scholarship fund to support study in Europe and events *charged at all times with a bona fide artistic atmosphere.* He also hoped it would help elevate what he saw as the dismal quality of work being produced at that moment: *I have not the slightest doubt that such an art center would have a constructive effect upon our present-day so-called Negro classics and semi-classics, now being manufactured almost exclusively from backwoods, cornfield, and waterfront material.*

An autobiographical essay Gumby wrote some two decades later for the January 1957 edition of the *Columbia Library World* makes no mention of his art center dream. By then, Gumby was again working at Columbia and had arranged for his scrapbooks to become part of the Special Collections department of the university's Butler Library. A brief article appeared in the *Columbia Daily Spectator* to publicize the holdings. Gumby's ambition was now more modest, or possibly toned-down and misreported by a student journalist who perhaps could only see Gumby's creation in terms of what it meant for white observers. *I want the white people to judge themselves on the Negro problem by reading both sides of the question,* Gumby said of his collection. The reporter noted, *Mr. Gumby hopes that his history of the Negro…will stimulate interest in Negro history and culture and act as a basis for greater cooperation and understanding among the races.*

An anemic account of Gumby's scrapbooking activity is given, along with mentions of the highlights of the collection now housed in the library. These included nine volumes on Joe Louis, three volumes on lynchings, and scrapbooks on Booker T. Washington and jazz. Gumby is said to be currently *making scrapbooks on Columbia, the Negro and Communism, and many personalities such as Dr. Bunche.* Gumby was also occupied with cataloguing his collection. No details are given about the fate of Gumby's rare books and other items. Perhaps he retained them, never having established the art center of his dreams. Or perhaps he'd had to continue selling them off, in order to survive.

The remains of Gumby's scrapbook collection are still at the Rare Books and Manuscripts department of Columbia's Butler Library, but the holdings have been photographed and put on microfilm; special permission is necessary to handle the pages he painstakingly compiled. Gumby relinquished his collection with the agreement that it would be put on regular display, but that hasn't happened. The scrapbook pages are promoted more as secondary sources on the celebrated figures and important topics that Gumby catalogued, rather than seen holistically as the brilliant and strange production of the man himself.

In that same 1957 memoir, Gumby basically concedes this vision of his scrapbooks' future, saying, *Whether or not I have succeeded, I do sincerely hope the collection will be useful for serious historical research, and an abiding incentive to those who try to make scrapbooks on any subject.* This hope was elsewhere stated somewhat differently when, in December 1929, a *New York Times* article noted:

> "My greatest ambition," remarked Gumby, his brown face beaming with the patient enthusiasm of the collector, "is to write the history of the negro in scrapbooks. Perhaps there are others who will come later to put what I have collected into a more concise form."

A page on the microfilm preserves Gumby's personal book plate. His name, L. S. Alexander Gumby, is written in a calligrapher's copperplate hand on a prominent scroll. The words *EX LIBRIS* support the composition from the bottom of the frame. Flowers and foliage festoon the perimeter, while the center is occupied by the muscular figures of two men. One has his back turned against the viewer and his face turned away; the other is positioned slightly below the first, reaching across in assistance. Together they lift a giant, partially opened book, grimacing under the labor.

Eventually I passed 2144 Fifth Avenue when the front door of the lamp repair shop was open. Music played from a speaker above the threshold; outside was a shallow tub filled with water in which two small turtles swam. To the side of the door, a small potted plant was in bloom. This tableau, and the fact that I was walking with a male friend, beckoned me toward the place I had for so long avoided. Inside, I found the proprietor of the shop. He was at work, repairing a table that was turned on its side. The wall of the storefront was lined with shelves that held dozens of lamps of all sizes and designs. I told him I was glad he was open, because my house was full of broken lamps I had never managed to fix. This was true, but seeing that I had nothing with me that would bring him immediate business, the owner must have known that I was merely making conversation. He did not react much beyond a remote *Oh?* before continuing with his task. Since he didn't turn us out of the store immediately, I looked all around the shop. Besides the shelves of lamps, the walls were covered in a metallic paper whose pattern looked like something from the 1970s. There were also scattered artifacts that drew my attention, a poster of Malcolm X, an antique-looking jug that advertised a southern brand of whiskey. Like a visitor to a curiosity shop, I marveled aloud at each object, exclaiming in a manner that the owner must have found irritating. Continuing my attempt to make conversation, I told him what a nice plant he had outside, and said it looked like a jasmine. Without looking up, he said he didn't know what it was. I told him I was pretty sure it was a jasmine because I had one at my house that never blooms, and he offered just as little interest as before. Discarding all niceties, I told the owner I'd always been curious about this shop because it was the same building where a man named Alexander Gumby had lived. Did he know anything about that man?

He stopped working, patient with my intrusion. He didn't know anything about Alexander Gumby, but I must have the wrong place because this space had been a lamp-repair shop for many years, and before that it was a hardware shop. When I told him I was certain it was the same address, and that Alexander Gumby had lived upstairs, he said, *Nope, no way,* and went back to his business with the upended table. I conceded that maybe I had the wrong place, and thanked him for his time. I told him I liked the jazz he was playing through the speaker above the door. He smiled at that, and then my friend and I were gone.

Not long after, I passed 2144 Fifth Avenue again. The lamp shop was closed, as it had been so many times I'd passed before. But things were different. The windows of the upper floors—including the large plate-glass window which had been Gumby's Book Studio—those windows whose darkness had halted my approach—were all covered with wooden boards.

Recently, I began to record my dreams. It was not an effort at self-help or psychoanalysis; the idea was to have a catalog of the realms I sometimes visit at night, often repeatedly. The landscapes in my dreams combine certain elements of some places I've been: the gently undulating hills of the English countryside; the winding waterways of southern India; the steely gray and rich green of the Scottish highlands; the angular spires of cypress trees in Tuscany; and the flat horizon and open skies of the West Texas high desert—where one isn't able to hide. Added to this topography is a distorted version of my everyday scenery. Of this territory I wrote in my notebook, *I arrived in a dream Harlem. Things were much different.*

In this dream Harlem, I visit a library whose magnificent architecture is a more appropriate shrine to Schomburg's endeavor than the forbidding red brick fortress where I spend so many waking hours. It is located on one corner of a dream version of Marcus Garvey Park. The hill of Mount Morris still commands the center, but the plaza formed by the streets around the park resembles some squares where I've lingered in London's Bloomsbury. Inside the dream library is a magic volume that solves all the enigmas that follow me from the real library into my sleep. In this dream Harlem, the avenues are even wider and more grand. I visit elegant lounges that have mahogany fittings and floor-to-ceiling windows that open onto the avenue — striped silk curtains billow in the breeze. In that dream Harlem, that nowhere Harlem, I reach the campus of City College by ascending the face of a ragged cliff many times more treacherous than the steps of St. Nicholas Park. In these settings unfold various plots of which I am not exactly the author.

In the morning, before the tyranny of daylight has imposed itself, when the dream world and the real world are still entangled, some images from the night's travels are still available. More often, they slip back toward the dark, toward the blackest of mysteries; perhaps to be visited again in a future passage, perhaps to be altered, perhaps to be lost.

The collision of real world and dream world may tell me something about the choices made by the writers I have loved. When I was young, their words introduced me to Harlem and to writing. Their challenges were not so different from the fevered operation by which I try to record my dreams before they are exiled from the dominion of voluntary recall and rational thought — that rush to transpose a dream into words, at once preserving the vision and altering its reality. This nowhere, between dream and reality, between what one sees and what one imagines, between what is happening and your attempt to describe it, is the territory we wander while awake. It forms a montage of deferred dreams that couldn't be transcribed accurately before disappearing into the dark.

Soon after arriving in Harlem, I heard a man giving a talk at the museum on 125th Street. In an aside quite removed from the rest of his subject matter, he exclaimed, *Harlem is a city of dream books!* I didn't know what he meant, but I was intrigued by the sound of it. Later, when I came to know about the numbers racket, I learned—from my neighbors and from the library—about the books that make symbols of dream imagery and daily happenings and attach them to numbers. One book offered the following "Harlem Hunches" for the year 1944:

Colored woman calling first thing in the morning	655
Colored man calling first thing in the morning	622
White woman calling first thing in the morning	852
White man calling first thing in the morning	258
Black cat crossing path	142
White cat crossing path	318
Dog barking at you	466
To meet a cross eyed colored man	659
To meet a cross eyed white man	752
To meet a cross eyed white woman	775
To be approached by a beggar early in the morning	336
Carrying stick around Black Jack game	668
To hear a man play the dozen	912
To hear a woman play the dozen	012
To see a car hit a colored man	312

To see a car hit a colored woman	621
To see a car hit a white man	972
To see a car hit a white woman	749
To meet an old girl friend	133
To meet an old boy friend	355
To see cats fighting	345
To see dogs fighting	545
To see a funeral procession	371
To see a wedding	234
To see a mule	555
To see a crowd	882
To see a riot	222
To see a gang fight	228
To see cops chasing bandits	299
To see a hold-up	613
To see a fire	424
To see fire engines rushing	302
To see two men fighting	797
To see two women fighting	798
To see an automobile accident	112
To see a trolley car hit a person	511
To see an Elks parade	888
To see a communist demonstration	615
To meet your sweetheart unexpectedly	757
To trip while walking	481
To shout for joy	327
To meet a colored number runner unexpectedly	718
To meet a white number runner unexpectedly	757
To meet a circus parade	711
To meet a colored actor on the street looking for work	510
To see an organ-grinder	103
To pass a person smoking reefer	028

To have a barber cut your face   367
To see a man thrown out of a speakeasy   641
To see a woman thrown out of a speakeasy   580
To see a crap game on a street corner   238
To see a speakeasy raided   679

These numbers are said to be extra lucky because they are bolstered by prophetic power.

You could say: I dreamed I was trapped in a house with a gargantuan wild beast pacing hungrily outside the window, and I raced around that house slamming doors behind me while running through a series of rooms that were arrayed in a circuit. Then I dashed to the top of a winding staircase where there were no more floors to ascend. Or, I dreamed I was in a house where the floor kept falling out from beneath me, caving in without giving way completely, so it seemed as if I was sinking and gaining ground simultaneously. Or, I dreamed I was visiting friends in a house on a dream version of Striver's Row, when suddenly it started tumbling around so that we were not inside a house after all, but locked within a sphere whose movements we could not control.

Consultants of a dream book would not use those details to venture an interpretation or diagnose an affliction. Instead—by fixing my dream images with certain numbers—they'd invent a diversion to bring temporary release. Upon hearing such scenes a knowledgeable person might say, without hesitation: One. Two. Five.

5

Messages

I GREET MY neighbors in the street. I come from a place where you speak to people when they cross your path, stranger or friend. I had to learn the particular greeting common to this place, as I have done in other places. On the streets of the Faubourg Tremé in New Orleans, there is a luscious formality: one says *Good morning* and *Good afternoon* and *Good evening*; your salutation is a sundial that tells the time of day. Walking country footpaths in England, I learned to proclaim *All right!* cheerfully, authoritatively even. It is at once a query and a declaration, but there's never enough of a pause to discover if things are, in fact, all right. Here, I learned a greeting more familiar, almost intimate. You say: *How you feel?* Or, *How you feeling?* This question seeks out the inner state. Said in a certain languorous tone, it leads one to pause on the sidewalk exchanging minor confidences. It is not a question from which you can rush away.

There are other manners of speaking that are not so easy to adopt. For instance, when a person refers to the street toward which they are walking, or the street where they have just been, or a place where a third party can be found, should any of those streets be located above 110th Street, in Harlem it is customary to make a graceful abbreviation. 133rd Street would be called *'33rd*, 125th Street, *'25th*, and so on. This manner is not easy to mimic. A stranger should not try to emulate it.

But a stranger to this place can take comfort in knowing that even the locals were once strangers, too. *Where is your home?* I have often asked. Or, *Where are your people from?* The answer will be someplace in Alabama or Georgia, the Carolinas or Mississippi. From asking such questions I have come to learn the names of small towns throughout the South that I never had cause to know about or think of: Scotland Neck, North Carolina; Denmark, South Carolina; Yazoo City, Mississippi. At first, I hoped that, being from a place not so far away, I'd be met with slightly less suspicion. In the course of such conversations, my tongue slides across the meridian toward those places we call home. The rhythm of speech is a password; shared laughter sweeps you across the threshold.

Crucial facts of my existence raise eyebrows and alarms. *You're up here all by yourself?* Or, *You're not married yet?* Or, *You don't have any children?* And, *You don't belong to a church?* The questions I ask — *Where is your home? Where are your people from?* — search out origins. The ones people ask me seek to establish my position in the present order. My answers reveal that I am decidedly adrift.

A stranger stops to ask if I require directions. I have lingered too long before stepping into an intersection, or I look uncertain as to where I am headed. The reason is this: I am looking up at a building or down the avenue or scrutinizing a sign that refers to some place no longer there. I shake my head no, insisting I am not lost, or even very far from home. I offer thanks for their kindness, then resume staring or hurry along in imitation of someone with a purpose.

Often enough, my attention is carried off by something I have

not sought. Walking west on 125th Street approaching Seventh
Avenue, I hear garbled sounds carried by a bullhorn and wonder if
there's a rally at African Square. I arrive to find an evangelist occupying the median in the shadow of the Hotel Theresa and calling
out in Spanish, *¡Jesus viene!* Further up the avenue, I notice that the
address of the headquarters for the Five Percent Nation of Gods and
Earths, known as Mecca in Harlem, is 2122 Seventh Avenue. The
address bears auspicious numerology: when added up, the building's
number equals seven; the street name is seven; and, according to the
Five Percent philosophy of Supreme Mathematics, the number seven
represents Allah. Perhaps it is just a providential sign confirming the
supremacy of the poor righteous teachers, the five percent who know.
I saw a street vendor squatting close to the ground beneath a red,
black, and green flag on 125th Street. I thought he'd be hawking
revolutionary tracts, but he was selling packs of batteries.

There are churches that used to be synagogues, churches that
used to be casinos, churches that used to be movie theaters,
churches that used to be bank buildings, and churches that used
to be houses. Many churches are locked during the week, throwing open their doors on Sundays to parishioners who live in other
boroughs and tourists from Europe and Japan. On 134th Street
sits a small church built of slate-colored stone. It looks as though
it should be in the Welsh countryside, atop some craggy moor,
not in Harlem next to an abandoned lot. It has a red door, and its
steps are covered in green Astroturf. The doors are usually locked.
There is a mural on the side of the church next to the lot, which
says *The Open Door,* invoking John's vision in the Book of Revelation about the establishment of New Jerusalem. (*I saw a door
standing open in heaven, and the same voice I had heard before spoke
to me with the sound of a mighty trumpet blast. The voice said,
"Come up here, and I will show you what must happen after these
things."*) The mural shows a group of people with Afros standing

in two lines awaiting entry. The doors in the mural are red, just like the ones at the front of the church, but unlike the actual doors of the church these are crowned by the variegated colors of a stained-glass fanlight. A dazzling light draws the faithful through the doors, but the artist offers only a mystical suggestion of what lies beyond. Other than the lettering invoking *The Open Door,* the only writing on the mural is a dedication that begins: *To the memory of...* You cannot read in whose memory this work was made — the facade is crumbling and a great chunk of plaster has fallen off the side of the building. Remnants of that name must be concealed by the thicket of weeds in the abandoned lot below.

I used to walk by that church regularly, imagining what was inside. I pictured an austere, formal interior to match the cool gray stone. When I finally did enter, the occasion was a political meeting. We didn't use the sanctuary. Its doors were closed, and I pressed my face against a diamond-shaped window but could not see anything in the dark. The preacher let us use a basement meeting area that looked like it normally hosted postworship luncheons: there were folding tables festooned with red plastic party tablecloths, arrangements of fake flowers, and a number of decorative plates lining a display shelf against a side wall. The preacher said the building was a hundred years old but they were going to tear it down because the structure was no longer sound. I have passed there since; they have not started the demolition. A sign advertises the fund-raising activities of a building campaign.

For a long while, two lampposts just in front of the church bore signs whose message related to what the seekers would find beyond the open door. *MAP TO HEAVEN,* the signs read. But the Map to Heaven isn't a map at all. The shape of heaven is not described by a sphere or a spiral or an island of clouds hovering above the earthly realm. There are no streets, mountains, or rivers. The Map to Heaven is a series of Bible verses. A brief summary is given for each item of the list, along with a reference to the necessary chapter and verse: *All have Sinned* (Romans 2:23) and *God's Pay check is Death* (Romans 6:23) and *God loves you* (John 3:16) and *The Gospel saves* (Romans 10:9) and *Receive Christ today* (John 1:12). A passerby in search of salvation, redemption, or deliverance from peril, but faced with the chain around the red double doors, could find guidance from those two signs, like pillars at either side of the strait gate.

Other signs nearby show how to take a day trip to Atlantic City, how to reach your full earning potential as a self-employed travel agent, how to make life easier by engaging the services of dog-walkers, babysitters, or handymen, or how to join a medical study if you are a crack-addicted female. In the summer's heat I note an increase of signs in search of the disappeared—Alzheimer's patients and teenage girls—but also invitations to hip-hop rooftop parties and yoga classes in the park. There are signs advertising apartments for rent—lately it seems these are not in Harlem, but in the Bronx. You will see signs that say *Se renta cuartos.* The phrase is at once straightforward and in code: the language and the words tell quite a lot about what kinds of rooms are being rented and to whom. Recently, a photocopied sign with ornate lettering appeared. It publicized an open house and proclaimed an incredible real estate bargain: the price of a town house on historic Striver's Row had dropped by $400,000. The new, discounted price was $2,550,000. *All are welcome.*

A cell phone company that must have hired a culturally sensitive advertising firm promoted itself with the following corny ode:

Harlem You Rule. How do you stay so fly? From the old heads in the fedoras to the shorties rocking uptowns, Harlem, you never disappoint. Culturally no one has given us as much as you have. From music, to art, to dance, to literature, you're a renaissance community. You've changed the world. We've followed your lead by offering cell phone plans without annual contracts. Just use one of our plans with unlimited 7 pm nights and weekends to get at us. Like everyone else, we just want to be in the place to be.

Not far from there, a less coherent appeal cries, *HARLEM UNITED. Scatted sided of 306 Lenox Avenue and North General Hospital Need to be Investigate for discrimination with the latinos. I got wistnesses -n- evidence Colón, M.* From a bus crossing 116th Street I saw a sign that said *DANGER*, but I did not go back to that spot to investigate. There are signs to free the Jena Six, signs for a people's tribunal on the government's role in Hurricane Katrina, signs to stop the war in Iraq, signs to stop a war from beginning in Iran, signs for a new 9/11 commission. Around Thanksgiving appeared this impassioned plea:

Come Help Me Capture the Water and the Fire, So it Will Not Overflow or Burn When We Slip Through to feed the Hungry, Needy, Children and Forbidden. FOR "Thou Walkest through the fire, thou shalt not be burned neither shall the flame kindle upon thee" ISAIAH 43:2.

Before Christmas, I saw a sign for a food and clothing drive sponsored by the New Black Panther Party, a benign implementation of the original ten-point party platform, with which even Boy Scouts or the Junior League could agree. A more militant articulation could be found on the sign advertising a boycott that never gained much support: *The Peoples Committee says to BOYCOTT JIMBOS: McDonald's, Burger King, White Castle Hire Blacks in Harlem. Why not JIMBO's?*
Other signs ask other pressing questions. A document of several

pages was posted to a lamppost on my block. The first page was titled *BLACK INVENTORS...EXTRAORDINARY INVEN-TIONS*. The subsequent pages contained a list detailing those inventors and their inventions. At the end of this dossier, as if the names were evidence at some tribunal of what used to be called "racial feeling," there was a plea that was both damning and sorrowful: *WHY ARE THE GRANDSON'S OF THESE PEOPLE NOT EVEN WORKING IN THEIR COUNTRY???*

The very last page was either a cryptic answer to the question, or "exhibit A" in a separate charge. It was a poorly reproduced photograph of a lynching; amidst the crowd of spectators, a little white girl in a white frock flanked the charred and mutilated corpse. She was squinting, looking at the body with her head cocked to one side.

WHY DON'T YOU LOOK AT ME? Thus began a screed posted on 125th Street, the work of an anonymous latter-day pamphleteer:

Attention New Residents of Harlem (AKA Washington Heights etc) please be aware that you are contributing to the active displacement of the historic Harlem community. YES gentrification, which is a pretty word for modern day colonization.

You cannot blame the politicians or real estate brokers as long as YOU are willing to pay exorbitant prices for the same residential property that was once affordable. As you see more white, Asians, and others of economic advantage you will see less Blacks and Hispanics. Economic racism, are you the problem or the solution? There is no neutrality.

BUT do you see us? Because this is a neighborhood (specifically I refer to where you are reading this sign) we look at each other here and even greet the people we see daily. WHY aren't you looking at us? IS it guilt, are you purposely ignoring me are you afraid of me? This is often seen as a sign of disrespect and if you are afraid it would behoove you to look at people. How will you know who is an actual threat to you? Learn about and respect the places you decide to live!!! BUT even better would be for you to DECIDE to live elsewhere because where are we supposed to go?

Those advertisements, indictments, and supplications are rained on or ripped down or covered up or ignored. At the base of the same lampposts someone has stenciled messages in spraypaint. All along Lenox Avenue, Seventh Avenue, and Eighth Avenue are reminders of a struggle that elsewhere has gone underground: *WE DEMAND REPARATIONS FOR SLAVERY* and *THEY STOLE US THEY SOLD US THEY OWE US. REPARATIONS FOR SLAVERY. NOW! NOW!* and *THE HUEY P. NEWTON READER: THAT'S WASSUP!!* and *WE DEMAND UNIVERSAL HEALTH CARE AS REPARATIONS FOR SLAVERY* and *WE HAVE NOT FORGOTTEN REPARATIONS FOR SLAVERY* and *WHY ARE YOU SCARED OF REPARATIONS?* These near-permanent ciphers have begun to fade, covered with layers of grime. They have the effect of a subliminal message, quickly flashing at the edge of consciousness. You must be looking down to see them, or be otherwise disconnected from your surroundings. They are quick enough to read as you are just about to step into a busy intersection. (*Now! Now!*) But there is no information about how the goal will be achieved or how to join the cause. Some are exhortations, some are demands, and the placement of the signs at various intersections in Harlem suggests that the audience of the exhortation and the target of the demand is the same, or overlapping, or otherwise indeterminate.

Once, I crossed 139th street as an alternate path, walking that way just in order to see the street. It was a street in which I had no business, and this was obvious as soon as I entered the block. I looked down and saw at the base of yet another lamppost a sign that was not an exhortation or a demand or some part of a ten-point platform, but a message altogether more mysterious. It was also written in spray paint, but the words were scrawled by hand. *LOOK OUT,* this lamppost warned. I did look out, edgy and vigilant, until I reached the end of that block.

But by the time I received their notice, the words at the base of that lamppost had likely fulfilled their mission. The message had already been delivered—from and to emissaries of a realm whose boundaries are not visible by the light of day, or, perhaps, of a realm that exists only in the mind of a solitary spray-can scribbler. My eyes falling upon those words, and my mind later racing to attach some unverifiable meaning—or the eyes of another scanning the same spot without taking notice—all this was an unintended, meaningless consequence.

On Lenox Avenue, someone has taken to sending messages that are more direct but offered in a less permanent medium. It was late summer when I first saw the sidewalk messages, elaborate communications written on the pavement in brightly colored chalk. Every few days, in locations up and down Lenox Avenue, these messages appear.

Hi, Little People
Life is no joke

1) *Love yourself and respect others*
2) *Love your family*
3) *Care more and hate less*
4) *Try to THINK better so that you can act better*

5) *EDUCATION,*
6) *Trains your mind*
7) *Knowledge builds things*
8) *Reality will outlive you*
9) *Learn to have respect, good training and discipline in your life*
10) *Bad thinking will cause you to do bad things to others and especially yourself THINK WELL*

From the carefully rendered lettering and the artistic flourishes (hearts and flowers and sparkles shining out from certain words), I presumed the writer was an old woman, a retired schoolteacher, continuing her educational mission with these sidewalk signs. New ones appeared on a near-weekly basis:

Youngsters can you print and spell?

1) *I love myself and my family*
2) *Believe in school*
3) *Respect older people*
4) *Study and practice*
5) *Life is not a joke*
6) *Listen and pay attention*
7) *Think better to be a better person*
8) *Give more and hate less*
9) *Your life is worth saving*

I would stop and get out my notebook to copy down these messages, adding them to pages of notes from political meetings and transcriptions of signs posted on lampposts and windows. I wished I could reproduce in my lined notebook and with my imprecise hand the careful design of the words, the fanciful swirls and embellishments. I wished that I carried around crayons to reproduce the chosen color scheme. I would stop and write these messages down whenever I saw them: even late at night or in the rain. At least once when I was copying the sidewalk messages a man stopped, wanting to speak with me. Because I did not pay him any attention, but continued with my task, he stopped to read what was on the sidewalk. Then he said he was going to write it down, too.

EVILNESS DOESN'T LOVE YOU!
LOVE YOURSELF!

Little People Can You Read?

1) *Life is not a joke*
2) *THINK! Well*
3) *Think better to become a better person*
4) *Bad thinking leads to bad things*
5) *Love yourself, family and respect others*
6) *Education is the right step to move ahead*
7) *You must value your life*
8) *Knowledge makes things work*
9) *Think always and think safely*
10) *Make your life mean something*

STUDENTS
ALWAYS LOVE YOURSELF

EDUCATION

1) *You must have it*
2) *You must WANT it*
3) *Do not be afraid to learn*

4) *Love your family*
5) *Respect other people*
6) *Respect your teachers*
7) *THINK! POSITIVE*

STUDENTS! PUT LOVE IN YOUR HEART

EDUCATION

1) *Love yourself*
2) *Love your family*
3) *Respect others*
4) *Your mind needs knowledge so you can become more intelligent*
5) *THINK. Try to be more positive*
6) *Schooling is very serious*
7) *Life is no joke*
8) *Do not take a person's life if you want to live your life*

HI! LITTLE FOLKS

1) *Love yourself always*
2) *Love your family*
3) *Respect others*
4) *Let school be your best friend*
5) *Practice your reading*
6) *Study as much as possible*
7) *Challenge arithmetic (don't be afraid)*
8) *Being good is better for you*
9) *Being bad is not good for you*
10) *Respect senior citizens*

LIFE IS NO JOKE. THINK.

Other versions of the messages offered academic lessons, as if the street were a classroom chalkboard. Spelling lessons had letters eliminated, challenging students to fill in the blank; arithmetic problems asked passersby to complete equations. The other messages repeated variations on an unchanging theme: *Life is no joke. Read. Be good. Think better. Respect others. Love yourself. Your life is worth saving. Reality will outlast you.* These were commandments, on a tablet significantly less enduring than stone. They were the kind of thing that might be affixed to a classroom bulletin board in bright paper letters at the beginning of a school year. Here on the street, there was even less opportunity to gauge their effect. And although they were designed to be destroyed, I felt compelled to preserve them. Often when I stopped to write, someone would walk across the words, temporarily obstructing the view.

When I met Sister Doris Littlejohn, she told me she was also known as Pastor Dorcas Lynn, but that her name was now James because she was married, and before James she was married to a man called Cook, until she found out he was a bigamist. I was walking east across 125th Street with my notepad in hand when I paused to write something down. I had reached the row benches in front of the State Office Building at 125th Street and Seventh Avenue. In weather fine and foul people gather there to exchange news, talk politics, or stare into the street. I was already seated when I noticed the woman next to me, sitting with a notepad and pen already in use. After I saw the notebook I noticed her feet: they were bare, her toes were cramped, and her toenails were long and dirty. The skin on her feet and shins was covered in a gray dust.

Some time passed, me scribbling in my pad, she in hers, before we looked up at each other and smiled. She asked if I was a writer, and I said yes. I asked her the same, and she said yes. We both smiled again, and laughed, and she told me her name and its variations. She told me that she wrote poetry and music about spiritual things and about political things. She asked whether I liked political things, and I said yes, so she flipped a few pages in her yellow legal pad and explained that the following concerned the condition of alienation in our community and was addressed to people of means, people like Oprah Winfrey, Bill Gates, and certain singers and sports celebrities. First she began to read it aloud, and then she stopped to ask if I wouldn't prefer to read it on my own. By the time Sister Doris Littlejohn and I had begun our exchange, I had stopped taking notes, so I cannot tell you any details at all of her piece of writing. I only remember that her words ran across the page like fugitives from sense while at the same time possessing a power by which some meaning pierced through. Eventually, this feeling of comprehension and confusion receded, and I was able to grasp her bigger meaning.

A man came up to the row of benches and began dashing back and forth in front of us, and then into and out of the street. He was dressed in athletic clothes and possessed by a remarkable purpose: he was shadowboxing while delivering rhyming couplets. The dexterity of the jabs and blows to his invisible sparring partner was matched by the staccato cadence of his words. Sister Doris Littlejohn and I laughed, and then we got out our notebooks and began writing. *A boxing poet!* she exclaimed, and began recording his antics. Her feet danced as she wrote; she dangled them with the flicking movement of a delighted child seated at water's edge. I felt somewhat comforted by her, writing down the same thing I was observing. We must have formed a strange picture, both looking up and out and into the world and then looking down into our pages. The result might have been books that were mirror images of each other.

When the boxing poet had gone, Sister Doris asked if I would like to hear one of her songs. She began to clap out a dirgelike rhythm. The only lyric that I can remember was a paraphrase of scripture: *You are more than a conqueror.* This line was repeated in an unchanging chorus, though Sister Doris did not seem to tire of singing or accompanying herself with clapping hands. When her song was complete, we chatted about her songs and poems, and at some point I asked her whether she lived in Harlem. She said she lived in the streets. After this revelation, she gave me a history of how that had come to be so. It involved the men whose names she had borne in succession, and also the interference of a treacherous mother-in-law connected to the church Sister Doris had belonged to until recently. This church was the scene of rampant factionalism, and Sister Doris had been its victim due to jealousy over her own ease of communication with the higher power. The cause of this strife in her personal and ecclesiastical life was not surprising to Sister Doris. She told me that a lot of territorialism exists in the physical and spiritual realms right now, an observation that caused our talk to veer from the personal to the world-historical, with Sister Doris giving her opinion on spiritual territorialism as demonstrated by the wars in the Middle East.

The imminence of warfare in both the spiritual and terrestrial realms prompted Sister Doris Littlejohn to produce a phone number on a wrinkled sheet of paper and press it into my hand. It was the number of a prayer line, and she said I should call it at any hour when in need of assistance, and that I should not mention her name. This discretion was necessary because the number belonged to the same church that she had just told me was persecuting her, the scene of the spiritual factions and territorialism.

We had been together for some time, mostly facing the street, Sister Doris talking while I listened, when she turned to face me squarely and declared that our meeting had been the working of a providential power and that she wanted to tell me that there are such things as angels. After this speech, she asked in words more exact than any I had seen written on her pages what I had gained from this time with her. I stammered something utterly unequal to our encounter and said I was glad that we met.

Not long before we parted, I asked, in the most delicate way possible, whether she was in need of shoes. I had decided that we would get up right then and go to the nearest shoe store. But she said she had shoes, and that she had only removed them because her feet ached. She gestured to the bag she was carrying as if to confirm the existence of the shoes.

We said good-bye and agreed that we were sure to meet again. And we did. When I saw her next, it was on Lenox Avenue in front of the Mormon Church. It seemed like a great sign that we should meet again so soon. And whether or not it actually *was* a sign, the crucial thing is that we were both willing to see it as such. This time our conversation did not include the existence of angels or field reports from the front line of spiritual battlefields. Sister Doris needed money. She did not ask. She managed to express that need without explicitly making a request, and I gave her two dollars, all that was in my purse. She reached into her purse and gave me two pieces of paper. On each was printed a prayer. It seemed like an unequal exchange, with my contribution being of lesser value. I was not buying the prayers, and she was not selling them. She had given me what she had to offer.

I presumed that would be the beginning of a series of encounters between us. The reason for this expectation is simple: such is life on Lenox Avenue. There is some predictability as to whom you will meet and when. As always it is necessary to stop and speak, to collect the latest bulletin or a hug. It is not possible to pass from an exchange such as the one I had with Sister Doris Littlejohn back into anonymity.

But I never saw Sister Doris Littlejohn again. The weather changed; I was going out less and staying inside more — and that was not entirely to do with the weather. When I did go out, it wasn't to amble along Lenox Avenue or 125th Street, and I did not stop with my notebook at the benches near the State Office Building. I went out only to rush onto the subway and go downtown, or to walk a few blocks and into a political meeting (often enough, these were *inside* the State Office Building). My thoughts returned occasionally to Sister Doris. I wondered why we had not met again, not knowing whether her disappearance had to do with spiritual warfare or whether, owing to her intimacy with the esoteric domain, she had disappeared in order to avoid being written about.

I had seen the sign: *Come Help Me Capture the Water and the Fire, So It Will Not Overflow or Burn When We Slip Through to Feed the Hungry, Needy, Children and Forbidden.* Most likely, her disappearance had to do with the reality of living in Harlem — on the streets — as the weather grew cold. It is possible that we did meet again, but perhaps one or both of us had not noticed the other. Perhaps I had been in a hurry to get downtown, or in a hurry to get to a meeting. Perhaps, because it was winter, one or both of us had been tightly bundled and therefore unrecognizable.

Not long after I saw Sister Doris in the second and final instance, and before I stopped going out, I saw a pair of women planted at the intersection of 133rd and Lenox, right near my building. They were preaching and singing, holding a two-woman revival without a tent and without an audience. Their congregants were the people passing by. Their production was broadcast into the night by a microphone and portable amplifier. They are often there on summer nights, so I walked briskly by them, scarcely looking up as I passed. Their song followed me from behind, accompanied by the tinny syncopation of a single tambourine: *I have a feeling, I have a feeling, I have feeling everything is gonna be all right.* I turned the corner quickly because I did not share the sentiment.

It was springtime when I finally met the creator of the chalk messages. I would like to tell you his name, to tell you about the way he dresses, to tell you about his eyes and the way he cocks his head to one side when he pauses to listen and also when he speaks. But the most important thing about our first meeting is that he didn't want me to write about him at all. Because I had already been recording the chalk messages whenever I saw them, I had thought it would be a good topic for a local-color story I could pitch to the *Times* or a radio station as an "only in New York"–type segment. Now that I had met the creator, the story had a protagonist. I told him I wanted to write about him, but he immediately brushed me off. He said he did not want to be written about, he did not want publicity. He said he had just met another girl who was a journalism student and wanted to write about him for a school project. He patted the pocket of his trousers and said it was full of cards from people who tell him to call because they, too, would like to write a story about him. I felt a bit rebuked. I wondered whether it was, in fact, a question of "publicity."

You will ask why I am writing this anyway, only without mentioning his name. I have asked this, too. The man who writes the chalk messages (I will call him the Messenger) perhaps offers the clearest answer to us both. A while after our first meeting, when we had become friends, when I told him that my hands were hurting and I could not write, he scolded me because I had not been to see a doctor. He said that he hated to take a stern tone with me, but he had to because I had to get serious about my business. And once, when I complimented him on what he was doing, and how the messages were so important and so urgent, he shrugged and said that he was only trying to make his *contribution,* and that this was something we all had to figure out how to do. He often says that he is in touch with the reality of existence, and that this is what compels him to his task.

I'd seen the Messenger once before that first meeting. He was crouched down on the sidewalk working on a new creation, oblivious to anything going on around him, and much of what was going on around him reciprocated the oblivion. This time, he was not in the middle of work; he was perched on a standpipe in front of the hospital surveying something he had just completed. At first, I had passed him by because I was on the way somewhere else and was late, but I stopped and doubled back. Once I'd reached him and we had finished our salutations—we didn't shake hands, but bumped elbows because his hands were covered in chalk—he said he'd watched me pass and watched me pause and watched me turn around to come back, and that he was glad I had done so.

When we spoke that first afternoon, the Messenger told me some of the things he has again told me since: that he writes his messages because the children have *an emptiness inside,* an emptiness because they are not nourished at home. He says his mission is to share his wisdom and understanding. He tells me about the children he meets who are thrilled by the mathematical problems he writes on the sidewalk, and he also tells me how some of the adults who used to scorn him and make fun of him now offer nods of approval.

The Messenger said he wanted to expand his territory; he thinks of moving over to Seventh Avenue, for instance. But I have only seen his messages on both sides of Lenox Avenue in the blocks between 125th and 136th Streets. The Messenger spoke of a gang member who'd asked him to write a few chalk messages on his block, to inspire the children there. He decried the attitude of the young man, especially the way he insisted on the territory being *his block,* as if it were his sole dominion. The Messenger said this was evidence of a damaged mentality, but he took up this strange commission anyway, going beyond his normal area on the avenue and into a side street. He planned to write a message on the sidewalk before a small storefront that was boarded up, choosing that spot because it wouldn't obstruct the traffic of a business. But in the midst of setting his words down, the cops stopped him. He mentioned that it was a black female cop in particular who talked to him like he was a dog. He said he wasn't doing anything wrong and that if the cops had actually stopped to read what he was writing, they would have agreed with him and congratulated him and encouraged what he was doing. It was another instance of the *damaged mentality* he'd spoken of.

Along with his inspirational statements, the Messenger includes certain symbols that appear repeatedly in his creations. He makes hearts held aloft by wings, shooting stars, and birds that soar over the words. Lately I've noticed another symbol among his messages, an embellished cross that resembles an image found by archaeologists in abandoned slave cabins in Texas, among other places. Some researchers have related the sign to the Kongo cosmogram, a "map" of the world that can be traced back hundreds of years to the kingdom of Kongo in West Central Africa. Its lines and quadrants could be mistaken for a simple compass showing the four directions, but in fact they mark the boundaries between night and day, life and death, past and present, male and female, matter and spirit. When the sign was made on the ground, the spot was consecrated; it sealed an oath, made in the presence and under the authority of God and the ancestors. To stand in the center of the circle that surrounds the crossing lines is to stand at the center of the world, safe within the boundaries of the community. These symbols have been found etched into shell or brick, but many more have vanished, having been etched into dust.

The Messenger asked me the title of the book I was writing. I began by telling him the title was borrowed from Ralph Ellison, but he hadn't heard of Ellison. He mentioned that when he was in school there were *so many things they didn't teach,* and he said he'd never had much opportunity to visit the library. When I said the title would be *Harlem Is Nowhere,* his face formed a pained expression, as if the very pronouncement of the words had erased us from the spot where we stood. Quickly I added that Ellison was talking about *mentality,* and immediately he seemed soothed. I tried to explain that Ellison's essay spoke of the same things he wrote about on the sidewalk.

I imagine him inside whatever walls he calls home, listening to the sound of the storms that come almost daily in late summer. But that is a worry of mine, not his. Probably he doesn't think of it at all; the one time he mentioned a message that disappeared in the rain, he waved it off like it was without consequence. He has told me only once about having written something twice. The first time, it had been washed away. He said that normally he doesn't repeat himself, but this particular phrase had stuck with him

Once, he stopped me to present a riddle he had not yet committed to the street. He said that he had tried the same thing earlier in the day with another female friend and that she had been stumped, so he wanted to test my wits. The riddle was: *What is the first thing that happens when a child comes into the world?*

I hesitated before venturing an answer, and of course my attempt was wrong. The Messenger said the question was very simple, and so was the correct reply. The first thing a child does when it comes into the world is take a deep breath. He said people seemed to not grasp the importance of this, but that was a simple fact gleaned from being in touch with the reality of existence.

When I meet him on Lenox Avenue, I never leave without thinking that I should like to make my task adhere to the Messenger's simple mission: to share his wisdom and understanding. To make things simple so that people can see. To fill what is empty inside us. When I see the Messenger, we do not talk about the rezoning of 125th Street. We do not talk about land. We do not talk about politics. When I see him we stop and chat; if he sees me first, he always calls out my name as I am walking down the avenue. Recently he was perched on a standpipe beneath a tree at the corner by Liberation Books. One of his friends had recently brought him a whole bag of chalk that she'd gotten on sale at Target. *When it's blue it's blue all the way through,* he said, *when it's pink it's pink all the way through.* He pointed with insistence toward the sidewalk, really *through* the sidewalk, and with such force that I did not doubt the possibility of those pigments penetrating the earth's crust. Noting the vibrancy of his new, better-quality colors, he wondered aloud whether maybe what he writes will last a bit longer. As I left, he told me he loved me, and I told him the same. He told me to check out the latest thing he'd written and tell him what I thought when we next met.

I walked a block down Lenox and saw his latest message. I didn't write it down because I was in a hurry, or I didn't have a pen, or I thought I would pass that way again later in the afternoon or even on the next day. But I did not leave the house at all the next day, and the day after that it rained.

Land Is the Basis of All Independence

WE COLLECTED OUR flyers from the Record Shack and spread from there across Harlem. I began my shift at the corner of 125th and Frederick Douglass Boulevard, as I had by then begun to refer to Eighth Avenue. This was a result of going to meetings: it was now necessary to call things by their correct names. So, Seventh was always Adam Clayton Powell Jr. Boulevard, and Lenox Avenue was Malcolm X Boulevard. At one meeting, a woman interrupted every time someone used the term 125th Street, instead of calling it by its official designation, Martin Luther King Jr. Boulevard. The name mattered, she said. How could we be serious if we didn't invoke the spirit of Martin Luther King Jr. by insisting that Harlem's most famous thoroughfare be called by its right and proper name? The meeting was stuck on this point for a few moments. Eventually it was agreed that since no one ever called 125th Street by its longer name, and because we were fighting for its future, we shouldn't confuse people by speaking about and passing out flyers referring to Martin Luther King Jr. Boulevard.

I walked east, attempting to interest passersby in the fact that the city was pushing a new plan to turn 125th Street into a valley of high-rise luxury apartment buildings. Would they care to have a flyer? Did they know about the rezoning? Had they heard about the upcoming protest? But I lacked technique, unable to mimic the rapid, florid gestures used by the other hawkers on the street—I could match neither the showmanship of Nation of Islam members selling *The Final Call* nor the rush-hour urgency of the people who distribute free newspapers at subway entrances. Instead, I surveyed the crowd streaming by and set upon anyone who looked vaguely sympathetic. My canvassing focused at first on mothers with children. I quickly abandoned an imprecise assessment of political commitment based on hairstyle or accessories (anyone wearing dreadlocks or African garb was an instant target). More often than not, people passed me by without even pausing. They did not show a fleeting interest in the fact that in a few days' time, the Coalition to Save Harlem would attempt to form a human chain across 125th Street to protest the city's plan to rezone the main street of Harlem. My partner for the shift observed that *people were so broke down, so scared, so indifferent, they couldn't even take a flyer.* But a few already knew about the demonstration, and a few others said they intended to join. One older man refused to take a flyer, not because he was indifferent or because he was broken down, but, he said, because we were *jiving the people*—that no demonstration across any length of 125th Street would ever change the outcome of the city's plan. He said we were too late; but actually, he was saying we were worse than late, we were dishonest and self-serving.

I stopped for a break at the base of the monument celebrating Reverend Adam Clayton Powell Jr. The statue of Powell, who was pastor of the Abyssinian Baptist Church from 1937 until 1970, and Harlem's envoy to the U.S. House of Representatives between 1945 and

1971, guards the southwest corner of 125th and Seventh Avenue, which was renamed in his honor. When the monument was first erected a few years ago, I thought it seemed flamboyant. Powell is depicted as a kind of superhero. He trudges up a treacherous incline of shiny metal, the path as steep as it is slick. The figure is ill-clad for the ascent, wearing dress shoes and a formal suit with coattails sculpted to flap permanently in an allegorical wind. His only tool for this trek up the mountaintop is a Bible tucked under one arm. Engraved around the plinth is a list of all the legislation the congressman passed while serving Harlem. On one side is a quote from Powell: *Press forward at all times, climbing forward toward that higher ground of the harmonious society that shapes the laws of man to the laws of God.* Around the other side in large letters is Powell's trademark phrase, *Keep the Faith.* The designer of the statue had sanitized the particular cool-cat phraseology of Harlem's suave representative. Both a race man and a ladies' man, he was actually known to encourage his constituents with the saying *Keep the faith, baby.*

My thoughts about the statue changed when I started attending political meetings in Harlem, where Powell's name and memory are invoked with the frequency and veneration usually accorded a saint. I heard a woman talk excitedly about marching with Powell as a little girl. Another woman sometimes passed out flyers bearing his portrait and the words *Harlem: Then, Now, and Forever.* Other flyers reminded *As Adam Clayton Powell, Jr., proffered knowingly, "What's in your hand?" THE VOTE. Do not be afraid to exercise it. Vote out politicians who do not protect you as Adam Clayton Powell, Jr., did!*

The statue is in the shadow of the State Office Building, a nineteen-story office tower built as a pet project of then Governor Nelson Rockefeller. But this great public work was controversial even before it was built. First proposed by the governor in 1966 to revitalize Harlem in the wake of the 1964 riots, the building is located where Lewis Michaux's famous nationalist bookstore once

Lewis Micheaux's National Memorial African Bookstore, also known as the "House of Common Sense and Home of Proper Propaganda," 1964. (Courtesy of Bettmann / CORBIS)

stood. The propagandist and agitator accepted compensation from the state for the loss of his property and was promised a new retail location inside the new tower, which never materialized. For three months in 1969, a group called the Harlem Community Coalition blocked the construction effort by occupying the building site with a continuous sit-in; a two-day long convention between Rockefeller and community groups led to the outright rejection of building plans. At least one chronicler of Harlem recalls that Powell himself was outraged by the project: *Congressman Powell averred that if the office building was erected he would quit Harlem and leave the country. "I fear even to state what's going to happen if the Governor does not reverse his decision," declared the Harlem Congressman.*

The story is probably more complicated than what that historian offered—all this was happening around the same time that Adam Clayton Powell Jr. was being run out of Congress. In the eyes of his detractors, he was already spending a great deal too much time outside the country. But some version of the ominous outcome predicted by Powell did come to pass. The long-delayed construction recommenced in 1970, just weeks before Powell lost his seat to Charles Rangel (a supporter of Rockefeller's building project). Powell moved to the Bahamas and died in 1972, at the age of sixty-three. Two years later, the Harlem State Office Building was dedicated; the ceremony attracted a thousand protestors. Barely a decade passed before the building Powell detested was renamed in his memory. The building and the statue honor the leader while upholding a tradition of controversy being smoothed over by tokens and symbolism.

Some years before I started passing out flyers near the Powell statue, I was receiving them. *BUY BLACK* was the message of that earlier afternoon. The bearer of the message sat at the base of the statue, with an attitude that deserved its own mount. Interested takers presented themselves before him like supplicants; he did not make any pursuit.

I approached him for a flyer and read it. I don't remember why we started to speak or what we said. Maybe it was an exchange based on presumed familiarity—perhaps he thought we'd met before, and, as usual, it was not true. I want to tell you his name, but I'm sure he wouldn't want me to, so I will say that he is known by the name of a heroic African warrior. I will call him the Chief, because the flyers he passed out show a picture of him from forty years ago in the upper right-hand corner. "Chief" is the title that appears in the caption giving his name. He is a member of the African Nationalist Pioneer Movement. A photo in the upper left-hand corner of the same flyer shows one Carlos A. Cooks, the founder of the African Nationalist Pioneer Movement (ANPM), but no special title precedes his name. I can tell you the name of Carlos A. Cooks because he is dead. I already knew his name when I met the Chief because I'd read about him in the library. He is not one whose name is immortalized by way of a street sign.

On the flyer, in those pictures from the 1950s or 1960s, both Carlos A. Cooks and the Chief wear leopard-skin hats and black military dress jackets with epaulets and leather braces strapped across their chests. I'd seen the same picture of Cooks in a book at the library, where the caption identified him as

the nation's number one Black Nationalist, and the foremost proponent of the Marcus Garvey postulations; Administrator of the African Nationalist Pioneer Movement, editor of the erstwhile *Street Speaker* magazine, and one of the two deans of the Harlem street speakers. He contended that black men had nuclear weapons in ancient Africa and by the use of them desiccated the land, producing the Sahara Desert.

The same book explained that this claim was part of Cooks's effort of *convincing Negroes of their innate ability to do big things now and in the future.* Cooks and his fellow orators at African Square *speak of great Negroes of long ago, and tell of magnificent performances by dark souls in African states of antiquity.* Commenting on the excavation of pharaonic tombs in Egypt, Cooks noted the deaths of several scientists involved. They were not, he said, the result of the "Pharaoh's Curse" or some word-magic effected by inscriptions on the tombs. According to Cooks, the reason was the presence of nuclear fission within the burial chambers. *When the explorers opened and entered them, their bodies became radioactive and this brought about their death.*

Cooks's ideas on ancient nuclear physics were a minor part of his presence and influence. Born in the Dominican Republic in 1913, Cooks immigrated to New York, where he founded the ANPM in 1941. He led the group until his death, in 1966. During his quarter century as a political personality, he seems to have enjoyed a level of local celebrity that, despite his penchant for the world-historical, never transcended the borders of Harlem. Indeed, most writing about Cooks by his acolytes emphasizes the lack of attention paid to his work while he lived and to his legacy in death. He is mourned as one who never got his due and described with a level of hyperbole intended to assert his place in history: *Carlos Cooks was to Black Nationalism what John Coltrane was to the so-called avant-garde "jazz", and what Aretha is to soul music; the prime progenitor among their respective peers.* But he was robbed of this recognition because *he was denied national coverage—by white and "Black" press—and was bound by an oath (the sacri) not to seek publicity for himself.*

Perhaps Cooks would not have tolerated that coverage—that publicity—if it had been granted him, and certainly he would not have trusted it. His own newsletters, *Street Speaker* and *The Black*

Challenge, would have been publicity enough, providing an outlet for Cooks and his cohort to write on various topics both contemporary (one issue reprinted a speech of Sékou Touré to the United Nations on the subject of the sovereignty of African nations) and historical (*Zimbabwe was in its noonday of culture and refinement two thousand years before the Germanic Tribes abolished the gruesome practice of feasting on the flesh of their conquered dead*).

The latter-day African Nationalist Pioneers strive to keep the memory of Carlos A. Cooks alive. *The Contributions of Carlos Cooks* include, apart from founding the ANPM and its newsletter: a merchant organization known as the African Pioneering Syndicate, Inc.; a resettlement organization, the African Colonization Society; the Universal African Relief, a charity arm; an African Communities League; the African Nationalist Legion, which was *the military arm of the race;* the School of African Culture and Fundamentalism; the Nationalist Social Club; and the production of Orthodox African Nationalist Literature. Cooks also presided over annual celebrations of Marcus Garvey's birthday; an African Freedom Day held in January to celebrate the Emancipation Proclamation and the anniversaries of various African independence declarations also celebrated in that month; and the Miss Natural Standard of Beauty Contest, held in conjunction with the Marcus Garvey Day celebrations, *a unique and rare contest designed to help restore pride and self-confidence in the heavily inferior-minded Black woman who falsely believes that the white woman (and all other women) is more beautiful than the Black woman.*

Some of these accomplishments were achieved only in theory. Their fate as part of Cooks's legacy is sealed in another of his contributions: the Marcus Garvey Memorial Building. Planned as a headquarters for the African Nationalist Pioneer Movement, the building was to serve as *a stone monument that will spiritually testify to the admiration and respect that the Black people of Harlem and throughout the world have for the life, efforts, deeds, doctrine and memory* of Garvey. The date, day, and time of a 1962 ground-breaking ceremony is recorded, along with its position *on a site located on the south side of 141st Street, approximately 100 feet east of Eighth Avenue, Harlem, New York.*

After breaking ground, Cooks postponed the official launch of all ANPM programming until the building's completion. But by the time of Cooks's death, it was only two-thirds constructed. The building, a ruin before its time, was demolished by the city in the 1970s. *Consequently, the programs of the ANPM were never launched and remain unfinished business for the African National-ists. The erection of the Marcus Garvey Memorial Building or its equivalent is also unfinished business for the African Nationalist.*

Lacking a physical home, Cooks's movement found shelter under the still-erect pillar of his most frequently articulated aim:

We submit that the Black people of Harlem and all other Homogeneous African communities, have the same natural and moral right to be clannish in their patronage as all other people have dramatised that they are. We advocate as a matter of sound racial economics, the BUY BLACK CAMPAIGN.

Patronize the merchants of your own race. Build a solvent foundation for your children. Help create employment and independence for your race.

Buy Black was the enduring cause of the African Nationalist Pioneer Movement, and in Harlem, the Chief was its main booster. He could be found most Saturdays at the same spot beneath the Powell monument, passing out flyers and holding court before a posse of supporters and protégés.

When we met, the Chief explained that the campaign was only the first action of an extensive movement for self-determination.

He asked me which movement I was a part of. I told him I was not a part of any movement. He asked what my platform was. I fumbled for an answer, saying something about liberation, and then confessed that I had none, but that I was a writer and that I was from Texas. One or both of these facts caused him to pursue his initial line of questioning with greater fervor — the Chief was even more convinced that I should have an urgent and articulate platform. I was, after all, from a place where a black man had recently been tied to the back of a truck and dragged along a country road until his limbs were torn from his body. I was from a state where a small-town drug bust had resulted in the arrest of 15 percent of the town's black population on suspicion of involvement in a drug ring. These more spectacular and egregious acts, the Chief informed me, could be joined by other more mundane atrocities. But since my place of birth and my chosen vocation had not inspired in me a form of political engagement that could be expressed as a slogan, the Chief gave up and began to give me a history quiz.

He asked me what I knew about Juneteenth. I told him it was the day, celebrated in Texas, when slaves finally learned the news of the Emancipation Proclamation, more than two years after it had been ratified. I told him how, as a child, I'd been taught (or had been half-listening and misheard what I was taught) that it had taken two years for the news to reach Texas. I did not tell him that this was a holiday about which I'd always felt ambivalent. Two extra years of slavery had always seemed a dismal cause for celebration.

That last bit would not have impressed him any more than the first part of my answer did. He told me I was wrong. He told me I had absorbed a rather benign if not fraudulent version of the events of June 19, 1865. The belated emancipation in Texas could not be blamed on the poor service of the Pony Express. Confederate slaveholders in Texas had refused to recognize Lincoln's proclamation, so Juneteenth celebrated the date when a general of the Union Army landed at Galveston with a phalanx of 1,800 soldiers to take possession of the state and enforce the order. The Chief lingered on this last detail, emphasizing the necessity of military force to assert the liberty of my ancestors in Texas.

I thanked him for the corrective history and said I'd read up on it. He told me that when we next met, he expected me to have a platform.

A person in search of a platform could hardly find a better spot than the setting of my encounter with the Chief. The Adam Clayton Powell statue faces southwest, across from the Hotel Theresa. The hotel is famous for hosting Fidel Castro during his postrevolutionary visit to New York, after Castro was unsatisfied with his reception by a downtown hotel. The Theresa was briefly the headquarters of the Organization of Afro-American Unity, founded by Malcolm X about a year before his assassination, after he broke with Elijah Muhammad and returned from Mecca. Its mission was modeled after the Pan-African platform of the Organization of African Unity, connecting the U.S. struggle to the circumstances of blacks across the diaspora.

Before Nelson Rockefeller's office tower was built, the corner had been a congregation point for soapbox orators. The confluence of those speakers and Michaux's National Memorial African Bookstore had earned it the name Harlem Square or African Square. Aside from a regular cast of street speakers, the intersection was also the setting for mass rallies featuring speeches by Powell, Malcolm X, and Kwame Nkrumah, among others.

Currently, African Square is also the place where the Brooklyn-based Pan-Africanist group the December 12th Movement and the Malcolm X Millennium Committee each year convene a "Black

Power March" on the leader's birthday, May 19, enforcing a three-hour shutdown of all businesses on 125th Street (and boycotting those establishments that refuse to close). On the same day, the Malcolm X Commemoration Committee organizes a caravan of buses that leave from African Square on an annual pilgrimage from Harlem to Woodlawn Cemetery in Queens, where a graveside ceremony is held to honor the man, who, after pilgrimage to Mecca, took on the formal designation of El-Hajj Malik El-Shabazz.

Just a few blocks away, on 129th Street, is the former Elks Lodge where, in 1925, A. Philip Randolph held a meeting of five hundred railway workers, organizing them in defiance of the Pullman Company. The men became the Brotherhood of Sleeping Car Porters, the first African American labor union, under the motto Fight or Be Slaves.

Adam Clayton Powell Jr. launched one of his most famous crusades a few blocks from the spot. The "Don't Buy Where You Can't Work" campaign was a boycott that forced white merchants on 125th Street to hire blacks as shop attendants. And in the 1940s, Powell led a "black-out" boycott against Consolidated Edison Electric and Gas, successfully forcing them to hire blacks by organizing Harlem residents to abandon the use of electricity once a week. Participants in the campaign lit their dwellings with candles. Later, the effort culminated by converging on the Con Ed premises on 125th Street in a "Bill-Payers' Parade," where marchers appeared at the office en masse to pay bills with pennies.

But that was all in the past. In the present, I could find a platform on posters covering store windows, and from flyers pressed into my hands or picked up from the pavement. All of these beckoned toward protests, demonstrations, and boycotts, but most of all, they announced meetings. They offered urgent information bulletins:

The Frederick Samuels North End Merchants store owners between 142nd and 147th on Seventh Avenue are losing their stores!

They put forward fiery exhortations:

Fight to Save the Record Shack...We say Harlem is ours, we will not be moved! The Record Shack Must Stay! Renew the Lease!

They suggested boycotts and mass actions that never took root:

Don't buy at H&M.
Every item you purchase at H&M helps to evict black shoppers and their families from Harlem. 10,000 Black families have been evicted from Harlem in the last ten years.

SAVE HARLEM!!
To protest the destruction of the black capital of the world and the cruel, heartless evictions of our poor black brothers and sisters from their homes, apartments and small businesses in Harlem,
HANG A TOWEL IN PROTEST OUT OF YOUR WINDOW TODAY!
Shame America! Let the World See an Ocean of Towels Hanging from Every Apartment and Every Black Business in Harlem

There were signs posted in front of Bobby's Happy House, where the ninety-year-old proprietor of the oldest black-owned business in Harlem had been evicted, along with several other commercial tenants, as a result of the largest single-parcel real estate deal in Harlem, valued at about $30 million. The high dollar value was not the only remarkable thing about that transaction. At meetings activists exhorted the public to investigate rumors that the real estate broker behind the deal and the property owner benefiting from the sale and the evictions were one and the same person. That person was also president of the 125th Street Business Improvement District, an organization of business owners with strong ties to Harlem politicians.

KIMCO MUST GO
PROTEST CORPORATE TAKEOVER OF HARLEM
Rally against ethnic cleansing of long standing black owned business on 125th and throughout Harlem

In Unity and Militancy we can save the soul of black businesses in Harlem and end the economic siege of our community. Show your support its now or never.

Another sign carried an unusually plaintive call to action, notable because it was unattached to any specific building under threat. Besides the "NYC Council" and "Your House of Worship Leader," it did not identify any particular actors to blame. It did not bear the name of any organization to join, or the date of a rally to attend—the crisis was general and the siege ongoing.

A Plea to the tenants of Harlem
Don't let yourself be pushed out of your apartment by the constantly increasing RENT Hike
Call your House of Worship leader
Or call the NYC Council
Tell them "The extortionist rents and mass eviction warrants must stop now!"

You Vote!
You Pray!
You have power
Use your power
To save your home in Harlem

It was because of such signs that I began to attend meetings.
They were held in church sanctuaries and anterooms, school audi-
toriums and community centers.

PUBLIC HEARING
"HARLEM IS NOT FOR SALE"

Sale Price 1 million @ 10% Down
Can you afford to live here?
NO!
STAND UP AND FIGHT!
SAVE HARLEM'S HISTORY, CULTURE,
SMALL BUSINESSES AND HOUSING
LET YOUR VOICE BE HEARD!

The Oberia Dempsey Multiservice Center was nearly filled to
capacity. It was the first presentation of the city's plan to rezone
125th Street, an initiative known as the River-to-River plan
because the changes would sweep the corridor from Broadway to
Second Avenue between 124th and 126th Streets. The meeting
was hosted by the Community Board representing Central Harlem (no. 10) and attended by representatives of the Department of
City Planning. The thousand-page rezoning document was dis-
tilled into a slide presentation. The main objective of the rezoning
was to transform the commercial district into a residential area and
to revise prevailing codes restricting density and height, allowing

the construction of high-rise luxury condominiums. By the city's own estimate, the rezoning would increase the residential capacity of 125th Street by 750 percent. The majority of this housing would be market-rate, but developers had the option to include affordable housing, with the incentive that any developer offering a certain number of affordable housing units would be rewarded with permission to build even more luxury or market-rate units.

Another incentive offered to developers was an "arts and culture" bonus, in which developers were similarly rewarded with more market-rate units if their buildings included space that could be rented as galleries, performance spaces, studios, or offices for artistic organizations. The representative from the city planning department put it thusly: *We've been told that arts and culture are important up here, so there are going to be restaurants and cultural venues.* A community member in the audience grumbled in response: *Arts and culture don't pay the bills.* Another suggested that the arts and culture bonus would lead to a situation where black culture was celebrated in Harlem but no black people actually lived there anymore. A long line of residents stood at a microphone to denounce the plan, the testimonies growing more and more heated. One man suggested that *there have been riots before in Harlem's past, and there can be riots again.* Another man wore a T-shirt that read *HARLEM IS NOT FOR SALE BECAUSE HARLEM'S ALREADY BEEN SOLD.* He named the local politicians and businessmen he claimed were responsible, then left the mic to hover close to the urban planners seated at a dais in the front of the room. He looked each in the eye and then said: *Whatever you build, we'll burn it down.*

The auditorium erupted in shouts. The community board member at the helm of the meeting admonished the crowd like a bunch of unruly children, threatening to shut the meeting down. No one settled down. The meeting was abruptly ended. A young woman from city planning was in tears.

A small sign on West 138th Street just off Lenox Avenue marks the spot where Marcus Mosiah Garvey convened his first gathering on American soil. The location was a meeting hall of St. Mark's Roman Catholic Church. The sign itself is unassuming, hardly doing justice to the aims Garvey unveiled there in May 1916. *I told them in Harlem that it was my duty to reunite the Negroes of the Western world with the Negroes of Africa, to make a great nation of black men.* Garvey had founded the Universal Negro Improvement Association and African Communities (Imperial) League (UNIA) two years earlier in Kingston, Jamaica, soon after returning from a stint in London, where he'd polished his political chops as an orator at Speakers' Corner in Hyde Park. Within a few years of arriving in America, Garvey claimed UNIA membership had reached the millions, galvanized by the soaring rhetoric on display in such writing as "An Inspiring Vision":

> So Negroes, I say, through the Universal Negro Improvement Association, that there is much to live for. I have a vision of the future, and I see before me a picture of a redeemed Africa, with her dotted cities, with her beautiful civilization, with her millions of happy children, going to and fro. Why should I lose hope? Why should I give up and take a back place in this age of progress? Remember that you are men, that God created you Lords of this creation. Lift up yourselves, men, take yourselves out of the mire and hitch your hopes to the stars; yes, rise as high as the very stars themselves. Let no man pull you down, let no man destroy your ambition, because man is but your companion, your equal; man is your brother; he is not your lord; he is not your sovereign master.

Other political actors in Harlem made less lofty appeals. The Friends of Negro Freedom was founded in 1920 by union organizers A. Philip Randolph and Chandler Owen. They openly reviled Garvey. Their magazine, *The Messenger,* carried the following notice:

PREPARE TO DEFEND YOURSELF!
Negroes are rapidly coming North. Already large numbers are here. It is foolish to think that they can come from the ignorant, backward South, where even white people are "far behind the times," and step right into a new heaven, as it were, in the highly complicated and specialized industrial system they find at their journey's end.
THE FRIENDS OF NEGRO FREEDOM OFFERS A WAY OUT.
The F.N.F. Program for 1923: Organize 100 Councils; Help Unionize Negro Migrants; Protect Tenants; Push the Cooperative Movement Among Negroes; Organize Forums for Publicly Educating the Masses.

The imperial ambitions of Garvey and the socialist project of the Friends of Negro Freedom took opposite approaches to a common plight. There was, as Garvey's vision suggested, *much to live for,* and, as *The Messenger* warned, much to lose.

———————

Walking down Lenox, going from the library to a meeting, I saw the Chief again. He was resting on the walker he uses to move around, planted on its seat, with his back against the plate-glass window of a variety store. It calls itself a department store, but it is really an overpriced ninety-nine-cent shop, and probably not a location where one could Buy Black. He was not passing out flyers.

I did not ask why he had paused there; he didn't ask whether I'd acquired a platform. Instead, the Chief stared across the street and began to speak aloud the words that must have been filling his head before I interrupted him. *I see fleeting images,* he told me. *Fleeting images,* he said again. The images before his eyes did not stand up to those in his mind. He told me that when he arrived here from Chicago, he was a young man who'd been hanging out around the University of Chicago. I told him that my grandfather had been a student there around the same time. He said he might have known him, but that he was not attending the school but mixing with its black intellectuals, trying to become one, too. He'd come to New York to study theater, and a trace of this train-ing was still evident in his diction and his bearing. I tried to imag-ine him in his pre-African Nationalist Pioneer days. With tones that mixed contempt for his past ambitions with slight wistful-ness, he mentioned that he'd wanted to go to Paris.

Chicago, he said, had fostered in him what he called *the Booker T. mentality.* It was a quality the Chief felt was lacking among New York blacks. He said the source of the distinction was that in Chicago the ruling white ethnic groups (Germans and Irish) had left the blacks more or less to their own devices; thus, he said, they had a kind of independence. According to the Chief, in New York a black man could not move without having to ask *the white man and the Jew* for permission.

Upon arriving in New York, his Booker T. mentality was stim-ulated by what he called the *dynamic, revolutionary, charismatic* leadership of Carlos A. Cooks. Thus did he assume his African name and dedicate his life to the cause of Pan-Africanism. From his early days with the ANPM, the Chief recalled to me a fellow member who was from Texas. That place of origin had not only made him prone to the platform of the ANPM, but this Pan-Africanist Texan was also a vicious political operator, known for murdering his foes. I was curious to know more about that. But the Chief changed the subject. He wanted to talk about my hair.

My hair was relevant because, as the Chief went on to explain, I would not be wearing my hair in its natural, unprocessed African state if it had not been for the dynamic, revolutionary, charismatic leadership of Carlos A. Cooks, who, in addition to the Buy Black platform had also arranged the Natural Standard of Beauty contests, through which the beauty of African hair in its natural state was promoted, during the 1950s, long before the Afro was in vogue. He pointed out this legacy with pride and also with some bitterness, for the genius and originality of Cooks's ideas about black being beautiful had been usurped by a subsequent decade. Other women passed by as we spoke: their braids, dreadlocks, and other natural styles supported his standards, as those wearing weaves and wigs of various shades, from blonde to fuchsia, defied them.

Next, he complained about my name. Why did I have an Arabic name? Why didn't I drop that name and find one from an African queen? I did not take time to explain that my parents had chosen the name Sharifa from that classic of 1960s and 1970s cultural nationalism *Know and Claim Your African Name*. It was still on the bookshelves of our home in Texas. As children, my sister and I used to take it down occasionally to study its pages, which featured line drawings of men and women with Afro hairstyles, with great reverence. When we needed to find names for new dolls or our puppy, we consulted the worn pamphlet that had been the source of our own names.

I did not explain how, in that publication, the origin of my name had been given as Swahili for "honorable" or "distinguished," which is how I always explained my name growing up. At that point, neither I nor my parents were considering, as the Chief was now, the problem of the Arab trade in salt, gold, and slaves. Swahili, the *lingua franca* of southern and eastern Africa, is a language born of commerce and invasion and other inconvenient aspects of cultural collision. It contains many words and names that are Arabic in origin, including my own. Only as an adult did I learn that, according to a more strict definition, my name was a title referring to direct descendants of the Prophet Muhammad and was thus objectionable to the anti-Islamic sensibilities of the Chief. I didn't protest. He probably wouldn't have been satisfied unless I had announced just then on Lenox Avenue that I was taking the name Hatshepsut. And I didn't point out to the Chief that his own second name was taken from an Egyptian pharaoh who had probably enslaved Nubians to work his mines, and was likely the pharaoh during the time of the Exodus.

A family of West Africans passed us. The little girls—claiming the sidewalk with the self-possession evident in their ram-rod posture—wore long skirts and hijabs, a walking tableau of all the Chief had just been speaking of. They did not escape his scrutiny. He did not understand, he said, why so many African immigrants were now crowded into Harlem, clamoring to live in America. He predicted that *they will curse the day they brought their children here, when their daughters are treated like prostitutes and their sons are rotting in jail.*

The Chief said the condition of black people in America amounted to genocide, *but everybody's walking around like everything's cool.* He repeated that phrase a few times as we spoke. I looked around us, where everyone was milling around like everything was, indeed, cool.

I left him there on Lenox Avenue. I was late for another meeting.

HARLEM TOWN HALL MEETING
"Building a movement to Save the neighborhood,
soul and spirit of the village of Harlem"

Let us take this stand together so that history will record that the people of African Descent who turned Harlem into an international showcase of Black pride, political struggle and achievement fought against their own demise!

The purpose of this meeting was to discuss strategies against Columbia University's plan to expand its campus into seventeen acres of West Harlem. The meeting featured several speakers explaining different aspects of the situation. There was the historical context of Columbia's earlier incursion into Harlem during the 1960s, when a plan to build an athletic facility by taking over public land from Morningside Park was scuttled by community outrage. There was the complicity of various black politicians who were either past or present employees of Columbia, and who were either supportive of the university's plan or would remain silent. There were the Columbia students organizing in solidarity with the community, a few of whom would later go on hunger strike. There was Columbia's decision to ignore the expertise of at least one scientist who issued urgent warnings about the catastrophe of building a subterranean research facility—where potentially hazardous experiments would take place—in an area known to be at risk of submersion during storm surges. And there was the awkward twist that the scientist was a member of Columbia's own faculty. There was, above all, the doctrine of eminent domain, which allowed the seizure of private land for the construction of buildings or infrastructure to enhance the public good. The expansion of Columbia University's private dormitories and private research facilities could be deemed, after an exhausting stretch, to enhance the public good, but it would also continue a dangerous precedent, following a Supreme Court decision that essentially extended the definition of "public good" to include dispossessing swathes of the public if rich and influential private entities found it good.

As part of a public relations campaign waged with the assistance of a well-connected black lobbying firm, Columbia placed advertisements in the *Amsterdam News* featuring black and brown faces promoting the university's benevolence as an employer and institutional neighbor. At the meeting, someone suggested taking up a collection to fund a counteractive ad campaign. It would feature the black and brown faces of people who would be displaced, or whose jobs would be lost, because of the Columbia expansion. Some people at the meeting contributed money right away, but those funds were reimbursed only a few moments later. It soon became clear that no entity claimed or wanted to claim the authority to collect the cash. No actual plan had been devised or would be executed.

That meeting was the first time I'd heard of the city's plan to rezone 125th Street. It was the next struggle coming down the pipeline. But at that moment, it all seemed distant and theoretical. Everyone was exhorted to go to a hearing on the Columbia case that was to happen in a few days. Many people did go; it was so crowded that most who wished to testify could not even get inside. I did not go to testify. I walked around among the people milling outside, asking questions and taking notes.

I spoke with one man who didn't know why he was there. He was passing out materials from "the Coalition for the Future of Manhattanville." That organization's name and reading materials were oddly similar to that of the Coalition to Preserve Community, the group of neighbors and activists who led opposition to Columbia's plan. But the Coalition for the Future of Manhattanville was in favor of the expansion, and it was not, exactly, a grassroots organization. It was launched by the same political consulting firm that placed the pro-Columbia advertisements in the *Amsterdam News*. The man passing out the pro-Columbia materials told me he didn't know anything about the plan. He'd been brought in a van of residents from a facility for recovering addicts in East Harlem. Upon arriving, they'd all been given stickers and told to pass out flyers in support of Columbia's expansion.

Seeing my notepad, an older man approached, eager to be recorded. He wore a wrinkled suit and white socks with his black dress shoes, but he had not arrived early enough to be allowed inside the hearing. At first he spoke to me in a mix of Spanish and English, and then he leaned close and said in a low voice: *They are going to drive us into the river.*

———————

I saw fleeting images, too. Long after they had ceased to refer to any existing program or administration, I saw signs from the Koch and Dinkins mayoral regimes hanging from the fire escapes of buildings. These announced the successes of *alternative management programs, empty building projects,* or weatherization upgrades according to the latest standards of two decades past. Nearby were newer signs, offering condominiums for sale. I saw the names of James Weldon Johnson and Martin Luther King Jr. and A. Phillip Randolph attached to public housing projects. I remembered James Weldon Johnson's prophetic questions:

What will Harlem be and become in the meantime? Is there danger that the Negro may lose his economic status in New York and be unable to hold his property? Will Harlem become merely a famous ghetto, or will it be a center of intellectual, cultural and economic forces exerting an influence throughout the world, especially upon Negro peoples? Will it become a point of friction between the races in New York?

Some have suggested that the mere presence of the projects in Harlem is the reason black people will, as James Weldon Johnson put it, *hold* Harlem. But there are condominiums going up directly across the street from the projects, and like the public housing buildings from the past, the condominiums are given names that are meant to inspire. The condominium Dafina neighbors the St. Nicholas houses; its name is Swahili for "a thing of value." Residents with southern-facing units in the Kalahari have an intimate view of the Martin Luther King Jr. houses. The Kalahari is named for the desert into which the Herero people of southwestern Africa were driven after the murderous exploits of German imperialists who usurped the most fertile land of what is now Namibia, a genocide known as Germany's first Holocaust, for which the Herero seek reparations. Other new buildings look to Harlem's cultural heritage for naming inspiration, so we have the Ellison, the Langston, the Fitzgerald, the Lester, the Renaissance, and the Rhapsody.

A. Philip Randolph Square, a triangle formed by the intersection of Seventh and St. Nicholas avenues with 116th Street, is marked by a quote from Randolph: *The idea of separatism is hearkening to the past, it is undesirable even if it could be realized, because the progress of mankind has been based upon social, intellectual, and cultural contact.*

Two blocks away, on 114th Street, a row of tenement buildings now serves as public housing. The housing development also bears the name of A. Philip Randolph, while failing to uphold his ideals about the progress of mankind. The block between Seventh and Eighth Avenues was taken over by the city in the 1960s as an innovative experiment in slum clearance intended to preserve the original housing stock and the intricate community network by renovating houses without displacing their occupants. The block went from being slums to being a jewel of the public housing system, but now it is slums again. Many of the houses on that street are boarded up. It is not possible to tell if they are in a state of abandonment or a state of suspended renovation. The effect is the same: no one lives there.

At one meeting about the rezoning of 125th Street, a speaker shouted out, *And you know what happened to Eighth Avenue!* What happened to Eighth Avenue was that in 1998 a private developer acquired several city-owned vacant lots and buildings for "middle-income housing," a proposal that passed the local Community Board with reservations: *Some members were concerned that it could lead to gentrification of the neighborhood. That is one reason they are asking the developers to include community groups in planning and construction.* This included promises of *locally based general contractors, workers and handymen on the site.* What happened on Eighth Avenue was a rezoning, specifically, forty-four blocks of Frederick Douglass Boulevard were rezoned in 2003 to abolish height restrictions and *enhance development potential.* The area now boasted a strip of upscale condominium developments from just above the park to 125th Street, along with the requisite amenities: dueling wine shops, a few cafés, choice places for Sunday brunch, a boutique selling pet accessories, and new satellite offices for New York's most exclusive real estate brokers.

On West 115th Street, near the corner of Eighth Avenue, a sign invites passersby to attend a meeting. The location of the advertised meeting, to have taken place in 2002, is the building to which the sign is affixed. But most of the windows and entrances of that building have been sealed over. In strange contrast there is no exterior door on the building. The vestibule is exposed to the street and its once fine tile mosaic is in disrepair.

Not far from there is the home of the Bilalian Center, a black Muslim outfit consisting of a barbershop and a convenience store, among other enterprises. The place gets its name from Bilal, the freed black slave who, after the prophet and his followers captured Mecca, was chosen by Muhammad to sound the first call to prayer from atop the Kaaba, the black rock in the center of the world, with the gate of heavens directly above. The Bilalian Center is closed. One sign announces a meeting from several years ago. The theme of the meeting was *Keeping the Promise*.

I have been to Promise Land.

It is a building at the corner of 146th Street and St. Nicholas Avenue. *Promise Land* is spelled out on the glass door of the building with carefully placed individual decal letters. Every time I pass it, I admire the unusual shape of that building. It sits on a corner, meeting the intersection with a gracefully rounded tower that goes up the side of the building like a turret. Just a few blocks up St. Nicholas Avenue is the brownstone where Ralph Ellison lived while writing *Invisible Man*. Its significance is not commemorated. When I last walked by, there was a sign offering it for sale through an exclusive real estate firm.

Whether or not Promise Land is occupied is a mystery. The door looks to be in regular use, but the windows are mostly boarded up — though at night, one partially obstructed window gives off a light from the lower level.

It all comes down to a point that is as simple as it is terrible. It is a fact that closes in on itself, like the mythical serpent that devours its own tail: This is our land that we don't own. At times the terrible simplicity of that fact was expressed at those various meetings, as the case for the moral claim to Harlem asserted by black people was detailed, with eloquence and power, in staggering litanies of abuses, triumphs, and betrayals, both historical and contemporary. But having enumerated such sorrows to the chairwoman of the New York City Planning Commission, most would have been met with a semirobotic smile before she said, as she did to me at the two hearings where I and many hundreds of others gave testimony opposing the city's plan, *Thank-you-will-you-please-submit-your-written-testimony-for-our-consideration.*

At meetings, people often say, *We have sweat equity in Harlem.* The reason for this is, *We have paid for it with our blood.*

But a blood payment and sweat equity were not what the Reverend W. W. Brown of Metropolitan Baptist Church had in mind during the earliest days of the Harlem Renaissance, when — according to James Weldon Johnson — Reverend Brown's Sunday sermons began to instruct his parishioners not only on the dimensions of the kingdom of heaven or the mystical capacities of sin-cleansing blood, but on one simple necessity of their lives as black people living under white supremacy and American capitalism: *Buy Property!* It was a sacrament that mixed spiritual salvation with the earthly deliverance of the race.

A few decades later, another minister, Malcolm X, said it differently in his "Message to the Grassroots": *Revolution is based on land. Land is the basis of all independence. Land is the basis of freedom, justice, and equality.*

Revolution was not launched from the land mentioned in a recent article in the *Amsterdam News,* where the ongoing political-cum-theological debate over property and equity and blood and deliverance arrived at a quite different resolution. Suddenly, the commandment was not to acquire land but to relinquish it, to the highest bidder. The pastor of the Church of the Master, on Morningside Drive in the 120s, announced the demolition of its 115-year-old premises. The land beneath the church was sold to the developer of a condominium block whose residences would likely be out of reach for the minister or his flock. The announcement included date and time of the demolition, promoted as a spectacle.

During that winter of meetings, a woman known as Arapha Speaks, who sometimes refers to herself as the Cussin' Preacher, established residence in a series of cardboard boxes fixed together near the base of the Adam Clayton Powell Jr. statue in front of the State Office Building. She identified each house by its number, according to the order in which it was built and the order of its destruction. She was continually being turned out of her houses, their contents seized and the structures demolished. At a community meeting convened to mourn and respond to the police murder of a young unarmed man shot in the back on the grounds of housing projects named for Harlem's congressman at the time (who remained silent on the Columbia expansion and the rezoning of 125th Street), Arapha Speaks exhorted the assembly to take a stand. *Are you willing to come up out of your houses?* she asked. We were, she said, in as much danger of being turned out of our brick-and-mortar houses as she was from her cardboard ones. We had to be willing to be out-of-doors, without refuge, in order to preserve Harlem. She envisioned a movement in the form of a spiritual Exodus; she would lead midnight prayer meetings in the State Office Plaza, by the Powell statue. It was, she said, the only way to turn back the malevolent forces behind the destruction of her homes and the threat of Harlem's obliteration.

At one of those hearings, I met a man who grew impatient when I expressed incredulity at his casual anecdote about a church that, in the 1980s or early 1990s, had been entrusted with the development of its own plot of land in addition to a number of brownstone houses. The houses had been acquired during the mythic era—immortalized by real estate journalists and speakers at community meetings—when brownstones in Harlem were being sold by the city for a dollar. The construction of that particular church had never come to pass—supposedly, the money was embezzled. The shell of the church's half-built future home was still standing on Lenox Avenue at 131st when I arrived in Harlem—it resembled the ruin of a cathedral I'd seen in Berlin. Bombed during the Allies' air war, its rubble was left standing as if the strike had just occurred yesterday, both a memorial and a reminder to the German people of their sin. But on Lenox Avenue, there was no trace, no atonement: the property was developed into a condominium. For a few months, the tenant in the building's ground-floor retail space was a black-owned car dealership specializing in Bentleys and other exotic luxury cars.

When I pressed for details about the spectacular failure of that ruined church, he shrugged his shoulders and gave the vaguest details about who absconded with the money. *It's all well known*, he said, *this is all common knowledge.* But the era of profligacy had come to an end. He invoked an image from the Bible that was equal in force but directly opposite to that earlier mention of Exodus. He said it was as if we had been forty years in the desert and our time in the wilderness was just about to end.

All of this leaves quite a few unanswered questions.

Which is more valuable, "sweat equity" or actual equity, such as the kind mobilized by that preacher when he sold his church's land to developers?

Does the legend of the one-dollar brownstone bring shame upon all in Harlem who did not purchase when the getting was good, or does the story unravel when you consider the minor detail that many would not have been able to afford to renovate or insure such a building because of red-lining practices by mortgage and insurance companies?

Do the people of Harlem stand with forty years of wilderness stretched out in front of us, or is deliverance close at hand, the Exodus already at our backs?

Brothers and sisters, countrymen
You'd better get on board.
Six steam ships want to sail away

Loaded with a heavy load.
It's gonna take us all back home.
Yes every native child,
And when we get there
What a time . . .
Get on board the Countryman
Get on board to leave this land
Get on board the Countryman
Come along 'cause the water's fine
Flying home on the Black Star Line.

Depending on who tells the story, the Black Star Line was either Marcus Garvey's most visionary Pan-African program or his greatest hoax. In 1919, Garvey launched his dream: the first black-owned shipping line to ply the seas, with black captains at the helm. It would refigure the old triangular trade between Africa, the Caribbean, and America. This new version would bypass Europe, and its cargo would be liberatory economic self-determination instead of slaves, cotton, rum, and sugar. Beyond goods, the Black Star Line would carry Garveyites back to Africa. Members of the UNIA flocked to support the endeavor, pledging at least $500,000 in stock certificates purchased at $5 apiece. The first ship was the SS *Frederick Douglass*. It was a reconditioned World War I navy ship, and it was a poor beginning for the shipping company. Worth only $25,000, the ship was sold to Garvey's agents for $165,000 and then required a further $200,000 in repairs. In his own defense, Garvey later asserted that his appointed captain had profited from the payment on the ship. Another vessel, the SS *Antonio Maceo,* named for the Afro-Cuban general, was inaugurated with a celebration at one of Harlem's piers. During its maiden voyage, it suffered a mechanical failure at sea that killed a crew member; it had to be towed into port. As for the Black Star Line's contribution to commerce, one voyage allegedly carried a cargo of tropical fruit that rotted because Garvey insisted that it make ceremonial stops at ports of call around the Caribbean. Another ship made a dramatic embarkment from the Hudson River, only to deposit its passengers a few miles north on what was deemed *the cruise to nowhere.*

A letter published in the October 1921 issue of *The Crusader,* a magazine published by the Afrocentric, Marxist-influenced Hamitic League of the World, bore the headline *Salvation of the Negro.* The correspondent was writing from the South during the most virulent era of lynching, mob violence, land seizure, voter disenfranchisement, and debt peonage. But he did not believe—as Alain Locke did when he called Harlem *the Mecca of the New Negro* just a few years later—that salvation was located north of the Mason-Dixon Line:

No 121 Harris Street,
Vicksburg, Miss.
Sept 12 1921

Mr. Editor of the Crusader:

[I am a] gentleman and a man of race pride and of very deep and broad thoughts:
    After reading the indictments in your valuable magazine for September, I now answer your question.
    The salvation for the American Negro is to organize a Territory Corporation.
    There may be one more; that is the great act of God in our behalf.

The corporation should be led by the best men as promoters. These promoters should agree on the price for a share and request the twelve millions of Negroes to take out shares.

The Public Corporation funds should be deposited until organized to do business, on interest, under an agreement that all money should be returned if not organized and used for said purpose.

We must colonize somewhere.

Yours truly,
NATIONAL STAR

———

I next saw the Chief at the library. He arranged himself across from me at a table in the reading room, and I knew my work for that day had come to an end. He eyed the books that were spread before me without offering an opinion on the selection. Then he produced his own reading material. This included photocopies of his Buy Black flyers and other ANPM literature I'd seen before. He laid them out as if entering exhibits into evidence. Last, he brought out a sheet bearing a brief passage. It had no headline, and gave no reference to its original source.

I asked if I could read that page, and when I finished, I asked permission to copy it down. He hesitated, and then—as if he were passing me a classified document, rather than a quotation that with a bit of effort I could locate in the pages of the ANPM newsletter, whose archives were available for public review right there in the library—he warily agreed, after insisting that *this is not meant for Europeans.*

It was a quotation from Carlos Cooks. In the passage, Cooks is outlining the end result of a successful march to African Nationalism in America. And, despite the injunctions of the Chief,

Cooks's words and his aims would have been familiar to certain Europeans of the twentieth century:

> With the establishment of a solvent economy by the group comes self-reliance, racial clannishness, mass cooperation and a common-cause psychosis which invariably leads to the erection of racial standards and the formation of a distinct and exclusive sense of value, evolving into an original racial pattern, reaching its climax in a deafening mass claim for nationhood.

Once I'd finished copying those words, the Chief began to lecture me on the details of this historical unfolding. His approach was familiar from universal histories, where the world-spirit is seen to animate different civilizations, doggedly aiming at its most exalted expression. He told me that Jewish girls in Israel are crying out for Jewish nationalism; Chinese girls in China were crying out for Chinese nationalism; white girls here in America were crying out for white nationalism. According to this pattern there was only one avenue for the political consciousness of a young woman like me, and it had nothing to do with attending meetings in Harlem, or my vision of going back to my hometown to do community work in Texas. *Damn Harlem!* he told me. *Damn Texas!*

By then his tone had abandoned any hush appropriate to a library and ascended the soapbox. Like a practiced rhetorician, he shifted tack, abandoning emotional appeals for empirical ones. *Gold, bauxite, rubber, cobalt, uranium, silver! The natural resources of Africa—that should be your battle cry!* Though I didn't interrupt, I was, in fact, interested in the natural resources of Africa, especially since I had learned of the deals between various African governments and various Chinese companies transferring fishing rights, mining rights, and logging rights, and allowing the construction of hydroelectric dams, among other forms of resource extraction. I had also learned that the construction of new roads and railways in Africa, while beginning to alleviate the dangers of travel in some parts of the continent, was also funded by the Chinese, in order to better facilitate their program of resource extraction.

The Chief told me that I needed to go to Africa and join the struggle, but he made clear that this struggle was not a matter of attending meetings. I mentioned that perhaps people in Africa did not want me showing up to interfere, and maybe they had their own ideas about their destiny. The Chief said this was part of the problem. Just as the conversion of much of West Africa to Islam had taken place under the threat of death, said the Chief, it was only by threat of death that this process would be reversed, so that Africans would *get in line* with the program delineated by his battle cry. To make his point, he drew another example from history, noting that it was the threat of death that had motivated *50 million Uncle Tom Chinamen to give up Christianity, Islam, and Buddhism* in order to *get in line* for Mao's Long March. It was only the threat of death, he said, in the form of *Jewish firepower,* that had halted the *killing of Jewish people, the rape of Jewish women, making lampshades out of Jewish skin, experimenting on Jewish babies.* Not having the use of our own firepower, black people were still suffering such traumas. The last affliction, the Chief reminded me, had been exposed in recent years just across the street from the library, when doctors at Harlem Hospital were found to be using black foster children for unauthorized experimental drug treatments. He was going on about the A-bomb and its necessity for black liberation when I pointed out that the nationalism asserted by *Jewish firepower* meant the suppression of Palestinian people's sovereignty. He told me the problems of the Palestinians were none of my business. My business, in case I had forgotten, involved the natural resources of Africa. I asked him what business was it of Frantz Fanon to travel from Martinique in order to struggle with the Algerians against their common imperialist oppressor, France. His answer was simple. *Fanon was a fool,* he said, sneering. His anticolonial brotherhood with the North Africans was misguided, since it put him in allegiance with the very Arabs who had delivered black Africans into slavery. This point led the Chief to remember his quarrel with my Arabic name, which received a smirking aside before he continued.

All of this was secondary. The Chief thought I was changing the subject and missing the point. I had to *get in line,* he told me. *You only get one shot.*

He invoked *the spirit of Winnie Mandela* and told me, *You need to be a part of that spirit!*

He invoked *the spirit of Harriet Tubman* and told me, *You need to be a part of that spirit!*

He paused and pointed over my shoulder to a painting on the wall, one of several brightly colored works by Haitian artists. It showed the three main heroes of the Haitian Revolution: Toussaint L'Ouverture, Jean-Jacques Dessalines, and Henri Christophe.

After I had looked over my shoulder, the Chief asked me, *Do you know what that represents?* I said that I did, and he asked me to name the figures. After I had correctly identified them he said, *You got that right.*

Then he asked me what they had accomplished. I told him they had fought for liberation and he said, *You got that right.*

My history being correct, the Chief he didn't see why I *couldn't understand the liberation of our people.* I ventured that I did.

The Chief pointed to the button pinned to his shirt; it was a small black-and-white photo of Patrice Lumumba. Continuing my examination, he asked me if I knew who it was. I said that I did. I had even read an article from the African Nationalist Pioneer newspaper, written before Lumumba's murder, in which

Carlos A. Cooks wrote an editorial, "There Is Going to Be a New Day: Lumumba Foils Colonialist Plot to Partition the Congo." The same edition also included a poem, "The Awakening Call":

Hail Lumumba! Man of Africa
Who stands like a mighty dam
Against the floods of oppression
A granite wall of reality before
The white man's dream of madness.
To keep the African his slave and Africa
His feasting ground of exploitation.

Hark! The Congo is free
The heart of Africa beats again at last
The pulsating throb of Freedom is felt
Throughout the land
The giant awakens and lifts His mighty hand
To smite the leeches who sucked
His blood while so long he slept.

The poem continues with a plea from a weakened Father Africa, *for centuries his blood having flowed to foreign lands,* crying out, *"Arise Black sons of Africa on foreign soil / Decaying tools of empires created by your blood and toil."* The sons of Africa are implored to come home and:

"Bring my daughters with you
To work, to build, to teach, to bask
In the glory that is due."
Blackmen from every point across the sea
Send back their answers to this plea:

"FATHER AFRICA, OPEN WIDE YOUR DOOR THIS DAY FOR WE ARE READY—WE ARE ON OUR WAY!!"

The author of the poem is listed as one R. Waldo Williams, of New York. I imagine him as a sensitive, poetic, and politically charged young man, much the way the Chief had described himself to be upon arriving in Harlem from Chicago—eager to answer *the awakening call,* but perhaps not yet free of his artistic aspirations.

But it was not a new day. Congo was partitioned. Patrice Lumumba was spirited away by treacherous countrymen to the breakaway province of Katanga, whose main town was then and is still a mining center bolstered by rich deposits of copper, cobalt, tin, uranium, radium, and zinc, among other minerals. The Belgian-owned mining company Union Minière du Haut Katanga had supplied uranium to the United States for the development of the atom bomb.

At Katanga, Lumumba and two companions were executed by a firing squad operating under Belgian command with American knowledge and assent. After Lumumba was murdered, his corpse was buried behind an anthill. Later, Belgian officers returned with orders to destroy the evidence. They exhumed the bodies, chopping them to pieces and dousing those pieces in sulphuric acid also supplied by that same Belgian-owned mining concern. There was not enough acid to consume what was left of Lumumba and his two companions, so what remained of the body that had been *one of the greatest African personalities to appear on the stage of world affairs today* was set ablaze.

The Chief did not use the small pin on his lapel showing Lumumba's face as another exhibit in the tribunal on my political commitment. He only mentioned that the murder of Lumumba had happened when he was a young man. He didn't say anything more. I figured it was probably the kind of thing that led him to acquire a platform.

I returned to my work, and the Chief went over to the computers where he had an appointment to use the Internet. Once again, the reading room was quiet, so I was confronted by my own silence in the face of firepower, the A-bomb, getting in line, the natural resources of Africa, the revolutionaries of Haiti, Lumumba, Harlem, and Texas. Long after that day I recalled some words of Frantz Fanon that I wished had come to mind at the library, despite Fanon's having been denounced by the Chief. They express an ideal of physical and intellectual freedom—which means they are, perhaps, the closest I will ever come to having a political platform:

Oh my body, make of me always a man who questions!

We were protesting on a picket line in front of Melba's restaurant on Eighth Avenue, a relatively new establishment celebrated for its upscale version of chicken-and-waffles and its ebullient hostess. We were not protesting the cuisine or hiring practices of the restaurant. On that afternoon—just a week after the 125th Street rezoning proposal passed the city council with only two dissenting votes—Melba's hosted a political fund-raiser for the councilwoman from Harlem who had recently made headlines as a staunch and impassioned defender of her neighborhood. In a speech in City Hall chambers, she had styled herself as a latter-day Harriet Tubman, just before brokering a deal to pass the proposal virtually unmodified from the version put forth by the Department of City Planning. This intervention was lauded because 46 percent of projected new housing would be "income-targeted" for residents of varying incomes. But only 200 of the projected 4,000 new units to be built on 125th Street would be affordable to that overwhelming majority of Harlem residents who make less than $30,000 per year.

I did not have a notepad and pen, I had a sign. I stood in the picket line, I joined the chants, and I tried to invent a pithy but nonpoetic chant of my own to express the fraud perpetrated by the vote. The council was full of self-congratulation for having passed a proposal with more affordable housing than ever accomplished in previous development plans. *Two hundred units!* I yelled. It didn't catch on. We all shouted until our voices grew hoarse.

Many people passed by in buses, in cars, and on foot, taking flyers and nodding in support. Most didn't join the line, but they stood at its perimeter or shouted from cars, *She sold us out!* A group of three young boys came up to ask what was happening. I stood by as one friend explained to them that we were protesting the councilwoman for representing Harlem so poorly. Another protester patiently tried to give a definition of gentrification appropriate for a third-grade level. Taking all of this in, one boy looked at the others and said: *Don't you know that's why they're planting trees on our block?!*

Most likely the child had not heard about the *arts-and-culture corridor;* he was not aware of various requests for proposals about monuments that were meant to celebrate his heritage. Most likely he had not been to the "open session" in which invited members of the community and several members of the city's urban planning staff discussed the intricacies of sidewalk furniture, among other things. (Meetings were held on a variety of subjects; none were held to discuss the question of housing.) But the child had noticed trees turning up where before there had been no trees. He'd seen trees where, before, his presence and the presence of everyone he knew had not seemed to warrant an occasion for trees. It is possible this child was only mimicking a tone of indignation voiced in his presence by an adult. But is also possible that he knew enough of this place and its landscape—and had observed enough changes in that landscape—to suspect that the new trees, and their beautifying, shade-enhancing, air-purifying qualities, were not necessarily for his own enjoyment or use.

———

I would like to reach for a more hopeful tone. I would like to write of legacies, of torches being passed, of mantles being worn, and of flags raised high after the standard bearer has fallen. I would like to feel uplifted by the monument to Harriet Tubman that stands at the intersection of St. Nicholas Avenue and 122nd Street, near a police precinct. Some controversy attended its unveiling when people noticed that the figure was facing south toward lower Manhattan instead of north toward freedom. *Well, there can't be a wrong direction for her because she came and went on many occasions,* a politician insisted, offering excuses for what was probably a careless mistake. *Yes, she was the Moses of our people, but she wasn't Moses who apparently led all of his people out at once and did not have to go back.* The monument shows Tubman with some kind of pocketbook strapped across her chest, but without her trademark rifle, which was used to ward off the bounty hunters on her trail and to urge on fearful escapees who wished to abandon their flight.

The artist who made that memorial reached for a hopeful tone. The words of an old Negro spiritual linking Tubman to the original Moses are inscribed as a plaintive incantation ringing the base of the statue, just below a strange sculptural feature meant to illustrate the proverbial ancestral roots. *When time breaks up eternity, O let my people go! We need not always weep and mourn, O let my people go! And wear these slavery chains forlorn, O let my people go!* In this artist's rendition, the physical portrayal of those meta-phorical roots connects the southward-facing, forward-lurching Tubman to the earth and to history. But they seem to reach out as an impediment, against the Exodus, pulling her down and back. *O let my people go What a beautiful morning it will be! O let my people go What a beautiful morning it will be! O let my people...*

Harold Cruse, the cultural critic and historian, came to New York as a child from his home in Virginia. He had been to many meetings in Harlem—including brief affiliations with factions of artists, communists, and nationalists—by the time he made the following assessment in his 1967 epic *The Crisis of the Negro Intellectual:*

> Harlem is a victim of cynical and premeditated cultural devegetation. Harlem is an impoverished and superexploited economic dependency, tied to a real estate, banking, business-commercial combine of absentee whites who suck the community dry every payday. In short, Harlem exists for the benefit of others and has no cultural, political or economic autonomy. Hence, no social movement of a protest nature in Harlem can be successful or have any positive meaning unless it is at one and the same time a political, economic and cultural movement. A Harlem movement that is only political or only economic or only cultural or merely a protest movement—has to fail.
>
> ...But the hour for Harlem is late, insofar as autonomous, self-directed social change from the *bottom up* is concerned. Under capitalism, the dynamics of time and tide wait for no one.

Late in the course of things, when the struggle over 125th Street had already been lost but I was still going to meetings, a leader from Harlem's chapter of the New Black Panther Party (NBPP) objected to what he saw as the underestimating of his group's contribution. In the midst of a discussion to plan yet another town hall assembly, someone suggested that the NBPP be asked to provide security. The request was met with mild offense: *We're not just security.* As an example of their other activities, he described an initiative that he called Affirmation Marches, in which members of the party march throughout the neighborhood in military formation while shouting uplifting slogans. They were, he said, *letting people know that black is still beautiful.*

I wrote this down in the margin of a page separate from the one I was using to record the meeting's minutes. The comment was not immediately germane to the agenda or to organizational business, but it seemed to summarize, quite deftly, the magnitude of the current crisis.

Every year, the birthday of Marcus Mosiah Garvey is celebrated on or around August 17 with a march that circuits central Harlem. One year, in advance of the parade, graffiti appeared on the plywood barrier to a construction site on 125th Street: *Happy Birthday to the "Honorable" Marcus Garvey.* The graffiti remained there long after the parade had come and gone, hailing the leader in perpetuity, but the construction taking place behind the plywood barrier itself seemed to be in a state of suspended operation. Before the most recent parade there was a schism between the organizers, and two different celebrations were taking place. I didn't attend either one.

The previous year, I did go. I had not yet begun to frequent meetings in Harlem, and I was not yet aware of the 125th Street rezoning proposal. I did not get in line. When I arrived at the meeting point in Marcus Garvey Park, I stood to the side with my reporter's pad and pen. Most people there were wearing black, and I was wearing blue. A tall man held a large red, black, and green flag above the heads of the assembly.

Just as the march commenced, it began to rain. We left the park, going west across 122nd Street, down Lenox Avenue across 116th to Seventh, up Seventh all the way to 135th Street. It began to rain harder, but the parade continued, its ranks a loose phalanx comprising the remnants of a number of Pan-Africanist and black nationalist organizations whose histories stretched back to the beginning of the twentieth century. In addition to representatives of the UNIA, resurrected as the Universal Nubian Improvement Association, there was a contingent from the Ethiopia World Federation, which had been founded in Harlem in the 1930s to support the cause of Haile Selassie against Benito Mussolini's fascist and imperialist encroachment. There were also the New Black Panthers, who, it should be said, have been disavowed by prominent members of the old Black Panthers, including the widow of Huey P. Newton. The assembled groups made a ramshackle pageant of the history of black resistance. Although these groups cannot claim a mass constituency, they still claim to speak for all black people, perhaps as much as they speak for the history from which their organizations were born. They are not obsolete, because many of the conditions that attended their founding persist and because many of the original aims have not been achieved.

But at that moment, the persistence of history was expressed through our persistence through the rain. Some bystanders stopped to cheer; others pumped Black Power fists from the sidewalk. People took pictures with their camera phones, and a few teenagers flashed the middle finger. The marshals in charge of the parade urged the marchers to continue. *Black Power!* they said. *Close the ranks!* I ran to keep apace. Soon there was no distinction between the sideline and main line.

The weather didn't stop the parade, but it did inspire an impassioned chant. At some point, instead of the typical cheers (*Black Power!* and *Buy Black!* or *No Justice No Peace!* or *Free the Land!* or *Africa for the Africans!* and *Freedom or Death!!*), someone began to lead the marchers with the shout *Look for me in the whirlwind or the storm!* This chant caught on, propelling the crowd across 135th Street to Lenox Avenue again, down to 125th Street, and then east to Fifth Avenue.

The words of that chant were taken from a 1925 letter from Marcus Garvey to his followers, written from an Atlanta prison when he was about to be deported for mail fraud.

Look for me in the whirlwind or storm, look for me all around you, for with God's grace, I shall come and bring with me countless millions of black slaves who have died in America and the West Indies and the millions in Africa to aid you in the fight for Liberty, Freedom and Life.

The marchers' inspiring battle cry was drawn from Garvey's clearest articulation of defeat. He answered the persistent charge that he was swindling his followers by means of messianic illusion with words befitting a messianic illusionist. At the moment of his deportation (which some say was carried out at the behest of or with the aid of black leaders as highly placed as W. E. B. DuBois), Garvey makes a rhetorical shift from the physical (land, economics, politics) to the metaphysical (an army of the dead, led by himself, whose powers match or outdo those of the risen Christ and the 144,000 at the Rapture). That day, the thunder and rain signaled that a reckoning was at hand.

Upon reaching Fifth Avenue at 124th Street, the parade completed its circuit and was once again at Marcus Garvey Park. The group stopped at the entrance of a condominium that had been built on an empty lot. The New Black Panthers fell into formation and raised Black Power fists in the air. The condominiums were the source of a controversy that was then overheating. After moving into the new complex, many residents were dismayed to discover that the park hosted a Harlem tradition of thirty years' standing, a drum circle that takes place in the park every Saturday during the months of temperate weather. (*African drumming is wonderful for the first four hours, but after that, it's pure, unadulterated noise. We couldn't see straight anymore,* one new resident was quoted saying in a national paper. *Some of these drums are prayed over, blessed in Africa,* countered a musician.) The police, not expecting the spontaneous protest, scrambled to the parade organizers, insisting that the crowd disperse.

We returned to the meeting point next to the park. A man introduced as an original Garveyite from Jamaica was ushered forward to conclude the occasion. His melodious delivery of a reverent invocation, which included gratitude to the police who escorted the march, was interrupted when a member of the New Black Panther Party grew impatient with his formalities: *Make it plain!* she told him, before snarling something about *crackers.* The old Garveyite, who stood with the assistance of a cane, began to bristle with indignation. The young woman had offended his sense of history as much as his sense of propriety. *But Garvey wouldn't have said that!* he protested, asking her to *remain cord-i-al for the rest of the evening,* but she continued to challenge him. The sadness and frustration of the old man collided with the sadness and frustration of the young woman for more than a few tense moments before the concluding remarks could proceed.

A celebration in honor of "The Redeemer" was held later at a nearby Masonic lodge. Dinner was available for a small charge. Libations offered to our ancestors inaugurated a long agenda of speakers—presenting in order of eldest first, according to the program handed out that night. The program also announced that there would be the annual edition of the Afrikan (*sic*) Natural Standard of Beauty Contest, but it was not held, and no explanation was given. Perhaps there had been too many speakers, or maybe there was no one present who deserved the honor.

When I arrived at the Masonic lodge, an older man was entering at the same time. I recognized him from the parade. Together we passed through the iron gate of the lodge. As we descended the stairs into the building, he paused, turned toward me, and posed a question I was not equipped to answer: *Harlem is a city of Masons,* he said. *How could we lose Harlem?*

A rock formation erupts from the center of Marcus Garvey Park. This is Mount Morris, after which the park was originally named and after which the historical district, the Mount Morris Park Historical District, and the neighborhood association, the Mount Morris Park Community Improvement Association, are named still. (It is, perhaps, the persistence of the original name on the historic district and the association that gives rise to recurrent rumors that wealthy residents of the area—white and black—are conspiring to have Marcus Garvey's name stripped from the park.)

The houses on the western perimeter of the park are some of the finest in Harlem, the focus of an annual tour of homes that takes place every spring. Around its northern limit are large apartment blocks—equally grand but less glamorous abodes. One, an ornate building called the Sans Souci, is an SRO. On one visit to the city, before I moved to New York, I was attracted to this building because it shared a name—which means carefree—with the palace built by Haitian emperor Henri Christophe. The Haitian palace, along with its nearby citadel, are on the UNESCO World Heritage list, touted as *the first monuments to be constructed by black slaves who had gained their freedom*. But the buildings were constructed by black slaves who had gained their freedom and then worked for a monomaniacal emperor who imposed the *corvée*, a system of unpaid labor also used in ancient Egypt to build the pyramids. When I went up the steps of Harlem's San Souci to ask if there were any apartments available, I was shooed away from its door by the security guard on duty. *Do you know what kind of place this is?*

A new building has risen just south of the park, where Fifth Avenue runs uptown and divides itself into the abbreviated avenues known as Mount Morris Park West and East before joining again to cross 125th Street. The vast tower is called Fifth on the Park. A *mixed-income* development featuring units valued up to $3 million, it is advertised as being located in *New Harlem* and *South Harlem*. Also touted is its proximity to *Mount Morris Park*. It sits on land that was owned by a church, and developers purchased the "air rights" from another piece of land owned by the church in order to achieve the building's thirty-story height, unprecedented in Harlem. The church received $12 million, a number of "affordable" housing rental units (one-bedrooms starting at $1,800), and a state-of-the-art worship facility inside the new tower. Development has also come to a former jail that occupied a purpose-built structure at 121st and Mount Morris West—now it's a condominium. On the same side of the park, two blocks north, the old house that was for many years the headquarters and synagogue of the black Jewish sect the Commandment Keepers is also being renovated, reclaimed for residential use. According to an article lamenting its fall, it was sold for development after a long-running internal dispute over the leadership of the community, and the temple was closed without the requisite religious ceremonies. The writer concludes: *Thus, the memory of that building has now become a monument to self-destruction.* In the course of construction work, to effect the desecration or resecularization of the old Commandment Keepers temple, the Star of David was removed from above the threshold. A large Dumpster parked nearby received the contents from within.

The summit of Mount Morris is the province of junkies and derelicts, or so I have been warned. A male friend who I'd always assumed would escort me to the top described a recognizance mission in which he successfully gained the height of Mount Morris. The plateau there is called the Acropolis, borrowing the word—meaning city on the edge—that ancient Greeks used to designate the citadels they built at the highest point in a settlement to defend against invasion. There, my friend met a scene of oblivion. Even in the light of day the place was full of people nodding off in different stages of sleep and intoxication. My friend said he *had no business up there.* On seeing him approach, someone had cursed loudly; he'd been mistaken for an undercover cop.

Because Mount Morris was the highest point in Harlem, a watchtower was installed there in 1857 (it was then known as Snake Hill), to protect upper Manhattan from fire. Already in 1896, about a decade before black settlement in Harlem began, the tower was considered a symbol of the neighborhood, with a former watchman sharing his lamentation in the *New York Times*:

It is a shame for the authorities to let the tower go to ruin, as it is one of Harlem's oldest and most historic landmarks. At one period it governed time in all of Harlem and the surrounding villages. All watches and clocks within sound of the bell were

Harlem Fire Watchtower, Marcus Garvey Park, ca. after 1968. (Photo by Stephen Zane / Courtesy of Historic American Engineering Record, Library of Congress)

regulated by it. It was proposed several years ago to tear the tower down on account of its shaky condition, but the residents raised such an opposition that it was left standing.

In the 1960s, concerned residents acted to preserve the watchtower as an emblem of the enclave, and it received landmark designation. In winter, the skeleton of the tower is visible from a distance, seen from below through bare tree branches.

I have not been to the top. Instead I imagine the view from there. In the late 1960s and early 1970s, absentee slumlords colluded with arsonists to set fire to their own property all around Harlem, driving tenants into the street and collecting insurance money. That scorched-earth campaign—along with the more common, more time-consuming, and less actively violent tactic of neglect, in which buildings were abandoned, boarded up, and left to rot for decades until they nearly collapsed—created the empty lots that pocked the neighborhood's landscape. This condition later came to be known by the passive, indeterminate, and oddly agricultural term "blight," and to reverse that blight, many of those empty lots would be developed as luxury condominiums. From the top of Mount Morris, high in the watchtower, it must have been possible to see the catastrophe blazing night after night—but no alarm could bring relief. Now, the preserved tower—an attraction for the intrepid tourist clutching a guidebook—is of little use as other dangers approach.

Back to Carolina

MS. MINNIE DIED. It was May 23, a Thursday. On or around that day, I'd fallen asleep thinking to slip a get-well note beneath her door, something her son could take to the hospital. I'd use the blank card propped up on my desk; the front showed an English still life from the 1600s. Its long and detailed title explained the subject matter: *An urn containing flowers, including tulips, roses, daffodils, narcissus, carnations, morning-glory, love-in-a-mist, hyacinth, larkspur, anemone and medick, with a butterfly and two birds and a goldfinch.* I didn't get around to writing the card or slipping it under the door. She had already been in the hospital for months, and I had not gone to visit.

Ms. Barbara delivered the news. I came out of the building, saying hello to everyone gathered near the stoop. Ms. Barbara pulled me aside and led me away from the group. We stood near the curb and she whispered, *Minnie is gone.* Not everyone knew, she said. The service would happen the following Thursday, at the funeral home less than half a block down Lenox Avenue.

We said to each other the things one says at such moments:

that we had not known how ill she was and that she would be missed. I thanked Ms. Barbara for letting me know and left her in front of the building. Walking up the block, I was guided by my familiarity with the path — my eyes had ceased to focus on anything in particular. What I did see was filtered through the operation that begins at the very instant one hears the news of death. The mind makes a frantic attempt to integrate the information into everything perceived, as if the most solid particles of the universe must rearrange themselves in the wake of the departed. There is the corner store, *Ms. Minnie is gone.* There is the stoplight, *Ms. Minnie is gone.* There is the subway, *Ms. Minnie is gone.* There is the hospital, *Ms. Minnie is gone.* There is the library, *Ms. Minnie is gone.*

In the next days, when I walked by the funeral home where her service would take place, I could not rush quickly past, knowing I'd be there soon with all my neighbors to say good-bye to Ms. Minnie. It was a place I passed on an almost daily basis, weaving around or through crowds lingering at the end of a service. This was necessary when passing any of the funeral homes on Lenox Avenue after a service: their doors flung open, and the crowd spilled out. Sometimes they were crowds of elders, full of dark suits, dress coats, and smart hats. But often they were crowds of the young, not dressed especially for the occasion. At least once, I passed a crowd where the mourners were being led out of the parlor by a man playing an African drum.

I cannot remember, in any occasion over several years, passing a throng filled with weeping people. I am certain of this because when approaching such crowds, preparing to weave around or through, I almost always braced myself. I was anticipating some flood of sentiment, in the presence of which — not having any connection to the people or the event other than just passing by — I should try to make myself nonintrusive. The emotion I expected among the mourners was never present. There was only a somewhat subdued calm and the sense that these people were bound together by what had just taken place. The only agitation was mine.

Once, Ms. Minnie greeted me in the street just after she'd emerged from such a crowd. Her declarations might have explained the absence of heaviness I'd seen before. *It was a beautiful funeral*, she told me. She praised the skill of the preacher and the selection of songs. She told me that the deceased wasn't someone she knew well, but I gathered that her attendance had been a function of custom: one pays respect to the dead, even the dead who are not well known to you. And, perhaps, going to the funeral that day had been an activity, something to do. This did not diminish the event, nor the impression it had made on her. She rhapsodized on its beauty, its feeling, the size of the assembled crowd.

A few days after Ms. Barbara told me of Ms. Minnie's passing, a flyer appeared on the door of our building. It gave details for the funeral and showed a picture of Ms. Minnie. I had seen similar flyers on others doors. Such signs alert the neighbors that one was now gone from their midst and that everyone will soon gather to pay respect to the dead. Some of the signs I'd seen on the doors of other buildings solicited funds to cover burial costs. If the dead had left behind young children, there might be a request to help provide for their care.

The news of death: I overheard it often, sitting on the bus while someone spoke on the phone, standing on a corner waiting to cross the street, watching the momentary meeting of two friends who had not seen each other in a while. Usually the angel of death swooped into an otherwise relaxed chat in the form of an assumption: *You heard about____, right?* But the other person had not heard. They had only just seen____; they did not know____ was ill; they asked how long ago it had happened; they were sorry for the family. I would exit the bus or crossed the street as the particles began to rearrange themselves and would not hear the rest of the mutual consolation.

The news of death was borne on T-shirts mass-produced by the local copy shop for the occasion. This seemed to be a ritual of young people mourning one of their own. A picture, taken during prom or a house party, showed the dead young man or woman looking full of confidence and age-appropriate immortality. The birth and death were given as *Sunrise* and *Sunset,* though the dates were too close together to have allowed the full passage of a day. I saw these T-shirts individually—when some people wore them incorporated into their normal wardrobe long after the funeral—and in groups, a uniform for those mourners stationed in clumps outside the doors of one of the funeral parlors on Lenox.

Newspapers or the radio sometimes announced the time and location of a funeral service if the deceased was a famous jazz musician or had been killed in a crime that had captured the attention of tabloids. Reading such announcements, or hearing them, the information first struck me as noteworthy. Perhaps I, too, should go and pay my respects, even though the dead person was a stranger.

I never did go to one of these public funerals. But once, walking home at night via 125th Street, I came to a gathering by the benches in front of the State Office Building. I thought it was a political meeting of some sort, so I stopped. It *was* a political meeting of some sort, but it was also a memorial service. Speakers took turns standing on a bench to address the small crowd which had formed a semicircle on the sidewalk. They were there to honor a man named Yusuf, who had been a regular occupant of those benches and had died of a sudden illness several months before. A poster-sized portrait of him leaned against one bench. I studied it, trying to recognize him from the many times I had passed the spot. Several of the speakers assured the small crowd that *even if you don't think you knew Yusuf, you probably did,* and they spoke of the kindness he showed to anyone he met at those benches, his commitment to his neighborhood, and his love of his people and his religion. Soon, the prayers and eulogies gave way to announcements: of various meetings, of an opportunity to join the bus caravan to Jena, Louisiana, to protest the treatment of the Jena 6. At the end, the man who'd organized the service handed out the melted remnants of tiny tea-light candles. Some had been burning throughout the assembly, but others had been snuffed out in the wind.

In the dark of one night I saw a collection of funeral flowers arranged behind a gate on 114th Street. There were a great lot of them, elaborate arrangements propped up on wire stands and on an arbor. Two were designed in the shape of numbers — 1 and 23 — but there was no way of knowing if these digits referred to the age of the departed, the number of a favorite sports jersey, or the date of death. When I passed some weeks later, all the flowers were gone but the wire stands were still there. The arbor was empty except for a piece of synthetic tulle wound about it, an invitation to pass through.

On Lenox Avenue a bouquet of synthetic yellow roses is fastened to a tree with strong cellophane tape. Above this offering is a photo of a young man who stares hard at the camera while embracing a pit bull. The image is laminated to withstand the elements, and it has survived for many months. Someone seems to be tending the empty cardboard box that, turned on its side as a makeshift altar, shelters the votive candles that are readily available from bodegas, botanicas, and ninety-nine-cent stores. Often they are blown out by the wind. One night, passing such an arrangement and seeing that all the candles had succumbed, I searched my purse for matches to light them again. Similar memorials are found on trees, on corners, near subway stations, in front of a building or a favorite hangout spot. Someone had been there, in that spot. That person was not there any longer. But the significance of location expanded in my mind when my neighbors told me, in the midst of our customary greetings, that a young woman had been stabbed to death the night before on the corner of our block, and a few days later, a wreath held aloft on a stand, festooned with red ribbons and roses, marked the spot where she fell.

Just across from there on 133rd Street, a black-and-purple swag draped the doorway of St. Andrew's Church, a small congregation whose sanctuary occupied the parlor floor of a brownstone. The banner stayed in place for months. When it first appeared, I assumed it announced the death of some member of the flock; later I wondered if it was the sign of some festival of the liturgical year. The decoration remained in place longer than would be necessary for a period of mourning or a religious season. A piece of paper appeared on the door. Seeing this from the sidewalk, I knew it announced — like similar signs on the doors of small churches I'd passed — that the church had stopped having services. I don't know if the congregation moved or was dissolved. Even after this, the black-and-purple swag remained above the threshold, greeting vanished congregants of the vacant church.

I almost didn't notice when the banner disappeared. The realization came when I finally registered that the blue-trimmed white facade that had set the church building apart from the rest of the houses had disappeared too. It was painted brown to cohere with the other recently renovated brownstones on the block. But there was one trace remaining of St. Andrew's. Even after its external transformation, the imitation stained-glass windows that had distinguished the building as a house of worship remained intact for months. Recently I saw they'd been smashed, some shards still held up by the window frame. They were probably destroyed by the construction crew that was working inside.

Raven Chanticleer died just a few weeks before I moved to Harlem, on March 31, 2002. I must have seen the notice of his death in the *New York Times,* but I don't recall having heard about the time and place of his funeral. I am no longer sure if I learned of his existence at the same moment I read of his death, or if I had arrived in Harlem having already heard of his African American Wax and History Museum. I do know that at some time during those first months of living here, after he had already died, I looked up the museum in the phone book, and even called, but did not get an answer.

Chanticleer's museum was celebrated as the first wax museum dedicated to the famous figures of black history. Established in the early 1990s, it was a completely independent endeavor. Its founder was also its chief docent, head fund-raiser, artist-in-residence, and maintenance man. From the very beginning, the museum garnered lots of media attention. In Harlem, Raven Chanticleer was already something of a celebrity. He was a theater director, performer, and fashion designer known for his *glamorous "garbage bag glamor fashions"* creating high fashion from plastic bags. Notables who had purchased his work were said to include Mahalia Jackson, Billie Holiday, Josephine Baker, Louis Armstrong, and Muhammad Ali. As an artist he enjoyed solo shows in Rome, London, Montreal, and Hawaii. In the 1970s, Chanticleer performed in *The Wiz, House of Flowers,* and *Cotton Comes to Harlem.* Long before he founded the wax museum, his notorious fashion sense was the stuff of legend. He made a memorable entrance at the 1971 "Fight of the Century" between Muhammad Ali and George Frazier at Madison Square Garden, wearing *an ermine and chinchilla cape and leopard skin briefs*. At a Harlem film premiere at the old Victoria Theatre, he was *immaculately attired in a Russian sable outfit, complete with cape, brocade boots and diamond bejeweled skullcap, alighting from an old-fashioned white carriage drawn by 2 prancing white horses*.

Chanticleer said the inspiration for the museum had come when he was living abroad. *I got into my wax thing in London, after seeing Madame Tussaud's*. He was immediately *captivated by this wondrous vibrant art form*. Another report tells the story differently. *I was impressed by Madame Tussaud's on a field trip to Paris but she had no black "herons or sherons"—they were all lily-white. . . . I said "I won't take this for an answer; I will open the first black wax museum in the world."*

The first figure immortalized by Raven Chanticleer's secret formula of plaster, papier-mâché, and beeswax was Raven Chanticleer himself. His effigy was soon joined by others: a figure of Harriet Tubman wearing aviator glasses; Fannie Lou Hamer in a leopard-print evening gown. The wax likenesses were not arranged by chronology or specialty—according to some reports, many were not even strict likenesses. There was Michael Jackson next to Magic Johnson next to Martin Luther King Jr. Malcolm X was next to Whoopi Goldberg, who was next to Josephine Baker. Local *herons and sherons* like Mayor David Dinkins, Mother Hale, and Adam Clayton Powell Jr. also formed a part of Chanticleer's pantheon, in addition to African leaders Nelson Mandela and Haile Selassie. A 1998 article in the *New York Times* reported that Chanticleer's wax renditions of Mike Tyson, Michael Jackson, and Biggie Smalls were on loan to an exhibition in Europe. The next year saw the unveiling of two new statues, Paul Robeson and Langston Hughes.

Many of the newspaper articles promoting the museum portray Chanticleer next to his creations, often surrounded by children from the school groups and youth groups that frequently visited the museum. In the photos, he always wears a broad and knowing grin. Besides the wax figures, the museum featured art in other media, much of it also by Chanticleer. There was a portrait of the singer Madonna, depicted with black skin. Perhaps not referring to that particular incarnation, Chanticleer had said, *Every black home should have a black Jesus and a black Madonna.* Other religious work included a version of the Last Supper featuring the likenesses of Malcolm X, Stokely Carmichael, Marcus Garvey, Elijah Muhammad, Mary McLeod Bethune, Frederick Douglass, W. E. B. DuBois, Thurgood Marshall, and Paul Robeson.

A group of oil paintings on the wall illustrated *the hardships in slavery.* One painting on the wall showed a picture of *cotton-fields in the south*; another showed *shanty-life in Haiti.* Not on regular display were *some skeletal bones that Chanticleer says are of African ancestors.*

When I first came to Harlem, I noticed the great number of funeral parlors. There were at least four on Lenox Avenue, and many more on the other main thoroughfares and side streets. This seemed to be a high ratio of funeral homes per capita. Perhaps it is a stable business, like beauty parlors and ninety-nine-cent stores. The signs in front of most were weather-beaten, as though they'd been operating for many years.

One of the funeral parlors on Lenox advertises its services on its awning with a slogan: "Where Beauty Softens Your Grief." Another one, just a few doors down, does not carry a sales pitch. Its sign reads Mickey Funeral Service, The Carolina Chapel. I always wondered about the origin of its name. Mickey's is located within a graceful mansion on Lenox between 121st and 122nd, near other fine town houses occupied by SROs and churches. Sometimes I would pass when a funeral was taking place, when mourners were arrayed along the stout staircase that curved gently from the front door to the pavement.

But mostly, when I passed, the parlor was empty. It was as if no one was dying. The windows of the Mickey funeral home were hardly ever lit, but I imagined the interior: heavy drapes, overstuffed sofas, thick carpet, faux-wood paneling on the walls, and the kind of sturdy potted houseplants that scoff at inattention. A small window in a door of the garden-floor entrance displayed the funeral home's OPEN or CLOSED sign. A WILL BE BACK clock alerted visitors when the owner was briefly away from the premises; if in need, one would know the undertaker was returning shortly, and thus not seek out the parlor a few doors down the avenue. Most times when I passed the Carolina Chapel the office was closed, so I began to take note of the clock's message. Other times, when the sign read OPEN I nearly went in, but never followed the urge.

This same absurd drama played out at a different location, the St. Helena Funeral Home on 136th Street. I have also paused out front on the sidewalk. I have exchanged anonymous and courteous hellos when passing its proprietor as he stands outside when I enter and exit the Countee Cullen Branch library across the street. The windows of its upper floor face 136th Street. They are long, narrow, and set high into the wall, so the only scenery visible from the desks is the line of cornices crowning the houses across the way. Sitting there staring out over the rooftops, I could pick out the blue cornice belonging to the funeral home.

I crafted my own version of its history. I assumed it was named for the barrier island off the coast of South Carolina, which is the stronghold of Gullah culture and the ancestral home of many Harlemites whose roots are in that state. It was also the location of the Port Royal experiment, an episode during the Civil War when the Union Army, having driven the slaveowners off the land, organized the freedmen to manage and operate the plantations they had already been running to create income that would help fund the Union's effort.

I became convinced, based only on my fantasies, that each funeral home in Harlem had a very specific following, determined not by quality of service or membership in a certain church or lodge, but by the place from which one's family came. According to my explanation, the services of each particular chapel included preparing the body, arranging the services, and then carrying the body back home. Attached to this last fantasy was a fugitive factoid from my earliest researches at the Schomburg Center as a student visiting New York. It crossed my mind whenever I passed the Carolina Chapel; though it was not exactly appropriate, the memory could not be suppressed. Back when I'd been frantically researching the Scottsboro Boys, and black madonnas, and eighteenth-century executions of slave children, I was also looking up the dramatic structure of old minstrel shows. I jotted down the following words, which were often spoken as the curtain was about to close: *And now, kind friends, as all good things must come to an end, so too must this part of our entertainment come to an end, and thanking you one and all, we'll say farewell, for we are going back to Carolina.*

Putting an end to all this speculation, one day I happened to pass the Mickey funeral home on Lenox and finally saw a man standing outside. His elegant dress and the way he commanded the expanse of sidewalk directly in front of the building's entryway made me certain he was the undertaker. I decided that instead of those unfruitful hellos with the owner of the St. Helena parlor, I would take my chance. I greeted him and asked if he was the proprietor. When he assured me he was, I explained my curiosity about the name of his establishment. Why was it called the Carolina Chapel? He confirmed my suspicion that the owners had come from the Carolinas. When I asked him what year they'd arrived in Harlem, he said he wasn't sure, maybe in the 1930s, but they had come to New York earlier and had gone to Brooklyn first.

After he answered my question, and I thanked him brightly for solving my riddle (*Oh, I had always wondered about that*), our conversation did not continue. There was no invitation beyond the gate. I proceeded up the avenue, proud of myself for having defeated my fancies, yet knowing I'd only produced a bit of trivia.

By then, having hesitated at the door of those two funeral parlors so many times without entering, without reason, I created a logic for my apprehension, or at least an excuse. One should not venture into a funeral home without cause, I told myself. It was a convenient superstition, invented especially for the occasion.

The Harlem rituals of death have parallels with those of the ancient necropolis of Egypt. They are in the continuum of those on the Nile of four thousand years ago. Thus begins Camille Billops's introduction to *The Harlem Book of the Dead,* which collects the funeral portraits made by James VanDerZee. In addition to the parade pictures and studio portraits for which he became famous, VanDerZee also made pictures of dead people in their coffins. It was a common practice at the time, and a good source of income.

In these pictures, death is recorded as yet another milestone of life—along with baptism, graduation, or marriage. At the time, a portrait was a common way to commemorate another rite of passage. A newly arrived southerner might pose in his finest clothes for a picture that could be sent to the family left behind. The photographs of the dead are also for the left behind. In VanDerZee's funeral portraits, the dead are sometimes pictured alone; sometimes their essential aloneness is pierced by the presence of mourners posed impassively nearby. The coffins are lined with gleaming satin and taffeta and piled with arrangements of mums, roses, carnations, and lilies. The corpses wear cakey makeup and fine clothes.

Usually, the portraits are enhanced with one of VanDerZee's special death portrait innovations. When producing the prints, he superimposed embellishments onto the picture. Sometimes these were stock images of angelic orders hovering above, unfurling scrolls that contained a few lines of poetry or a prayer. Sometimes he merged the past with the present, double-exposing the funeral image with an old portrait of the same person while alive. The death of a soldier is commemorated in a picture decorated with an American flag. At times VanDerZee's interventions are not technological, but merely a matter of arrangement. One picture shows a dead man with his arms folded around a newspaper that announces the 1927 death of Florence Mills. The funerals took place on the same day. *To make this dead gentleman look more natural, his family wanted the paper put in his hand, to make it appear he had been reading and had just dozed off.*

But sometimes, despite arrangement and embellishment, the pictures still told their own story. A father cradles a dead infant in his arms, as if the child is still alive. I wonder if this was according to VanDerZee's instruction. The father smiles ever so slightly, as if proudly admiring his child on the day it was born. The mother, perched on the arm of the photography studio's prop chair, leans over her husband's shoulder, also looking at the baby. But VanDerZee's carefully composed domestic scene failed to conceal the odd look on her face, which reads as derangement mixed with accusation.

In an interview featured along with the portraits, VanDerZee mentions Mickey's funeral home as one of the places where he worked regularly. It is only a passing detail among many passing details. At the prompting of the interviewer, VanDerZee recounts small snippets from the stories of the dead, whether the circumstances of their death, the repercussions of their death (an inheritance), or how he had come to produce a certain effect within the frame. Indeed, throughout the interview, he sometimes seems a bit annoyed by the probing questions of the archivist, Camille Billops. Perhaps for VanDerZee the book consists of photographs of people who have no relation to each other or significance beyond proximity of circumstance and time: They had lived in Harlem, they had died, and they had died in Harlem while James VanDerZee was making some portion of his living by fulfilling the demand for funeral portraiture, then in fashion.

VanDerZee offers the half-remembered details surrounding the death of one young beauty, her fair skin somewhat mottled by an exuberant application of mortuary makeup. Her fate is obscured by the satin ripples and mounds of flowers. She'd fallen ill at a party, complaining of stomach pain. When her friends took her to lie down, loosening her clothes for comfort, they discovered that she was bleeding from the abdomen. She'd been shot in the midst of the revelry by a silenced gun. Asked to identify her assailant as she was dying, all she said was, *I'll tell you tomorrow, yes, I'll tell you tomorrow.*

The woman's murder and her last words, giving her disgruntled lover enough time to escape, provided the point of departure for Toni Morrison's novel *Jazz.* The novel, an imaginary version of the circumstances surrounding the young woman's fate, does more than fictionalize fact. In weaving a complete story from the woman's fragmented deferral, Morrison unravels the trick this woman played on the living at the moment of her death. It is a commonplace that the dead tell no tales. But no cliché has been invented to capture just how troubled we are by those who take their truth beyond the grave.

On Lenox Avenue, a brownstone owner took special care, when restoring his property's facade, to uncover and preserve a sign. Thick black letters spelling "G&G Photo Studio" stand out against a white background that is streaked with residual brown paint. When the sign was first uncovered, it was a marvel: *That is VanDerZee's studio! That is where he worked!* The physical excavation of that sign made the fact more urgent than if I'd just found the address in a history book and then gone to stand at the door. I imagined the process of uncovering it, precise as the deft brushwork used at excavations to unearth a fossilized skull preserved by volcanic ash.

Until recently, the old VanDerZee studio housed a new real estate office specializing in condos and brownstone conversions. But the agent must have had poor business, because later I saw a sign posted in the window announcing that the marshal had taken possession of the premises. The customized awning that advertised the office is still there, but the name has been painted out. Elsewhere in Harlem, other long-gone storefronts also retain their signs. These are not acts of preservation or additions to the tourist trail, they are simply the last traces of failed enterprises. As with the sign above VanDerZee's studio, the letters are only meaningful to one who knows. And even then, they only mean so much. *That is where he was, he is not there any longer.*

In *The Harlem Book of the Dead,* when VanDerZee is asked why people had stopped taking pictures with their dead loved ones, he answers bluntly. *I didn't know they had stopped. They're still doing it today. Sometimes the family wanted to be there to show the other relatives just how the deceased had been put away.*

If funeral portraiture captured images of the dead that were of more use to the living, the traditional books of the dead for which the collection of VanDerZee's funeral pictures is named are oriented more insistently toward the hereafter. They examine not only how to manage the passage in a psychological and metaphysical sense, but actually how one might, by ritual, transcend earthly existence, defeat death, and penetrate eternity.

The Egyptian death rites cited in the introduction to *The Harlem Book of the Dead* are based on the epic lamentation of Isis, who scoured the four corners of the earth in search of the dismembered parts of her murdered husband, Osiris. In putting him back together again and achieving his resurrection, she helps him gain immortality, establishing him as Lord of the Underworld, Lord of Eternity, Ruler of the Dead. The incantation of Isis's lament formed the foundation of all burial ceremonies in ancient Egypt. Mourners, in preparing the body, also accomplished the resurrection of their dead. The belief was that each man buried according to those original rites would also live forever and, in death, become the risen god.

The *Tibetan Book of the Dead* is also a carefully conceived ritual for immortality, meant to be read aloud to a person who is dying; it includes a description of various regions of the afterlife, particularly the *bardo,* that territory between the end of one life cycle and the rebirth which begins the next. This description of the landscapes that one would pass through after leaving earth was preparation for the journey. This may be a kind of comfort, but it is also an initiation. Another important part of the Tibetan philosophy of death is that the soul must depart the body in a certain manner, so that the condition of the spirit in the next life could be elevated. A person had to know how to die in order to achieve this transcendence, leading to eventual liberation from the cycle of birth, death, and rebirth. Perhaps participating in the ritual deathbed reading, engaging the earthly part of the passage, was one occasion to learn.

In 1981, after living downtown and abroad, Raven Chanticleer returned to his native Harlem. *I had to come back,* he told one journalist. *I imagined myself as some kind of pioneer,* he told another. *And I figured that if those people in their covered wagons withstood all those Indians and the cold winters, then so could I.* He'd been working at Bergdorf Goodman when *crossing West 110th Street one day I felt the pulsation — the beat of the drums — call me forth to give my people the wax form.*

Chanticleer's pioneer homestead in Harlem was in the midst of a drug-infested block of West 115th Street. He purchased two town houses next to each other, living in one and turning the other into his museum. But he was spurred on by memories of his Harlem childhood, in a cultured home on Sugar Hill. His father was born in Haiti and was a school principal; his mother was from Barbados and had been a concert pianist.

It felt like Harlem was the center of the world, he recounted to one reporter.

Walking around his neighborhood he would see Langston Hughes and Richard Wright and Louis Armstrong. He recalled seeing Duke Ellington, Count Basie and Billie Holiday in the long-forgotten nightclubs and at the Apollo Theater. "White people would come up to Harlem then to see these black gentlemen and ladies who were the best in the world. . . . It wasn't hard then for a black youngster to dream of great things."

Once Raven Chanticleer had been around the world and achieved some of those great things, he felt compelled to return to his roots. *Harlem is coming back . . . and I'm doing my part. I could have gone anywhere and lived in luxury, but I've come back home where I belong.*

I discovered all this about Raven Chanticleer in a file at the Schomburg Center. After exhausting the limited sources available about him and his museum on the Internet and in newspaper databases, I'd asked a librarian if she knew where I could find any other details. She directed me to the typewritten index cataloging a collection of materials called the "vertical files." These files contain clippings of newspaper articles, an antiquated system from the pre-Internet days when the library had an entire department devoted to that task. I was delighted when I found that there was, indeed, a clippings file devoted to Raven Chanticleer's African American Wax and History Museum. It was overflowing with all the newspaper articles and ephemera from which I have constructed the story above. In one of those articles, attention was called to the existence of the file itself: *His work is cataloged in the Schomburg collection,* mentioned one article, in a reverent tone.

Later, when I went back to continue my research, one of the librarians handed me the file with an amused look on her face. *Oh yeah, I remember him.* She remembered Raven Chanticleer because he was a regular visitor to the library, where he spent many hours creating and maintaining the very file I was consulting. She described his fantastical outfits, his outré manner. And she mentioned having seen him outside the library on one occasion, when he dominated the proceedings of a meeting held about property ownership in Harlem, advocating for an elderly woman who was in danger of losing her home.

Another librarian also remembered Chanticleer's visits. She mentioned a woman who began to appear at the library after Chanticleer's death and spent many hours maintaining the clippings file. She said she didn't know the relationship between the woman and Chanticleer, but she remembered that this library patron often wept uncontrollably as she went about her task. This woman returned repeatedly, as if tending the flowers at a grave, but the librarian said she had not been seen there in a while.

At first I thought it would be wonderful to find and interview this unidentified weeping lady. I even managed, through some details found in the files, to identify her name. But after several visits with Chanticleer's file, I decided that I had enough information. I also decided not to contact his friend and unofficial executor, fearing my questions would somehow distress her and disturb her bereavement.

———

On the Thursday afternoon of Ms. Minnie's funeral, I emerged from our building feeling solemn and official in a black dress. I had never gone to a funeral outside of Texas — my attendance had always been within the context of family, or friends with family connections. I glanced around to see if anyone from the block was heading over. I didn't see anyone, so walked alone to Bailey's Funeral Home just a few doors down the avenue. I had passed there so many times, winding through its crowds and avoiding the path of its hearse, which used the city sidewalk as a private driveway. It was strange to now be greeted at those doors as a mourner. I was surprised by the pristine interior. The wood veneer of the wall paneling and benches shone under the room's bright lights. The employees of the funeral home gave great attention to formality, ushering guests in a manner at once sincerely tender and highly scripted.

It was time for the viewing. I slipped into a bench next to the nearest familiar faces, just behind Ms. Barbara and next to Ms. Freddie Mae Baxter. Ms. Freddie Mae was a childhood friend of Ms. Minnie's. I remember clearly the first time we met. I was talking with Ms. Minnie in front of our building, and this smartly dressed woman came sidling up to us with a mischievous look on her face. Something about their interaction let me know, immediately, that they had been girls together. Ms. Minnie often mentioned to me that her friend Freddie Mae had written a book about childhood in their hometown and her adult life in Harlem. At the funeral home, Ms. Freddie Mae sat with another friend, and they were talking. I said hello, but I didn't make an effort to join their conversation, because by then I'd looked to the front of the room and seen Ms. Minnie in the coffin, wearing a pink suit. When I saw her body I began to cry, and seeing that no one else at the wake was crying, I began to feel self-conscious.

Then, my response was only to try to suppress my tears. Now, when I think of it, I realize it was the kind of moment when belief, or lack thereof, exposes itself. I looked around at the other mourners, who calmly waited for the service to begin. There were no hysterics in the crowd. Maybe they'd gone to more funerals than I had, or maybe they'd had a chance to say good-bye to Ms. Minnie. Maybe it had to do with a faith I could not summon on command—a lack of certainty about the regions that the dead pass through.

More people arrived for the viewing, and I sat there a bit longer. Then I got up to attend a town hall meeting.

A shooting spree had taken place a few days before the funeral, the weekend after Ms. Minnie died. It was Memorial Day weekend. Eight people had been wounded on Lenox and Seventh Avenues in a maelstrom that progressed up the blocks between 125th and 131st Streets. No one was killed. Later, I heard rumors that the violence was part of a gang initiation or had begun with a fight after a concert in Marcus Garvey Park. The night of the shooting, I was at home, working at my desk. I made a note, *night—almost midnight.* Below that, enclosed within brackets, *[a helicopter is circling the area.]*

The reason for the helicopter's flight was revealed the next morning in the newspaper. Upon learning the news of the shooting spree, I made another note:

I had been thinking that the sounds were changing as summer approached. But last night, except noting the helicopter seeming lower and more prolonged than I'd ever noticed (had I ever noticed?) I did not hear any sounds from the street. I did not hear any shots, didn't hear any screams, didn't hear the noise of the crowds said to have formed on the avenue, with "scores" of cops dispatched to disperse them.

Not having seen this scene—only having heard the sounds of its consequence—and noting it, but not going out to investigate, then waking to read about it in the news: staying inside is safety; staying inside is to avoid being a witness.

It was this feeling of having avoided my duty that led me to rush over—in the interim between the end of Ms. Minnie's wake and the beginning of her funeral—to that town hall meeting about the shooting. Not much said in the meeting added to my understanding of the event, or helped to avoid its repetition. It was, like many meetings I'd been to, something of a ritual, a place for the community to come together to share shock, outrage, and sadness. I didn't take any notes. A preacher gave a long invocation; earnest and sincere teenagers of the sort who were involved in after-school programs, not in shootings, stood up to speak about the state of their peers; parents shouted anguished calls to action. After listening awhile, I slipped out of my seat to return to the funeral.

The program had already begun by the time I made it back. I

paused with another latecomer at the front door before we were ushered inside to seats at the rear of the chapel. I saw some of my neighbors in the pews, as well as people in the front row I assumed to be Ms. Minnie's relatives. There was testimony from a niece, and a message of condolence read aloud that had been sent from the family's home church in South Carolina. Ms. Barbara got up and spoke directly *to* Ms. Minnie and not *about* her, thanking her for being such a good friend. After the preacher gave his eulogy, the obituary was read. It was spare and gave basic details: the year she had been born, the year she came to New York, her work in the garment district, her having one son.

Ms. Minnie's son was seated in the front row with her sister and a niece, the ones she had always spoken of. The ushers began to direct us for the procession past the body, inviting one row at a time to the front of the room. Throughout all of this, I was aware of a struggle going on inside me. I was trying to stop myself from taking note of what was happening. I was trying not to be an observer but a participant: to participate in the prayers, the songs, the proper etiquette. Some part of this attempt to stop the recording instinct was successful, because now much of what happened is a blur that resists being shaped into words. What is certain: I did not know the words to the ancient lamentation. I was uninitiated in how to die and how to mourn the dead.

When the service ended, we all went outside and stood in front of the funeral home. We remarked upon how beautiful the service had been, the skill of the preacher, and the selection of the songs. Soon we were laughing, because Willie, who always flirts with me but is old enough to be my father, began to flirt again. I began to scold him as I normally do, and as Ms. Minnie sometimes did on my behalf. I told him that if Ms. Minnie had been there, she would've told him off. Someone pulled out a camera, and Willie,

Ms. Barbara, and I posed, smiling, against the backdrop of Lenox Avenue.

Afterward, and for the next several days, a line in a song from the service persisted in my mind. It picked up on a theme from the preacher's eulogy. The organist, who was also the singer, led the assembled mourners in several rounds of this repeating chorus. The song had the sound of a march, with descending and ascending chords. Its lyrics assume the voice of the dead upon reaching the gates of heaven, faced with that record of deeds written on the angel's scroll: *Let my life speak for me...*

Several copies of the *New York Times* obituary announcing the death of Raven Chanticleer are included in his carefully curated file. This was one element of the archive he could not control. At least one copy had been added by a librarian, bearing the date and source in neat handwriting. Other copies seemed to have been added later, perhaps by the friend of Raven Chanticleer. One of the librarians had told me that this mourning friend of Chanticleer had asked the library to start a file archiving her own life. She said that Raven had instructed her to do so. Strangely, some artifacts about this woman, lacking any information about Raven Chanticleer, were mixed up in the file about the wax museum.

The newspaper obituary included some details of his life that the other articles had missed. It serves as a corrective footnote to the official record on Raven Chanticleer as collected and preserved by himself.

Raven Chanticleer, who was *born and raised in Harlem and resides there to this day* was actually born James Watson on September 13, 1928, in Woodruff, South Carolina. His parents—mentioned in several earlier profiles as Henri and Abbie

Chanticleer, a Haitian-born school principal and a Barbados-born concert pianist and couturier respectively, who lived on Sugar Hill—were, according to the *Times* obituary, sharecroppers. He had not graduated from the Sorbonne or the University of Ghana. Most likely there were no *old mentors from the University of Timbuktu*. A niece is quoted in the obituary stating that she intended to keep the museum going, once the family had sorted out some of the *legalities*.

As early as 1993, one reporter was suspicious of Chanticleer's tale. Chanticleer gave an interview to the *New York Post* very soon after the birth of the museum. Pointing at the various items he'd created, he announced that one of his furniture designs had won a prize at the 1940 World's Fair. The reporter remarked that, according to the 1936 birth date Chanticleer had provided, the achievement would have been prodigious—he would have been four years old.

I could read and write when I was four, Raven countered sharply before changing the subject. The article proceeds with the reporter's tongue placed complicitly in cheek. *Pointing to an idealized rustic scene à la Woolworth's*—complete with utopian cabin—*[he] continues, "That's the house in Alabama where I lived when I joined Martin Luther King's Freedom Ride." Sensing the reporter's wariness, he asks, "You believe me, don't you?"*

I looked up the census on a computer program available at the library, used mostly by people searching out their own ancestry. I hoped it would yield other information about this James Watson. He appears in 1930 as the one-and-a-half-year-old youngest child of Henry and Abbie Watson. Henry was thirty-five years old in 1930, Abbie was thirty-three. Their family included Sam, age nine; Leroy, age seven; Irene, age six; and Fred, age three. Also listed in their household were two boarders, both twenty-three years old, by the names of Geneva Moore and David Watson.

Henry and Abbie Watsons were renters. Henry's occupation is listed as a laborer in public works, and Abbie took in laundry at home.

Looking at the facts of the Watson household as revealed by those few lines scrawled by a census taker, I began to understand why their youngest son might have embroidered his history. We are used to the idea that to forget, obscure, or embellish is to forsake. Such was the forgetfulness which Chanticleer tried to abolish with his museum, and that Arthur Schomburg tried to abolish with his library. But Raven Chanticleer's forgetfulness was also his transcendence. Forgetting, obscuring, and embellishing were vital to Chanticleer's self-creation. He transcended his earthly birth to become the first figure immortalized in wax at his museum.

Raven Chanticleer included his parents in his mythology — he mentioned them in those newspaper accounts, gave them new countries of origin, new accomplishments, and his new name. This could be seen as a disavowal, a rejection of his origins. Or it could be seen as an act of love. His invented Haitian patrimony provided Chanticleer with a strain of racial heroism, and the fiction of his mother's musical career gave him an artistically inclined pedigree. But he'd also provided his parents with an alternative existence, a different future.

But what about all of his siblings? Were they also given illustrious new biographies? And what of all the other sons and daughters of sharecroppers from the South among whom Raven Chanticleer lived in Harlem, and who were to be uplifted by his museum — had he transcended them, too?

I didn't find a specific moment when James Watson disappears from public record and Raven Chanticleer takes his place. It is not possible, from the facts available at the library, to know when this man — who was not, in fact, a native son of Harlem — actually arrived up north and uptown. It is not possible to know what he saw when exiting the subway station. The shock of it, the distance between the world he was entering and the one he'd been born into, might have been enough to make him want to rewrite his entire history. Walking those streets, where he did not—as a child at least—see Langston Hughes and Richard Wright and Louis Armstrong, may have given him the feeling of being born again. Life as he had lived it up to that point was obliterated. This new life was one in which he was the parent and the child, the artist and the creation.

The census document on the computer didn't unlock any door to the past. I left the Watson family in 1930 and considered the name Raven Chanticleer had chosen for himself. The last name is a word taken from Old French, meaning "clear song." Chanticleer is the merry and colorful rooster made famous in an episode of Chaucer's *Canterbury Tales*. This wily cock outwits the fox who hunts him, tricking death with a last-minute escape. Raven Chanticleer's first name honors another trickster bird. In many Native American stories, the raven's powers include shape-shifting and creation.

Or perhaps the new name stood for nothing but his transcendence. Maybe Raven Chanticleer just liked the sound of those words as they flew from his tongue. It would be reason enough. Keen to shake that suspicious *Post* reporter from his tail, Raven Chanticleer insisted on being known by his true name: *I'm an* artiste...*stress that. I'm not an artist, I'm an* artiste. *And flamboyant. Yes? Naw! The word is totally inadequate.*

———

Sometime before the day when she invited me into her apartment, I'd mentioned to Ms. Minnie that I might need to interview her to help with research for this book. The request was a truce, settling the war I was having with myself. I was not sure I wanted to interview anyone, but if I asked, I'd have to do it. An eminent essayist I respected said (in an interview) that she didn't trust interviews and did not conduct them. This supplied me an excuse, for I had the distinct suspicion that the very act of posing a question irrevocably alters the answer you receive. There was a difference—perhaps especially in Harlem—between what people told you from memory, unbidden and of their own volition, and the nostalgic tones that crept in when you asked them a question, no matter how specific, about The Past. Perhaps this discrepancy was a function of my interview skills, but I did not think it *should* be a matter of interview skills. I did not want to be haranguing my neighbors with a tape recorder and reporter's pad. When I asked Ms. Minnie, it was because I thought I should give interviews a try—in the name of a method more respectable than memory. I told her I'd slip a note under her door with a formal request.

My misgivings won out. I never slipped that note under her door. Instead, I continued to see Ms. Minnie in the ways to which we were accustomed: in the hallway checking our mailboxes, or crossing paths when she was coming in for the day after her morning excursion while I was just going out. We complimented each other, me remarking on how well she looked, her telling me about the secret product she used for smooth skin, or about making soap in her childhood yard with lye and lard, or about piling into a car with girlfriends, going from South Carolina to dances in Georgia. She pulled my coat closed as the winter approached, and was pleased when we met and I was properly bundled. We told each other how glad we were to be neighbors, we said hello, we said goodbye and that we loved each other. She would tell me about various characters on the street, and she told me to stop and stare.

None of these things are "material" of the sort I would have gained had I interviewed her. The archive of oral histories at the Schomburg is surely bursting with such material. Now that

Ms. Minnie is gone, the part of me that wants to be a more obedient student of history regrets not having conducted a formal interview. But there was something else gained in the conversations we did have. It was not just a transaction of information; there was also the care she gave me, and the care I hope I gave her. And, sometimes, in those moments we had together, something passed between us that could not have been caught on tape yet bears witness to something too vast to be contained on paper.

One day when we stood in front of our building, Ms. Minnie was telling me about her hometown, Denmark, South Carolina. She told me it was *a black town* and her sister-in-law was mayor. Then she shared a detail I had not known in our years as neighbors and acquaintances. It is a detail that I would not have necessarily asked about and that she would not necessarily have told me had I ever slipped the note under her door formally asking for her stories and her time. She told me that Davis was her married name. Her family name was Sojourner. I said it was a beautiful name, and she told me that not many people knew about her true name—only those who knew her from home. She looked me squarely in the eye before continuing. *That's not a slave name.*

———

I went to West 115th Street to see Raven Chanticleer's house. Finding it did not require the exact address. I recognized the building from a photocopy in the files, because the house had once graced the cover of Italian *Vogue.* For the occasion, Raven Chanticleer had posed outside, wearing a fur coat. The house is still painted with the exuberant mural. A dream landscape on the stoop shows a tropical scene—a beach, a little fish, an ominous shark. Another mural shows an Egyptian fantasia, with the Sphinx, the pyramids, and the same palm trees as shown on the beach. *I love beautiful things,* Raven Chanticleer once said. *I just*

have to make things around me beautiful. An example of his inclination was a pair of trash cans near his stoop, decorated with the
faces of a king and queen. Showing those same cans to a reporter,
Chanticleer had declared: *In the midst of ugliness, I find beauty.*

When I visited, the low, winding staircase leading to the front
door was blocked at the sidewalk by a high gate. The gate was
closed and secured by a chain. A fine cobweb drawn over the pad-
lock added the appearance of abandonment—perhaps the gate
had not been unlocked in some time. But the uppermost windows
facing the street were open, as if to ventilate the house during the
summer's heat. A fan was visible through one open window. I
could not see any lights inside. The only way I could have made
my presence known was to begin rattling the gate and shouting
up to that open window. I was not inclined to do so.

At that moment a man appeared from the garden level of the
house directly adjacent—a house built of sandstone, a staid aris-
tocrat beside its neighbor, the garish painted lady. The man asked
me if I needed any assistance, and I told him I was just looking at
the museum of Raven Chanticleer. He told me that I was looking
at the wrong house. His own building had been the actual
museum—Chanticleer had lived behind the elaborate facade
next door.

When I asked the man if he knew what had happened to the
contents of the museum, he shrugged. He thought they'd been
placed in storage after Chanticleer's death. When I told him I'd
noticed that the number for the museum was still listed in the
phone book, he smiled with mild embarrassment. He had always
intended to call the phone company to have the listing removed,
he said. He was responsible for the illusion that the museum was
still open.

He told me that relatives of Raven Chanticleer, a niece and
nephew, now lived in the house with the murals. Thinking of the

cobweb I'd just seen, I was surprised to hear this; it must have been the busy work of a spider earlier that morning. The man said Chanticleer's relatives were very friendly and would probably be happy to help in my research. He gave me their names, and I thanked him for taking the time to speak, apologizing for lingering outside his door.

I knew, even as he suggested it, that I would not leave a note at that gate or call the niece and nephew to get additional details beyond what Raven Chanticleer had so carefully curated at the library. I might have discovered more of the official story, but it seemed like a trespass. I had not been invited beyond the gate.

Perhaps it is an act of respect due the dead—akin to certain ointments applied to a corpse, or the proper prayers murmured beside an open coffin—to not want to know more than they cared to tell. *I'll tell you tomorrow...I'll tell you tomorrow...* Perhaps it is an act of love. Raven Chanticleer told the most crucial details of his story. The fact that he invented his origins is important, but it would be too easy to dwell on his flamboyant character and the sensational lies from which he sculpted his existence. Apart from all that, there was also the very simple, and very honorable, mission of his life's work.

I started the museum to bring our history to life, and to help people's self-esteem, he said. *I created these wax figures to keep alive their words and their deeds at a time when too many African Americans think we have no heroes.... The wax museum has been my dream since childhood.*

Still, I wonder about his wax effigies, immortalizing those heroes for eternity—or at least some fraction of eternity. No longer on display, perhaps they are preserved inside Raven Chanticleer's painted house, or maybe they are on loan to an exhibition in Europe, or in a storage facility, or destroyed. Do they keep alive words and deeds? Did his secret recipe involving plaster, papier-mâché, and beeswax endure? Or was the substance breaking down, unable to stop time? The *Times* obituary quoted Chanticleer's prophetic warning of what would happen if the museum did not outlast him. He'd made the wax sculpture of himself *just in case something should happen to me, if they didn't carry out my wishes and my dreams of this wax museum I would come back and haunt the hell out of them.*

It seems fitting that only the life lived by Raven Chanticleer should speak for him: *Matter of fact, I'm not creatively influenced by anybody but myself and my own dreams.*

We March Because...

EVERY YEAR I look forward to the African American Day parade. It happens the third Sunday in September, and it is the last of the ethnic festivals that dot the city's calendar. The Irish (and honorary Irish) and the Italians (and honorary Italians) have made the feast days of St. Patrick and San Gennaro into secular ethnic carnivals, but for me the parade in Harlem every year is a hallowed event.

When I first came to Harlem, it seemed the streets in summer were always full of parades. Hearing the sound of drums coming into my windows, I would tear out of the house on 120th Street to see who was making the music. It would be the Juneteenth parade, a procession carrying south on Lenox Avenue and terminating at Marcus Garvey Park; or a parade of African Muslims in flowing robes, celebrating the life of their saint. I saw an African Liberation Day parade that was not really a parade at all, but more of a picket line, with people marching in a small circuit on the sidewalk in front of the State Office Building, shouting slogans in support of Zimbabwe (*Free the land! Mugabe is right!*). Once, I came out of the house and discovered a long parade of young folks and older folks all dressed alike in uniforms resembling those of a scouting brigade. A color guard led them, but no signs revealed their group identity, and they shouted no slogans as they marched down Lenox in strict formation. I walked alongside them for a while, following the tense rhythm of their drummer's beat. I asked a few other spectators whether they knew the occasion for this martial display, but no one had any better notions than I did.

It is something of an accepted idea among some historians that Harlem began with a parade. The movement of blacks from other neighborhoods of New York or from the South did not take place as one unified march. Rather, these historians are speaking of the victory parade of the 369th regiment, the Harlem Hellfighters. The Hellfighters earned their name fighting in the trenches of World War I alongside the French (unable to serve with their white countrymen in a segregated armed forces) and were the first Americans to reach the German front. Perhaps the 1919 victory march of the 369th is a convenient place to begin the story, which relies on James Weldon Johnson's eyewitness account. Johnson describes how, once the regiment ascended Fifth Avenue, reaching 110th Street at the northern end of Central Park, they turned west to meet Lenox Avenue at its fountainhead and from there flowed into Harlem. The tight configuration they had maintained during their display to all of white New York scattered upon reaching Harlem into a loose and jovial swarm. The band gave up its military marching songs and started playing jazz tunes. One of the songs played was "How You Gonna Keep 'Em Down on the Farm (After They've Seen Paree)?"

A picture showing Lenox Avenue near the corner of 134th Street on Armistice Day, some months before the 369th made it home, provides an idea of what the crowd might have looked like at the victory march. The crowd is packed onto the sidewalks from the buildings to the edge of the curb, from the foreground toward the vanishing point on the horizon. Flags hang from every storefront and from a few upper-story windows. But in the picture of the Armistice celebrations, taken before the return of the Harlem Hellfighters, the crowd is oddly tranquil. It is as if victory in the Great War — fought for democracy and peace across Europe — was an abstraction. Whatever patriotic sentiment was not fully expressed in the crowd at news of the Armistice was finally released when the Harlem troops themselves returned from the front. Peace was declared, but another battle had begun. W. E. B. DuBois summarized (and perhaps helped to incite) the mood in a sober editorial from *The Crisis*:

We return.
We return from fighting.
We return fighting.
Make way for democracy.

I like to think the crowd that assembles for the African American Day parade each year matches that from 1919. It happens on Seventh Avenue, from 110th Street to 145th Street. The reviewing stand for distinguished onlookers is planted at the intersection of 125th and Seventh by the statue of Adam Clayton Powell Jr.

In the days leading up the parade, my neighbor Ms. Bessie always asks if I will be there and tells me that she will be situated near our street. She always watches from the same spot, and she tells me that I should come and find her.

The parade always starts behind schedule, and I've learned not to go out for the advertised start time of 2 p.m. By the time I arrive, the procession is already underway, so it is without any preliminaries that the urgent message of, say, the delegation from the Masjid Malcolm Shabazz greets me: *JAIL AIN'T NO GOOD*, declare their signs, and *We must establish businesses and industry to support quality education. FREEDOM JUSTICE EQUALITY* blare other signs, while the marchers in the group chant the words of Marcus Garvey: *Up you mighty race, you can accomplish what you will!* The faces of Elijah Muhammad, W. E. B. DuBois, Frederick Douglass, Marcus Garvey, Sojourner Truth, Harriet Tubman, and Malcolm X are borne on posters held high above the heads of the marchers, while dignitaries of the group creep along in the comfort of an off-road SUV. As they pass, a man imbued with the spirit of business and industry reaches across the police barriers to the crowd, selling flags with the African nationalist colors for two dollars. He says, *Salaam alaikum* as he offers his wares.

The businessmen and businesswomen of the Group of 100 Black Men and Group of 100 Black Women, their actual numbers amounting to many less than advertised, follow with signs of exhortation: *Protect it! Love it! Preserve it! Your home community, Harlem!*

Behind them come the Ki Egungun Loa Egbe Egungun of New York. Their marshal carries a staff with a skull upon it; he shakes this scepter at the onlookers. Another man walks on stilts, wearing a blank mask, eerie because it does not offer the logic of any facial features. They are accompanied by African drummers and attended by women in white. The leader brandishes a ceremonial whisk made from the tail of some animal. According to a sign carried nearby, this is the King of Oyutunji Village, His Royal Highness Oba Osejjeu Adefumi.

When the king and his retinue pass by, the first of the many marching bands imported from Baltimore quickly take their place. These include the Westsiders, the Christian Warrior Marching Unit, the New Edition Marching Band, the Baltimore Go-Getters, In Full Motion, the Edmonson Village Steppers, the Soul Tigers, and the Approaching Storm. These bands are, undoubtedly, the most important elements of the parade. They play regular marching tunes and souped-up versions of the current popular songs raucously transposed to brass instruments and snare drums. Their sounds fill the avenue, vibrating off the buildings on either side. The whistles of the drill sergeants punctuate the music and are matched by cheers from the crowd. The marching bands wear complicated costumes of bright colors, sequins, and gold or silver lamé. They range in age from the tiniest kindergartners to majorettes old enough to be grandmothers, proudly wearing the same revealing costumes of their younger cohorts, along with their silver hair. Effeminate teenage boys who confidently twirl batons and teasingly vamp for the audience are both praised and belittled from the sidelines. Attentive mothers follow the drill teams with towels to dry the sweaty faces of their children. They give water bottles to the thirsty and administer portable fans as performers succumb to heat stroke.

The rest of the march sometimes feels like filler between bands. There are the five members of the National Council of Negro Women, the modest three-person contingent of the Ethiopia World Federation, and the radiant and peaceful brigade from the Hindu-inflected Brahma Kumaris. Equally small are the delegations of black conservatives, black accountants, black social workers, black electricians, black nurses, and black engineers.

A long section of the parade features unions, as well as the black sanitation workers, black mass-transit workers, black parole workers, black corrections officers, black court officers, and black police and their protégés of the Police Athletic League, who follow close behind. The firefighters on their engine ladders earn rousing applause, and the school safety officers arrive in vans blaring menacing sirens. The men of 100 Blacks in Law Enforcement Who Care receive significantly more affection than the black state police troopers on their motorcycles and in sports cars. Many parade-goers seem to be familiar with the troopers, not because of family connections but from having encountered them on the highway when issued speeding tickets. Someone shouts at them from the crowd, *We don't trust y'all!*

This challenge is met by an officer who leaves her place in the parade rank to shout information about starting salaries, causing someone else to note, *That's a good unit to be in.*

A great stir is always caused by whatever up-and-coming pretty-boy rap sensation commands the epic speaker system of the Hot 97 float, which is always in competition with a similar display from a rival radio station. High above the crowd, like princes carried by bearers, they posture while lip-synching lyrics from their latest hit. The royal attendants of the entourage, street-team promoters enjoying their temporary celebrity, toss T-shirts, flyers, posters, and CDs to the screaming fans below. Teenage girls rush from the sidewalk to run alongside the float as it passes through the crowd. Some join the spectacle, dancing with jubilation and abandoning their friends at the sidelines.

More sober is the Five Percent Nation of Gods and Earths, who carry signs with their emblem of the crescent and the star. The number seven is prominently displayed. They march with a determined step, and their slogans are brief distillations of their complex theology: *The black man is God. The black woman is Earth*, and *What do we want? PEACE*, and *Let the babies shine!* Because no encounter with the Five Percenters is complete without some perplexing numerology, I note down—for future investigation—the message of one sign: *Psalm 86 vs. 6.*

I am no less dumbfounded by the long contingent of Freemasons and other fraternal orders. Their numbers have dwindled since the days when VanDerZee photographed their promenades along the same avenue, but their elegance has not diminished. With slight differences according to their affiliation and rank, the men wear dark suits, white gloves, and a white cloth hanging from the waist that looks like a kind of apron. Some wear fezzes, and their aprons are covered with embroidered patches showing pyramids and pharaohs' heads. Signs identify them as members of the

Prince Hall Grand Lodge, the Medina Temple, the Oasis of New York, the Desert of New York, as well as Elks clubs and the female Masonic counterpart, the Order of the Eastern Star. A man identified as *the most worshipful grand master* rides in a convertible sports car, wearing a Maltese cross and a hat with cascading plumes.

The Masons seem to occupy a special place in the parade—not only do their costume and ceremony link them to well-known images from Harlem's past, but everyone seems to know someone who is marching. The Masons always pause, ceremoniously greeting members of the crowd. I try to watch for secret handshakes.

The women of the Eastern Star wear comparatively simple outfits—white dresses, white hosiery, and white shoes that make them look like nurses. Some wear rhinestone tiaras. Usually they sing, and the crowd joins in with familiar songs like *This little light of mine / I'm gonna let it shine.* I sing too. Once there was a song I did not know at first, but I quickly learned its lyrics and have not been able to forget them: *We are soldiers, in the army / We got to pick up the blood-stained banner / We got to fight, or we got to die.* While much of their display is decipherable only by the initiated, a phrase on their banner points to the origin of their name: *We have seen His star in the east and come to worship Him.*

Once, the Masons had a challenger from the crowd. He yelled abuse above the drums that accompanied their stride. *You better not betray us! You better not betray us!* He shouted agitatedly, making demands whose urgency was obvious only to himself. His quarrel seemed to revolve around the Masonic iconography. *Turn the star right side up! TURN THE STAR! RIGHT SIDE UP!* At the same time he began to yell at the crowd: *Our last name is not our last name!* He resumed his accusations against the marching Masons. *Tell the truth! That means all of you!* He repeated his exhortation about the position of the star, but his rancor and persistence did not seem to fluster them. Suddenly he turned his attention to me, making notes nearby. *WRITE! IT! DOWN!* he yelled, with just as much venom as before.

I did write it down, but with certain groups I stop my notation. I put down the pen and press into the crowd. I always go to the parade alone so that I can move quickly. I begin on the sidewalk and then cross over to stand in the median, finding myself an unexpected guest among families who have come prepared for the day with folding stadium seats, coolers full of food and drink, and battery-operated personal fans. Unencumbered, I am free to push close to the barricades when my favorite marchers, the Panamanian drum and bugle corps, arrive. They wear crisply pleated guayabera shirts, woven straw hats, and khaki shorts or pants. Every year their costume is the same, and so is the disciplined precision of their steps, the rousing herald of their horns, and their crashing drums. Like the teenagers chasing after rappers on floats, I run along with the Panamanian musicians, matching my march to theirs, keeping them in sight in order to arrest their passage until I am tired out by walking. Then I find a space to sit and let the parade pass me by once more.

The group of Native Americans who march in the parade condense a complicated history. Most of the people who march as "Indians" would be identified as African American by the untrained eye, or by any eye. For the parade, they are dressed in fringed leather, headbands, moccasins, and other ritual costumes. A person with a very trained eye might note that these Indians do not necessarily seem equipped to perform any particular ritual at all; they adopt a "Hollywood Indian" look. But there are no authenticity police on the sidelines, just cheers and simulated war cries. I once heard someone comment that the Indians should have the biggest float of all.

The Mothers Against Guns carry signs in memory of children killed by gun violence. They are followed by Morticians Who

Care, whose contribution consists of a creeping hearse, with a coffin rolled behind. *HOW MANY MORE WILL IT TAKE?* their signs inquire. Members of the NAACP form a subdued flock, centered on dignitaries riding slowly in a Jaguar. Their signs emphasize the hallowed history of their organization (*since 1927*) and promote their latest campaign (*Bury the 'N' word*).

Attempting a more radical position are the New Black Panthers, who are joined by some of the old Black Panthers and hold up signs with the faces of heroes like Assata Shakur, Fred Hampton, and Huey P. Newton. They are supported by members of the Jericho Movement, who brandish posters with the names and faces of political prisoners. A member of the New Black Panthers shouts, *This is protected by the red, the black, and the green,* and exhorts the crowd to join in with chants of *Black Power!* A few white people in green hats walk along with them as legal observers; police cars trail close behind. This is because almost every year the New Black Panthers have a scuffle with the law. It unfolds at some point between 130th and 135th as if according to a script. The chants of *Black Power!* soon transform into choruses of *Fuck the Police!*

Decidedly more tranquil are the sisters of the black sororities, Alpha Kappa Alpha, Delta Sigma Theta, Phi Beta Sigma, and Zeta Phi Beta. A float trumpeting itself as *a salute to black college women* carries homecoming queens and pageant winners in tiaras and satin gowns who greet the crowd with the classic elbow-powered regal wave and blown kisses.

It is possible that when I am rushing to see my favorite parts of the parade, I miss the passage of certain floats and dignitaries. You will say, what about Pigfoot Mary and Porkchop Davis and Carl Van Vechten? But look, there they are marching, and there is the man who brings a van from North Carolina loaded with sausage links, boiled peanuts, pickled eggs, and peaches and sorghum syrup and collard greens, which he sells from the street. There are the girls playing double-dutch, there is that man who kept a tiger in his apartment, and yes, oh, there is Bill Clinton, we see him so infrequently at his office on 125th Street! There is this week's winner of Amateur Night at the Apollo, there are the Korean American owners of Harlem's most popular chain of soul-food buffet restaurants, there are those socialites going to the fabulous Harlem Renaissance parties, which I am quite tired of hearing about. They are all gathered at the parade. There is that man who asked me how long one had to live in Harlem before being allowed to write a book about it — implying, of course, that I had not lived in Harlem long enough to write a book about it. But what happened to the African hair-braiding ladies, what about the new boutiques, where is your gospel brunch with chicken and waffles, why didn't I mention the Collyer Brothers *y porque no digo nada sobre El Barrio?* I will say, *Oh, they are all there, you must have missed them marching by.* And I will say, *It is getting dark, I should be going home soon. See you next year at the parade.*

When the cowboys ride, that's the end of the parade. They arrive as night falls. These are members of the Federation of Black Cowboys, who have a ranch in Brooklyn. I met one of their members once, while waiting for the subway at 135th Street. Seeing his hat, boots, belt buckle, and other authentic gear, I must have had a hankering for home. I asked him if he was a cowboy, and he told me he was in charge of the chuckwagon. He invited me to the ranch in Brooklyn to ride, and when he learned where I was from, he was even more eager to have me visit. He warned me that the other women who run with the Brooklyn cowboys might be jealous because I am from Texas. I never went to the ranch, but every year when the cowboys finish off the parade, I run to keep up with them, trying not to let them out of my sight, whooping and hollering as they charge up the avenue. They actually do ride off into the sunset.

Once they pass, everyone begins to pack up their folding chairs and break through the barricades into the street. People who walked in the parade then mingle with the crowd, finding their way to the family and friends who'd come to see them march. The people who watched the parade from the perches of their windows and fire escapes above Seventh Avenue go back inside their homes; the out-of-town firefighters go back to the suburbs; my beloved Panamanian drummers and bugle players go back to Brooklyn. At the end of the parade, when everyone who has come from around Harlem to crowd onto Seventh Avenue from 110th to 145th Street goes back to their own blocks, when others who came from far away scatter back to their homes, it seems that Harlem is bigger than it was at the beginning of the day. All the spectators take a piece away with them, and they return every year to be renewed and restored.

Last year I would I have run with the cowboys all the way to the end of the parade, but their ride suddenly changed course. They made a right turn, heading east on 135th Street, missing the end of the parade route by ten blocks. I followed behind. At Lenox they turned south, galloping quickly, as if they were heading all the way back to the beginning. I couldn't keep up, so by the time I reached my corner at 133rd Street I gave up the chase.

Ms. Shirley was standing at the stoop. I asked if she'd been to the parade. She said that she never goes because *folks don't know how to act.* I stood with her for a while at the front door but did not go inside. The parade was done, but I wasn't done with the parade. After many hours out-of-doors, I still wanted to be in the street, among people. I crossed 133rd Street back toward Seventh. As I reached the end of the block, a view of the avenue opened up, revealing a scene much different from what I had just witnessed. It had not been very long since the cowboys' ride, but the uptown side of the street was already cleared of people, and where those people had been, discarded plates and bottles and flyers and many other varieties of trash lay strewn about. The median where many onlookers had just stood was empty, too. Only the trampled plants and debris indicated the agitation that had recently been.

But in this hour after the parade, a new event was about to start. Across the median, the downtown side of Seventh Avenue still swelled with people. They had all been there before—these were the teenagers who, during the parade, were too cool to take much interest in the main event. While the parade was on, this side of the street had the atmosphere of a fairground, with tables of food stalls and trinket vendors. All day long, young people had strolled the downtown side of Seventh. They were dressed in their finest gear for the occasion—the spectacle of each other. Their seemingly aimless milling was part of a courtship ritual. Small clusters divided by gender passed each other slowly, feigning indifference while making split-second appraisals.

During the day, the cops had been there, too, but I had not noticed the police tower that was planted on that side of the street, waiting for nightfall. During the day, the cops had been policing intersections so that people would not run into the middle of the parade. After dark, their force was redirected. Now, their task was to police the groups of promenading teens. At nightfall, by virtue of the force now dedicated to controlling their movement, those youth were transformed into a throng.

From where I sat on the median, it appeared that the throng had a purpose—or if not an actual purpose, then certainly a destination. The destination was south—this was where the police were herding everyone. As with the mysterious turn of the cowboys, at nightfall, the northward aspiration of the parade was reversed. Because everyone was being pushed and prodded in the same direction, the people in the crowd moved as a unified body.

My memory of the next thing has faded. I don't remember if I was ordered to remove myself from the median—taken as a stray who had escaped the pack—or if I joined the mass voluntarily.

Whether this propulsion occurred by an inner or outer force seems crucial, but the outcome was the same. Soon I was among them, being pushed along with them, goaded by the voices of the cops, if not by the threat of the nightsticks some twirled in the air and others held with both hands—each gripped at either end of the weapon, ready to engage. The police observation tower cast a bright light upon the street. Although the sun had long set, the scene was illuminated by a white glare.

We continued moving south, but just before we reached the crossing of 125th Street and Seventh Avenue where the statue of Adam Clayton Powell Jr., stands, gunshots sounded. This incident did not send panic through the crowd. There was no stampede. Instead among both the police and the young, there seemed to be an attitude that violence was to be expected. Paddy wagons formed part of the police retinue. As I moved with the crowd, I'd noticed that the teenagers and the cops seemed to regard each other almost with indifference. What was going on was, for both, business as usual. The teenagers were used to hostility from the cops, and the cops were used to hostility from the teenagers. The similarity in their attitudes did not translate to equity in power. This postparade roundup was probably also an annual event. I had never witnessed it before because I had always gone inside once the parade ended, when it was getting dark.

Although the mood of the crowd didn't change—and I am not sure how it could have changed, without releasing the coerced crowd into mayhem—the direction shifted. Once we had reached the intersection of 125th and Seventh, we were stopped from continuing south, diverted from the scene of the shooting. The course of our progress changed like a train spontaneously jumping its tracks—we were pushed west, across 125th Street toward the river.

On 125th Street, the arbitrariness of the police directives was exposed. Some groups of cops stood around telling people walking west via the sidewalk to get off the sidewalk and walk in the street, although vehicle traffic was still flowing. Cops in the street yelled at people to get out of the street and onto the sidewalk. A young man next to me, who had been ordered first into the street and then onto the sidewalk, protested the contradictions to one cop, but then he relented quickly, muttering to himself, *Man, y'all are trippin'*. People who wanted to go home but whose home was neither south nor west also tried to reason with the nearest officer, but walking in the wrong direction was cause for confrontation. I noticed a few people walking the opposite way, allowed to go in the direction we could not. These people were white.

It must have been when shots came from the west that I exited the crowd and wedged between a lamppost and a mailbox near the curb; I was barely on the sidewalk but not in the street. I continued to watch the people flowing in the direction from which the shots had come. It became clear that, in part, the violence that had broken out was related to the movement of the crowd. When we were herded south, shots rang out in the south. When we were herded west, shots rang out from the west.

Seemingly out of the way of the cops who wanted people on the sidewalk and the ones who wanted us in the street, I continued to note what I heard and what I saw. But this activity drew the attention of an officer. It isn't necessary for me to find new words to describe what happened after that, because the next morning I wrote it up when filing an official complaint.

In the aftermath of the African American Day parade on Sunday, September 16th, I was ushered south via Lenox Avenue and then West via 125th street, along with a large crowd of African American youth. I am a freelance reporter, so I had my notepad out to record the incident. I stepped out of the way of the crowd, and was positioned next to a mailbox

(i. e., not obstructing traffic or causing commotion) making notes when the community affairs officer came up to me and brusquely asked me what I was doing. He said that I had to leave and I said that I was a reporter doing my job. He became belligerent and said, "I'm very happy for you but you have to leave." He said that the area was closed. The area was clearly not closed because there were people walking back and forth in both directions. He said, "Do it while you are walking. I'm giving you a lawful order to move down the block." This "lawful order" was made in a snarling tone, with the officer imposing himself toward me in an intimidating manner. I was not disrupting police work or in any way involved with the crowd. Because of his belligerent, unprofessional, and discourteous attitude I asked him his name. He said: "I don't have to tell you my name." Because he was becoming increasingly hostile, I decided to move, but I told him I would find out who he was.

The officer's refusal to identify himself was a minor violation, but it is upon such a breach that greater abuses stand. Perhaps my indignation at the incident only reveals my relative innocence about such common, daily aggression. But I had previously noticed the police walking their beats in Harlem, standing four in a line on street corners. Their presence seems to increase in correlation to the number of new condominiums—raising questions about who is being protected and who is being patrolled. I had seen them stop a carload full of young black men on 132nd Street. I'd paused nearby to see what would happen next, only to watch as the men were released back to their car, having been stopped for no reason and having done nothing for which they could be detained. Witnessing that may have had no use; writing down my complaint may have had no use. Is it possible to confront a force that operates under the cloak of normality, a force that refuses to pronounce its own name?

Once, I needed scrap paper to make notes while at the library. I pulled a few sheets from the container provided for that purpose. Later, one of those scraps fluttered out from among my papers. It was sheet I had not used, so seeing its blank front, I turned to the other side to check for any notes before throwing it away. On the other side was a picture of a parade. It was a picture I'd seen before, a parade of Garveyites from the Universal Negro Improvement Association. The caption reads *A UNIA parade, Harlem, 1924...North-east corner of Lenox.* In the picture, one convertible moves down Lenox Avenue in a blur, exiting the frame. The only passenger visible sits in the backseat wearing a straw boater hat that matches those worn by almost everyone else in the crowd of onlookers. Another car, also a convertible, is just making the turn from 135th Street onto Lenox. It is in the middle of the intersection, at the crossroads, and the sign held by its passengers reads *THE NEW NEGRO HAS NO FEAR.* The straw boater hat of every spectator is pointed toward that oncoming car, as if all are reading the sign, absorbing its message, before the car and the parade continues heading south, down the avenue, followed by the cloud of exhaust already visible at its rear.

In 1917, two years before the 369th Regiment made its jubilant northward march returning to Harlem, a parade traced the same route on Fifth Avenue, only that time, it headed south. This display was not intended just for the pride of Harlem, it was also directed at the rest of New York, and the rest of the world. It was the "Silent March" organized to protest bloody race riots in East St. Louis and the lynch mob terror then rampant throughout the South. Its participants wore all white; they did not shout any slogans, they had no musical accompaniment except for a beating drum. They carried placards declaring their cause:

Universal Negro Improvement Association Parade, corner of 135th Street and Lenox Avenue, 1924. (Courtesy of Schomburg Center for Research in

Black Culture / Photographs and Prints Division, The New York Public Library, Astor, Lenox, and Tilden Foundations)

We march because the growing consciousness and solidarity of race, coupled with sorrow and discrimination, have made us one, a union that may never be dissolved . . .

We march because we want our children to live in a better land and enjoy fairer conditions than have been our lot.

Moving away from the hostile police officer, I headed west, rejoining the throng as it continued toward the river. I don't know what ultimately happened, how far they were pushed, or whether any more shots rang out that night. What comes next is not a metaphor. I had not reached the end of the first block when I turned around, heading back toward Lenox. I went against the crowd, against the command of the officer, determined to make my way home.

Acknowledgments

"It is the grace of scholarship. I am indebted to everyone."
—SUSAN HOWE

These pages owe so much to so many. My debts extend beyond scholarly matters, as these five years have found me sustained by a more generalized grace, while stumbling toward some notion of how to write and how to live.

Michael Vazquez, the executive editor of *Transition* magazine from 1995 to 2006, was very much involved with the genesis of this project. In 2002, soon after arriving in Harlem, I constantly regaled him with stories of the people I met in the street. Mike asked me to write an essay from those stories; our conversations were such an important part of my process that I could only begin to work after writing the words "Dear Mike." That essay, "Lenox Terminal" (2004), was the seed of this book. Writing for and thinking with Mike was a rigorous and singular apprenticeship, to say nothing of his place in my life as a treasured friend.

A number of other editors, including Kate Tuttle and Zakia Spalter of Africana .com; Jon Garelick of the *Boston Phoenix;* Jennifer Schuessler, then of the *Boston Globe;* Amy Hoffman of *The Women's Review of Books;* and Betsy Reed of *The Nation,* were also important teachers, pushing my limits while offering me a way to earn some fragment of a living as a writer. The editor Paul Elie encouraged this book before it was written. He understood what I was aiming at when I barely understood it myself.

At age seventeen, having traveled to Cornell University for a summer seminar called "Geography and Literature," without any idea what that meant, I met professors Barry Maxwell and Shelley Wong. They put Ann Petry's Harlem novel, *The Street,* in my hands; they taught me Walter Benjamin and the word *flâneur.* They demanded I be more precise with language and disabused me of a vague teenaged disdain for things political. It is only a slight exaggeration to say this book began that summer, under their influence.

I was fortunate to be mentored by several artists who were my teachers at Harvard: Adrienne Kennedy, Ross McElwee, and Isaac Julien each left a deep impression. Though I've ended up neither playwright nor filmmaker they remain guides for this work. Ewa Lajer-Burcharth advised me on an extracurricular research

Acknowledgments

project with devotion and intensity. In a class on Haiti, Laurent Dubois gave us Benjamin's "Theses on the Philosophy of History," which changed everything. I am grateful to my professors in the Department of Afro-American Studies for providing such a fertile ground during those heady years; pursuing a life of the mind seemed like the only possible option.

In more than seven years in New York, I refused to be called a New Yorker, partly to do with my allegiance to a great number of people in Texas—where I was born and raised and where I intend to return. Margaret Crawford and Nancy Eisenberg encouraged my writing at Episcopal High School and were great guides in the love of literature. The vibrant group of community-based and socially engaged artists who are my mother's contemporaries—including Vivian Ayers-Allen, Kimberly Lakes, Bert Long, Rick Lowe, and Floyd Newsum—provided a model of creativity and commitment. Jesse Lott is chief among them and a giant among men; his influence on my life is without measure. Texas is the land of my maternal family, so I honor the Williamses and Robertses of Cedar Creek, the Rhodeses of Fort Worth, and the Bradshaws of Austin. Gratitude is due to my extended / adopted families, the Zermeños, the Merciers, the Browns, the Newsums, the Allibones, and many more—all of you helped grow me up.

During work and lamentations for lack of work I received the generosity of so many organizations that I doubted my worthiness. The Lannan Foundation gave me ten weeks in Marfa, Texas, setting my Harlem thoughts to roam under the high desert sky, unveiling a hidden corner of my native state, and allowing me to plant a garden in which to putter when my pen would bear no fruit. The Rona Jaffe Foundation saw ahead to my next project with the honor of its award specifically for emerging women writers. I interrupted the earliest phase of writing to take up a scholarship from the U.S.–U.K. Fulbright Commission, landing me at the University of St. Andrews in Scotland as the only student in a historiography course. This quixotic pursuit and many walks across woods and fields in Britain were an unlikely proving ground for my notions about the streets of Harlem, thus I attempted the first words of this book while living in a hilltop cottage in Fife. Much later in the writing process the New York Foundation for the Arts; the Common Fire Foundation in Tivoli, New York; the Centre International d'Accueil et d'Échanges des Récollets, Paris; and A Studio in the Woods, New Orleans, provided monetary support and safe harbor.

Michael Henry Adams, Brent Hayes Edwards, and Thomas Wirth are scholars whose contributions to the study of Harlem are widely and deservedly celebrated; I am grateful to all three for conferring small nuggets from their vast treasuries of knowledge and resources. Michael and Brent also contributed gifts for the soul: Michael often demanded I abandon my desk to join him for dinners and parties, while Brent filled gaps in my musical library with generous donations from his own. CUNY Graduate Center PhD candidate in English Lavelle Porter did some

Acknowledgments

stealth undercover work to put me on the trail of a hard-to-locate photograph. Less concretely, this book is buoyed by near-invisible strands of lively conversations conducted over coffee, tea, lunch, dinner, loud music, long walks (and the very rare alcoholic beverage) with some formidable artists and thinkers who are also cherished friends: Naomi Beckwith, LeRonn Brooks, Sarah M. Broom, LaTasha N. Nevada Diggs, Ntone Edjabe, Leslie Hewitt, Arthur Jafa, Darryl Pinckney, Emily Raboteau, Greg Tate, and Shatema Threadcraft, among many others. Their wisdom and warmth have nourished me. On the very day I missed my first deadline and was deep in a pit of self-loathing, Emily arrived for tea bearing pastries and perspective, observing that I was not the first writer ever to do so.

My everyday life in Harlem was quite mixed up with writing about it, but plenty of times, when the writing offered no comfort at all, I was enveloped and protected by the friendship, care, and welcome of Barbara James, Bessie Smallwood, Julius Nelson, Ms. Shirley, Mr. Monroe, Willie, Rob, Sonny, Bing, Bobby, Ramadan, Marvin Lofton,Valerie Price, and many others, including those with whom, in the intimate informality of Lenox Avenue, I exchanged greetings on a daily basis but never exchanged names. Neighbors in my building, especially Donna Kiel and Ahmed Kiel-Kamil, Laaraji Nadananda, Nadi Burton, and Ernest Davis (son of Minnie Davis), at times made our five-floor tenement feel like a family house.

My landlord, Henry M. Greenup, rented me the last decently priced two-bedroom apartment in Harlem, in which an underemployed freelancer could afford to have a home office. For this I am eternally grateful. Mr. Greenup must also be publicly thanked for waiting patiently during the times when the underemployed freelancer couldn't afford the affordable apartment; under such circumstances he acted as an unofficial patron of the arts! A native New Orleanian, World War II veteran, and longtime Harlem businessman, Henry Greenup has been an education and a blessing to know.

When I returned to Harlem from Scotland, I found the neighborhood under siege by the onslaught of Columbia, the 125th Street Rezoning, and luxury condominiums. I attended meetings first to take notes and ended up taking minutes, becoming part of the organized resistance to a wrongheaded policy. By joining this struggle I benefited from the wisdom of many I am proud to call comrades and friends. Abdul-Kareem Muhammad; Katherine Adora Samuels, MD; Brenda Stokely; and M. Ndigo Washington must be singled out as particular inspirations during the months of the rezoning campaign. I am glad an early chapter of the effort brought me the friendship of Alana Atterbury and Barbara Smith Graves. I honor the steadfast commitment of Bertha Aiken, Peter Anderson, Nellie Hester Bailey, Carlton "Chuck" Berkely, Sharon Bowie, Francine Brown, Fatima Faloye, Imee Jackson, Patti Jacobs, Agnes Johnson, Akinlabi Mackall, Carole Nelson, Sandra Rivers, Shaka Shakur, Shikulu Shange, Ameena Shareef, the late Gloria

Acknowledgments

Swanson, Julius Tajiddin, and Alex Williams, among many others. All of these people were working for Harlem long before I arrived and continue to pursue a vision of beloved community where those who made the neighborhood famous, sustained it during difficult years, and have raised generations of families are not displaced, disinherited, and disenfranchised by supposedly benign market forces.

Rosten Woo, co-founder of the Center for Urban Pedagogy, and Mitch McEwen, founder of architecture and art enterprise SUPERFRONT, are both old friends. In the midst of the rezoning fiasco, their professional expertise gave me much-needed insight about the city's urban planning apparatus.

In the course of researching and writing this book, I spent countless days at the Schomburg Center for Research in Black Culture; it is as much a community center as a library, and a little bit of home. I wish to thank the librarians and staff of the Schomburg, including Sharon Howard, Sharon Jarvis, Betty Obadashian, Genette McLaurin, Michael Perry, Troy Belle, and Steven Fullwood. Many library assistants performed their repetitive tasks with smiles and diligence, and the security staff always ushered me in and out with kindness.

Other libraries and archives also aided my work. I wish to thank the following individuals and institutions: Louise Bernard, Moira Fitzgerald, and Nancy Kuhl at Yale's Beinecke Library; Anne Coleman Torrey of the Aaron Siskind Foundation and Barbara Puorro Galasso of George Eastman House; Eleanor Gillers and Jill Slaight of the New-York Historical Society; Tom Lisanti at the New York Public Library; Susan Hamson at the Rare Books and Manuscripts department of Columbia's Butler Library; Bruce Kellner of the Carl Van Vechten Trust; and anonymous workers of the Library of Congress and Bettmann / Corbis.

I thank the estate of Langston Hughes for permission to reprint his poetry; Craig Tenney of Harold Ober Associates and Jennifer Rowley of Random House helped facilitate this process.

I want to thank certain other friends for the love that has sheltered me over many years: Alice Albinia, Gini Alhadeff, Amiri Barksdale, Leslie Bennett, Jon Caramanica, Nucomme Davis-Walker, Cheryl Follon, Aaron Goldberg, Jamil Higley, Carmelo Larose, Jesse Lichtenstein, Rebecca Lubens, Brina Milikowsky, Beatrice Monti della Corte, Laura Moser, Miranda Pyne, Shirley Rumierk, Angela Shaiman, Claire Tancons, and Caecilia Tripp. Jomo K. Alakoye-Simmons has his own Harlem book to write. The instruction and guidance of Jill Satterfield, Ethan Nichtern, Sherene Schostak, and Margot Borden helped keep body, soul, and mind in one piece.

Although I have been among them for a very short time, I give thanks for several people in New Orleans, where I lived for a brief period while refining the proposal for this book in spring of 2005, and where I've returned as this work reaches its conclusion. Gia Hamilton of Gris Gris Lab, Melanie Lawrence, Pamela Broom of the Wanda (Women and Agriculture) Group, Greer Mendy of Tekrema Center

Acknowledgments

for Art and Culture, the founders and staff of A Studio in the Woods, the New Orleans African-American Museum, and the New Orléans Afrikan Film & Arts Festival have all welcomed me into a community where creative work, social justice work, and regenerative and necessary soul work exist on a powerful continuum. Living here has been restorative and instructive, and I am glad to call you all friends.

Jin Auh of the Wylie Agency has been a teacher, advocate, counselor, and friend; I marvel continually at her talent. I am grateful to her colleagues Katherine Lewis, Jacqueline Ko, Katherine Marino, Charles Buchan, and to everyone else at the agency who has worked on my behalf.

Little, Brown and Company took a chance on this book; for a good while after committing to write it, I was frightened into silence upon realizing how great a chance it was. A vast army of people make things happen there, many whose names I don't know. My friend Nneka Bennett was hired as a designer around the same time I began the book; the talent displayed in her cover design is only a sample of her multidisciplinary gifts. Helen Atsma and Vanessa Hartmann did important thankless tasks at the beginning of this process as has Vanessa Kehren at the crucial middle and end. Peggy Freudenthal and Peg Anderson heroically smoothed out my many wrinkled bits. As I write this, Elizabeth Garriga, Valerie Russo, Heather Fain, Amanda Tobier, Laura Keefe, and Brittany Boughter are helping this work make its way in the world. Above all, my editor Pat Strachan presided over the chaos of this book's creation with patient forbearance, waiting for me to get out of my own way. When there were finally pages to edit, her gentle interventions were revelatory. She offered precise and thoughtful guidance, cutting a path through the overgrown fields of my rough drafts toward a clearing at the end.

Finally, I bow in deep gratitude to my mother, Rhonda Rhodes, my father, Steven Pitts, and my sister, Syandene Rhodes-Pitts. My parents' journeys in art and social justice make my own explorations possible. Specific to the writing of this book you have each supported me materially, morally, and spiritually at crucial moments. Beyond the book and into life, your love fills a territory my words cannot describe.

For any whose names I have forgotten, your thanks are written in my heart. It has been a humbling passage to pursue this work. To quote a most eloquent Harlemite, El-Hajj Malik El-Shabazz, "Only the mistakes have been mine."

Notes

Epigraph

"The writer operates at a peculiar crossroads": Flannery O'Connor, "The Regional Writer," in *Mystery and Manners: Occasional Prose* (New York: Farrar, Straus and Giroux, 1969), 59.

Chapter 1: A Colony of Their Own

5   "Harlem: A residential and business district": *The Columbia-Lippincott Gazetteer of the World* (New York: Oxford University Press, 1952).

6   This volume reveals that a city called Hankow: *The Handbook of Geographical Nicknames* (Metuchen, NJ: Scarecrow, 1980).

6   *Harlem is blocked in*: *The WPA Guide to New York City* (New York: Pantheon, 1982), 253.

6   "Negro Harlem, into which are crowded": Ibid., 253–54.

14   *a haven for the clerks and small merchants*: Charles Henry White, "In Up-town New York," *Harper's Monthly Magazine*, 112 (December 1905), 220.

15   "The whites paid little attention": James Weldon Johnson, "Harlem: The Culture Capital," in *The New Negro: An Interpretation,* edited by Alain Locke (New York: Albert & Charles Boni, 1925), 303–4.

15   When the Hudson Realty Company: Ibid., 304.

15   A December 17, 1905, article: *New York Times,* "Real Estate Race War Is Started in Harlem," December 17, 1905. http://query.nytimes.com/mem/archivefree/pdfres=9B00E4DB153AE733A25754C1A96 49D946497D6CF (accessed May 5, 2010).

15–16   "An untoward circumstance": *New York Herald,* "Negroes Move into Harlem," December 24, 1905. Excerpted in Allon Schoener, *Harlem on My Mind: Cultural Capital of Black America, 1900–1968* (New York: Random House, 1968), 23.

16–17   "Their presence is undesirable among us": *New York Indicator* article quoted by unattributed author in "Opinion: Land," *The Crisis,* Vol. 8, No. 4 (August 1914): 176.

17   *We believe...that real friends of Negroes: Harlem Home News,* "Loans to

White Renegades Who Back Negroes Cut Off," April 7, 1911. Excerpted in Schoener, *Harlem on My Mind*, 25.

17   "In Harlem, Negro life is seizing upon": Alain Locke, "The New Negro," in Locke, ed., *The New Negro: An Interpretation*, 7.

18   *Harlem represents the Negro's latest thrust:* Locke, "Harlem," in *Survey Graphic* (March 1925: Special Issue, "Harlem Mecca of the New Negro"): 629.

18   *And there was New York City:* Charles S. Johnson, "The New Frontage on American Life," in Locke, ed., *The New Negro: An Interpretation*, 279.

18   In 1928, Wallace Thurman's: Wallace Thurman, *Negro Life in New York's Harlem: A Lively Picture of a Popular and Interesting Section* (New York: Haldeman-Julius Publications, 1927), 5.

19   "Harlem, like a Picasso painting in his cubistic period": Langston Hughes, "My Early Days in Harlem," in *Harlem, U.S.A.*, edited by John Henrik Clarke (New York: Collier Books, 1971), 85–89.

20   *Harlem, I grant you, isn't typical:* Locke, "Harlem," 630.

20   "The question naturally arises": Johnson, "Harlem: The Culture Capital," 308.

Chapter 2: Into the City of Refuge

21–22   *more determination than ever...what was that line:* Wallace Thurman, *The Blacker the Berry...* (New York: Collier Books, 1970), 66.

22   *again she had that strange transforming experience*: Nella Larsen, *Quicksand and Passing* (New Jersey: Rutgers University Press, 1986), 43.

22   *Harlem, teeming black Harlem:* Ibid.

22   *Oh, to be in Harlem again:* Claude McKay, *Home to Harlem* (Belmont, CA: Northeastern, 1987), 15.

23   *Oh, the contagious fever of Harlem:* Ibid.

23   *He stood up and his feet burned:* George Wylie Henderson, *Jule* (New York: Creative Age Press, 1946), 96–97.

23   *A sign on a lamppost said W. 135th St.:* Ibid.

23   *clean air, blue sky, bright sunlight:* Rudolph Fisher, "City of Refuge," in *The City of Refuge: The Collected Stories of Rudolph Fisher* (Columbia: University of Missouri Press, 2008), 35.

23–24   "Negroes at every turn": Ibid.

24   *In Harlem, black was white:* Ibid., 36.

24   *"Who you say sentcher heah, dearie?":* Zora Neale Hurston, "Muttsy," in *The Complete Stories* (New York: HarperCollins Publishers, 1995), 41–42.

24   *She wished herself back home:* Ibid., 45.

Notes

24   *flight—but where?:* Ibid.

24–25   "She got off the train": Ann Petry, *The Street* (Cambridge, MA: Riverside Press, 1946), 57.

25   "Up here they are no longer creatures": Ibid.

25   *Ay, Harlem! Ay, Harlem! Ay, Harlem!:* Federico García Lorca, "El Rey de Harlem / The King of Harlem," in *Poet in New York: A Bilingual Edition* (New York: Grove Press, 2007), 25–33.

30   a long, hand-wringing article: Adam Gopnik, "Saving Paradise," *The New Yorker* (April 22, 2002), 76–84.

30   More recently a plaintive piece: Trymaine Lee, "Harlem Pas de Deux," *New York Times,* February 17, 2008.

30   a housing deficit, lacking over 38,000 units: Danilo Pelletiere, Keith Wendrip, Sheila Crowley, *Out of Reach 2006* (New York: National Low Income Housing Coalition), 15.

31   the availability of a quality latte in Harlem: John Leland, "A New Harlem Gentry in Search of Its Latte," *New York Times,* August 7, 2003.

31   The article ended by celebrating: Michael Stoler, "The Sweetest and Best of Manhattan," *New York Sun*, September 1, 2005.

31   any land where the native people were not Christians: V. Y. Mudimbe, *The Idea of Africa* (Bloomington: Indiana University Press, 1994), 30.

32   nineteenth-century British architects of the plan: Diana Muir, "A Land Without a People for a People Without a Land," *The Middle East Quarterly* 15 (Spring 2008): 55–62.

32   The controversial "Harlem on My Mind" exhibition: The show was a groundbreaking endeavor for the Metropolitan Museum of Art, sparking debate and dissent on many fronts. It was a major exhibition at the nation's premier art museum, but it did not feature any art, instead offering multimedia displays, archival photos, music. This was seen as an affront to black artists such as Jacob Lawrence and Romare Bearden, and as anathema to cultural conservatives, who saw the museum as straying from its role; both sides deemed the show a sociological exhibit. Meanwhile, community representatives from Harlem who'd been brought in to bolster the show's credibility withdrew their support. Finally, the exhibition catalog contained an essay by a teenage Harlemite who was accused of anti-Semitism for her statements about the relationship between black Harlemites and Jewish shopkeepers. For more information about the historic exhibition, see Matthew Israel, "As Landmark: An Introduction to 'Harlem on My Mind,'" Art Spaces Archive Project, http://as-ap.org/Israel/resources.cfm (accessed August 29, 2010).

Notes

34   "A railroad ticket and a suitcase": Locke, "Harlem," 630.

35   *When I came out of the subway:* Ralph Ellison, *Invisible Man* (New York: Vintage, 1995), 159.

35   "This really was Harlem": Ibid.

35–36   "I spent as much time as I could in Harlem": Langston Hughes, "My Early Days in Harlem," in *Harlem, U.S.A.*, edited by John Henrik Clarke (New York: Collier Books, 1971), 57–59.

36   *youthful illusion that Harlem was a world unto itself:* Ibid.

36   "The arrival uptown, Harlem": Amiri Baraka/LeRoi Jones, "The Black Arts (Harlem, Politics, Search for a New Life)," in *Autobiography of LeRoi Jones* (Chicago: Freundlich Books, 1984), 202.

37   *the Negro's latest thrust:* Alain Locke, "Harlem," in *Survey Graphic* (March 1925: Special Issue, "Harlem Mecca of the New Negro"): 629.

37–38   "It's you young folks": Ellison, *Invisible Man,* 255.

40   *She eschewed the "Y" as too bare:* Larsen, *Quicksand,* 44.

41   "Beds with long, tapering posts": Ibid.

41   "Little by little the signs of spring appeared": Ibid.

42   *the dark, dirty, three rooms:* Petry, *The Street,* 12.

42   "The farther up they went": Ibid.

44   *I usedta live in the world:* Ntozake Shange, from *for colored girls who have considered suicide when the rainbow is enuf* (New York: Macmillan, 1977), 28.

44   *Black boy/O black boy:* Melvin B. Tolson, from "Alpha," in *The Harlem Gallery: Book I, The Curator* (New York: Twayne Publishers, 1965), 20.

44   *sometimes a few little Italians and Jewish children: New York Evening Post,* April 6, 1910.

45   "Although Mrs. Matthews was at the dock": Mary L. Lewis, "The White Rose Industrial Association: The Friend of the Strange Girl in New York," *The Messenger* VII (April 1925), 158.

45   *friend of the strange girl:* Ibid.

45   *Let us call it White Rose:* Hallie Q. Brown, "Victoria Earle Matthews, 1861–1898," in *Homespun Heroines* (Xenia, OH: Aldine Printing House, 1926), 214.

45   Mrs. Matthews and her collaborators took turns at the pier: Ibid.

45   *pleasant lodgings for girls:* Lewis, "The White Rose Industrial Association," 158.

46   *Some were well educated:* Brown, *Homespun Heroines,* 214.

46   By 1918, when the black population of New York: Lewis, "The White Rose Industrial Association," 158.

Notes

46 *one of the most unique special libraries:* New York Evening Post, April 6, 1910.

47 *a good stock of aprons:* New York Age, Advertisement, "Working Girls' Home," July 27, 1905.

47 *Our history and individuality:* Victoria Earle Matthews in Richard Newman, *African-American Quotations* (New York: Facts on File, 2000).

47 "Thus she hoped to inspire in them": Brown, *Homespun Heroines*, 216.

48 *decorated to the taste:* New York Amsterdam News, "White Rose Home Still a Refuge After 70 Long Years," March 4, 1967.

48 "The rooms retain their soft, nostalgic glow": Ibid.

Chapter 3: Searching for the Underground City

51 The comedy advertised: The play was *39 East* by Rachel Crothers. See John Corbin, "Drama: Wistaria Romance," *New York Times*, April 1, 1919.

51 The picture is titled: *Within Thirty Seconds Walk of the 135th Street Branch*, from the Franklin F. Hopper Harlem Scrapbook, 1920. NYPL Digital Gallery, Schomburg Center for Research in Black Culture / Photographs and Prints Division. http://digitalgallery.nypl .org/nypldigital/dgkeysearchdetail.cfm?strucID=465419&imag eID=1168424#_seemore (accessed May 20, 2010).

55 *Staff and Friends of the Negro Division:* Photograph, circa 1935, in *The Legacy of Arthur Alfonso Schomburg: A Celebration of the Past, A Vision for the Future* (New York: New York Public Library, 1986), 47.

56 *Instead of considering the Negro problem:* Celeste Tibbets, *Ernestine Rose and the Origins of the Schomburg Center: Schomburg Center Occasional Papers Series, Number Two* (New York: Schomburg Center for Research in Black Culture, The New York Public Library, 1989), 20.

56 *to preserve the historical records:* Elinor Des Verney Sinnette, *Arthur Alfonso Schomburg: Black Bibliophile and Collector* (Detroit: Wayne State University Press, 1989), 132–34.

58 *You would be surprised:* Ibid., 74.

58 His interest in black history was sparked: Ibid., 13.

59 *There is a Negro exhibit:* Marjorie Schuler, "New York Public Library Shows Exhibit of Negro Achievements," *Christian Science Monitor*, August 30, 1925.

59 "Not long ago, the Public Library of Harlem": Arthur A. Schomburg, "The Negro Digs Up His Past," in *The New Negro: An Interpretation,*

Notes

edited by Alain Locke (New York: Albert & Charles Boni, 1925), 232.

60 "Mecca of Literature": Richard B. Moore, "Africa-Conscious Harlem," in *Harlem, U.S.A.*, edited by John Henrik Clarke (New York: Collier Books, 1971), 37–38.

60 *Revealing volumes expressed the consciousness of Africa:* Ibid.

62 *When I first thought of opening a bookstore:* Abiola Sinclair, "Liberation Bookstore— 15th Anniversary," *New York Amsterdam News,* November 20, 1982.

73 "a three-way standoff": Rufus Schatzberg, *Black Organized Crime in Harlem: 1920–1930* (Sacramento, CA: Garland Science, 1993).

73 The book compiles the effort: The Civil Rights Congress, *We Charge Genocide: The Historic Petition to the United Nations for Relief from a Crime of the United States Government Against the Negro People* (New York: Civil Rights Congress, 1951).

74 *Mrs. Charles Turner of New York City:* Ibid., 116.

75 *One speaker, David White:* Lee A. Daniels, "City Proposal to Rebuild Harlem Gets Stony Community Response," *New York Times,* February 3, 1983.

75 "David White was a founding member": From author's private collection.

76 *Flashing through the streets:* Ibid.

76–77 "The American Negro must remake his past": Schomburg, "The Negro Digs Up His Past," 231, 237.

78 The original symbol once guarded: Eugène Goblet d'Alviella, *The Migration of Symbols* (Westminster: Archibald Constable and Company, 1894), 204–7.

78 *When we consider the facts:* Schomburg, "The Negro Digs Up His Past," 234.

79 *dust of digging:* Ibid., 237.

79 *So the Negro historian today:* Ibid., 231.

80 During the life of the Cheikh: See Allen F. Roberts and Mary Nooter Roberts with Gassia Armenian and Ousmane Gueye, *A Saint in the City: Sufi Arts of Urban Senegal* (Los Angeles: University of California Los Angeles, Fowler, 2003).

81 Their holy men minister with words: Ibid.

83 slum-clearance programs of the 1950s: See Committee on Slum Clearance Plans, *Harlem: Slum Clearance Plan Under Title 1 of the Housing Act of 1949: Report to Mayor Impellitteri and the Board of Estimate* (New York: Committee on Slum Clearance Plans, 1951).

Notes

Chapter 4: Harlem Dream Books

85   *The instructor said:* Langston Hughes, "Theme for English B," in *The Collected Poems of Langston Hughes* (New York: Knopf, 1994), 409–10.

86   *life for me ain't been no crystal stair:* Hughes, "Mother to Son," Ibid., 30.

87   *What happens to a dream deferred?:* Hughes, "Harlem [2]," Ibid., 426.

88   *Come, Let us roam the night together:* Hughes, "Harlem Night Song," Ibid., 94–95.

89   *I could take the Harlem night:* Hughes, "Juke Box Love Song," Ibid., 393.

89–90   *"I got the Weary Blues":* Hughes, "The Weary Blues," Ibid., 50.

95   *What you call a ghetto:* Bruce Davidson, *East 100th Street* (Cambridge, MA: Harvard University Press, 1970), n.p.

97   *I was a neighborhood boy:* Quoted by Ann Banks, "Introduction," in Aaron Siskind, *Harlem Document: Photographs 1932–1940* (Providence, RI: Matrix Publications, 1981), 7.

97   *I hung around playgrounds:* Ibid.

97   *they were black and themselves "on relief":* Ibid.

98   "So you want to know": Ralph Ellison, "The Way It Is," in *Shadow and Act* (New York: Random House, 1964), 284.

98   "I'm in New York": Ellison, "Railroad Porter," in Siskind, *Harlem Document,* 54.

99   "And you have to take care": Ralph Ellison, *Invisible Man* (New York: Vintage, 1995), 255.

101   *the low-down folks:* Langston Hughes, "The Negro Artist and the Racial Mountain," *The Nation* 23 (June 1926): 692–94.

101   *the limitations of folk art:* Babette Deutsch, "Waste Land of Harlem" (Review of *Montage of a Dream Deferred*), *New York Times,* May 6, 1951.

102   *I cannot truthfully state:* Langston Hughes, "Foreword: Who Is Simple," in *The Best of Simple* (New York: Hill and Wang, 1990), vii.

102   *Without me saying a word:* Ibid.

102   asexual: Arnold Rampersad, *The Life of Langston Hughes. Volume I: 1902–1941, I, Too, Sing America* (New York: Oxford University Press, 2001), 434.

103   *I hope my child'll:* Hughes, "Lament over Love," in *The Collected Poems of Langston Hughes,* 69.

103   *a basement to Hell:* Hurston quoted in Valerie Boyd, *Wrapped in Rainbows: The Life of Zora Neale Hurston* (New York: Scribner, 2003), 384.

103   *At certain times I have no race:* Zora Neale Hurston, "How It Feels to Be Colored Me," *World Tomorrow* 11 (May 1928): 215–16.

Notes

103   lied about her age: Boyd, *Wrapped in Rainbows,* 75.

104   *carefully accented Barnardese:* Zora Neale Hurston, "Research," in *Dust Tracks on a Road* (Urbana: University of Illinois Press, 1984), 175.

104   "Almost nobody else": Langston Hughes, "Harlem Literati," in *The Big Sea: An Autobiography* (New York: Alfred A. Knopf, 1945), 239.

104   *Research is a formalized curiosity:* Hurston, "Research," in *Dust Tracks,* 174.

104   *[to] many of her white friends:* Hughes, "Harlem Literati," in *The Big Sea,* 239.

105–106   "Bam, and down in Bam": Zora Neale Hurston, "Glossary of Harlem Slang," in *The Complete Stories* (New York: HarperCollins Publishers, 1995), 134–38.

106   arguing in favor of segregation: Zora Neale Hurston, "Court Order Can't Make the Races Mix," *Orlando Sentinel, The Public Thought,* August 11, 1955. In Waldo E. Martin, *Brown v. Board of Education: A Brief History with Documents* (Boston: Bedford/St. Martin's, 1998), 209–12.

106   *Since I wash myself of race pride:* Hurston, "Seeing the World as It Is," in *Dust Tracks,* 331.

106   *My old folks are dead:* Ibid., 332.

106   *Standing on the watch-wall:* Ibid., 333.

107   *Harlem, physically at least:* James Baldwin, "The Harlem Ghetto," in *Notes of a Native Son* (Boston: Beacon Press, 1984), 57.

107   *All of Harlem is pervaded:* Ibid.

108   *bounded by Lenox Avenue:* James Baldwin, "Fifth Avenue, Uptown: A Letter from Harlem," in *Nobody Knows My Name: More Notes of a Native Son* (New York: Vintage, 1993), 57.

109   *All of Harlem, indeed, seemed to be infected:* James Baldwin, "Me and My House," *Harper's* (November 1955): 54–61.

109   "Harlem had needed something to smash": Ibid., 61.

109   *Blackness and whiteness:* Ibid.

110   *walk through the streets of Harlem:* Baldwin, "Fifth Avenue, Uptown," 71.

110   *I have not written about being a Negro:* Baldwin, "Autobiographical Notes," in *Notes of a Native Son,* 8.

110   "To live in Harlem is to dwell": Ralph Ellison, "Harlem Is Nowhere," in *Shadow and Act* (New York: Random House, 1964), 295–96.

111   *This was not a city of realities:* Ellison, *Invisible Man,* 159.

111–112   "a vast process of change": Ellison, "Harlem Is Nowhere," 296.

112   *metaphoric space:* Monique M. Taylor, *Harlem Between Heaven and Hell* (Minneapolis: University of Minnesota Press, 2002), 18.

Notes

112   *How does it feel to be a problem?:* W. E. B. DuBois, *The Souls of Black Folk* (New York: Random House, 2005), 1.

112   *the grandchildren of those:* Ellison, "Harlem Is Nowhere," 296–97.

112–113   "A man ducks in and out of traffic": Ibid, 297.

113   "Not quite citizens": Ibid.

114   *throwing his typewriter:* Ellison, "No Apologies," *Harper's* (July 4, 1967): 4–20.

114   *how often white liberals:* Ibid., 12.

114–115   "respect the sacredness": Ibid.

115   *the most distinguished American novel:* According to a poll of 200 critics by *New York Herald Tribune Book Week.* Stephen Carl Tracy, *A Historical Guide to Ralph Ellison* (Oxford: Oxford University Press, 2004), 40.

115   *this is a world in which:* Ellison, "Harlem Is Nowhere," 297.

117   *One "is" literally:* Ibid., 300.

117   "How're you making it?": Baldwin, "Fifth Avenue, Uptown," 59.

118   "Heh, baby, how you doing?": Gordon Parks, "Foreword," *Harlem Document,* 6.

119   *became a New Yorker in spirit:* Alexander Gumby, Untitled Autobiographical Essay, *Columbia University Library World* (January 1957), 2. Manuscript in Gumby Papers, Columbia University, New York.

119   *pottery, bronzes, ivories, etc.:* Letter from B. Steiner, November 7, 1913. Gumby Papers, Columbia University, New York.

119   *I have been going to Europe:* Ibid.

120   "I decided to gather them": Gumby, Untitled Autobiographical Essay, 4.

120   *acquainted with a young man:* Ibid.

121   *I am a Count:* "Count DeGumphry," Gumby Papers, Columbia University, New York.

122   In a letter to his friend Bruce Nugent: Letter from Gumby to Bruce Nugent, quoted in *Gay Rebel of the Harlem Renaissance: Selections from the Work of Richard Bruce Nugent,* edited by Thomas Wirth (Durham, NC: Duke University Press, 2002), 29.

122   *young college men from the South:* Gumby Papers, Columbia University, New York.

122   *Young College Men from South Organize:* Southern Utopia Fraternity ephemera, Gumby Papers, Columbia University, New York.

123   *It is now that your help is needed:* Letter from Alexander Gumby to the members of the Southern Utopia Fraternity, November 26, 1917. Gumby Papers, Columbia University, New York.

123–124   "S.U.F. was organized": Ibid.

124   *May the banner:* Ibid.

124   other organizations were formed: Charles S. Johnson, "The New Front-age on American Life," in *The New Negro: An Interpretation,* edited by Alain Locke (New York: Albert & Charles Boni, 1925), 284.

125   *in the years from 1914:* Gumby, Untitled Autobiographical Essay, 5.

125   Gumby took out a lease: Ibid.

125   "for my personal use": Ibid.

126   Gumby's scrapbooks went on view: Ibid., 6.

127   *forget all those things:* Zora Neale Hurston, *Their Eyes Were Watching God* (New York: Harper Perennial Modern Classics, 2006), 1.

127   Gumby's Spode china: Wirth, *Gay Rebel,* 28.

128   In December 1929: "Negro History in Scrapbooks," *New York Times,* December 27, 1929.

128   That same month: Gumby, Untitled Autobiographical Essay, 6–7.

128   *Maurice Hunter, artist's model:* "Debutantes Play Hostesses at Sunday Afternoon Tea at Gumby's Studio," *New York Amsterdam News,* April 30, 1930.

128   *While much cannot be said:* "Book Studio Marks Fifth Anniversary," *New York Amsterdam News,* February 26, 1930.

128   *Not only does Mr. Gumby:* "Gumby's Studio Anniversary," *New York News,* March 1, 1930.

128   In 1930, Gumby also launched: *Gumby's Book Studio Quarterly: A Journal of Discussion,* in Gumby Papers, Columbia University, New York.

129   "The Gumby Book Studio, 2144 5th Avenue": *New York News,* May 31, 1930.

129   *The loss of my Studio:* Gumby, Untitled Autobiographical Essay, 7.

129   An advertisement for the benefit: Gumby "Arts Ball" Benefit ephem-era, Gumby Papers, Columbia University, New York.

129–130 *"Dear Gumby, just to say hello":* Ibid.

130   *certain first editions:* Gumby, Untitled Autobiographical Essay, 7.

130   *our gentlemen's agreement:* Ibid.

130–131 "I decided to remove all Negro items": Ibid., 8.

131   *Yes, thing have been different:* "The Road Back: Alexander Gumby Plans Comeback with New Art Studio," *New York Amsterdam News,* December 8, 1934.

131   "Now, I believe that there should be some place in Harlem": Ibid.

132   *charged at all times:* Ibid.

132   *I have not the slightest doubt:* Ibid.

132   *I want the white people:* Milt Feingold, "Negroana Collection Housed at Columbia," *Columbia Daily Spectator,* 1952.

Notes

132   *making scrapbooks on Columbia:* Ibid.

133   *Whether or not I have succeeded:* Gumby, Untitled Autobiographical Essay, 8.

133   "My greatest ambition": "Negro History in Scrapbooks," *New York Times,* December 27, 1929.

133–134   Gumby's personal book plate: L. S. Alexander Gumby, Ex Libris, in Gumby Papers, Columbia University, New York.

137–139   "Harlem Hunches" for the year 1944: See Rajah Rabo, *Rajah Rabo's 5-Star Mutuel Dream Book for Lottery and Lotto* (Mt. Vernon, NY: Vernon Book Sales, 1944).

Chapter 6: Land Is the Basis of All Independence

162   Seventh was always Adam Clayton Powell Jr. Boulevard: See Sanna Feirstein, *Naming New York: Manhattan Places and How They Got Their Names* (New York: New York University Press, 2001).

164   Other flyers reminded: Flyers from author's private collection.

166   The propagandist and agitator accepted compensation: George Barner, "Some Hurt as State Takes Over 125th St. Area," *New York Amsterdam News,* April 8, 1967.

166   the Harlem Community Coalition: Peter Siskind, "'Rockefeller's Vietnam'? Black Politics and Urban Development in Harlem, 1969–1974," http://www.gothamcenter.org/festival/2001/confpap ers/siskind.pdf (accessed May 18, 2010).

166   *Congressman Powell averred:* Samuel M. Johnson, *Often Back: The Tales of Harlem* (New York: Vantage Press, 1971), 206.

166   In the eyes of his detractors: See Wil Haygood, *King of the Cats: The Life and Times of Adam Clayton Powell, Jr.* (New York: Amistad, 2006).

166   the building Powell detested was renamed in his memory: Laurie Johnston and Susan Heller Anderson, "Name Change to Honor a Harlem Hero," *New York Times,* July 20, 1983.

167   "the nation's number one Black Nationalist": Johnson, *Often Back* (photo caption on an unnumbered page).

168   *convincing Negroes of their innate ability:* Ibid., 168.

168   *speak of great Negroes of long ago:* Ibid.

168   *When the explorers opened:* Ibid., 169.

168   Born in the Dominican Republic: Ibid., 168.

168   *Carlos Cooks was to Black Nationalism:* Robert Acemendeces Harris, "Carlos A. Cooks: A True Blackman," http://www.theblacklist.net/ CarlosCooks.htm (accessed December 18, 2008).

169   one issue reprinted a speech: "Sékou Touré Addressed the United Nations," *The Black Challenge,* 1961, 7.

169   *Zimbabwe was in its noonday:* "The Ruins of Zimbabwe," Ibid.

169   *The Contributions of Carlos Cooks:* Robert Acemendeces Harris, "The Contributions of Carlos Cooks," http://www.theblacklist.net/Carlos Cooks.htm (accessed December 18, 2008).

169   *a stone monument:* Ibid.

170   The date, day, and time: Ibid.

170   *Consequently, the programs of the ANPM:* Ibid.

170   "We submit that the Black people of Harlem": "Buy Black," *The Black Challenge,* 1961, 19.

171   tied to the back of a truck and dragged: See Dina Temple-Raston, *A Death in Texas* (New York: Henry Holt, 2002).

171   a small-town drug bust: See Nate Blakeslee, *Tulia: Race, Cocaine, and Corruption in a Small Texas Town* (New York: PublicAffairs, 2006).

172   Juneteenth celebrated the date: See Charles William Ramsdell, *Reconstruction in Texas* (New York: General Books, 2009).

172   The hotel is famous for hosting Fidel Castro: Christopher Gray, "Fidel Castro Slept Here," *New York Times,* April 30, 2009.

172   headquarters of the Organization of Afro-American Unity: Malcolm X, "The Founding Rally of the Organization of Afro-American Unity," in *By Any Means Necessary: Malcolm X Speeches & Writings* (New York: Pathfinder Press, 1992), 33–67.

173   a three-hour shutdown: Flyer from author's private collection.

173   the Brotherhood of Sleeping Car Porters: See Beth Tompkins Bates, *Pullman Porters and the Rise of Protest Politics in Black America, 1925–1945* (Chapel Hill: University of North Carolina Press, 2001).

173   "Don't Buy Where You Can't Work": See Cheryl Greenberg, *"Or Does It Explode?": Black Harlem in the Great Depression* (New York: Oxford University Press, 1997), 114–39.

173   "black-out" boycott against Consolidated Edison: Ibid.

174–175   the largest single-parcel real estate deal: The property at the center of this record sale was owned by "MPL LLC." At several meetings, activists suggested that MPL LLC was another name for Maxine Lynne Properties. Eugene Giscombe is listed in public records as the president/CEO of Maxine Lynne Properties. Giscombe, president of Giscombe Henderson Properties, was the real estate broker in charge of the sale.

178   *I told them in Harlem*: Marcus Garvey, "Speech by Marcus Garvey" (Ward Theatre, Kingston; 18 December 1927), in *The Marcus Garvey and Universal Negro Improvement Association Papers, Vol. VII: November 1927–August 1940,* edited by Robert A. Hill (Berkeley: University of California Press, 1990), 48.

Notes

178   UNIA membership had reached the millions: Garvey's membership claims were always in dispute. See Edmund David Cronon, *Black Moses: The Story of Marcus Garvey and the Universal Negro Improvement Association* (Madison: University of Wisconsin Press, 1968), 204–6.

178   "So Negroes, I say": Marcus Garvey, "An Inspiring Vision," in *Philosophy and Opinions of Marcus Garvey, or, Africa for the Africans* (London: Cass, 1967), 58.

179   "PREPARE TO DEFEND YOURSELF!": Advertisement in *The Messenger,* Vol. 5, No. 2 (February 1923), 589.

182   "HARLEM TOWN HALL MEETING": Flyer from author's private collection.

183   Columbia University's plan to expand its campus: Timothy Williams, "Land Dispute Pits Columbia vs. Residents in West Harlem," *New York Times,* November 20, 2006.

183   a plan to build an athletic facility: Stefan M. Bradley, *Harlem vs. Columbia University: Black Student Power in the Late 1960s* (Urbana: University of Illinois Press, 2009), 39–62.

183   the complicity of various black politicians: David Dinkins, mayor of New York from 1990 to 1994 and the first African American to hold that office, attended public hearings held by West Harlem's Community Board 9 on August 15, 2007. Dinkins testified in favor of the plan, and he was heckled by community members. See Sewell Chan, "Panel Rejects Columbia's Expansion Plan," *New York Times* City Room Blog, August 16, 2007. http://cityroom.blogs.nytimes.com/2007/08/16/panel-rejects-columbias-expansion-plan/ (accessed May 18, 2010). Dinkins's written testimony for a later hearing can be found at http://neighbors.columbia.edu/pages/manplanning/community/cctestimony/DinkinsTestimony.pdf (accessed May 18, 2010). Dinkins is professor in the Practice of Public Affairs at Columbia's School of International and Public Affairs (SIPA). Kenneth J. Knuckles, the vice chairman of the City Planning Commission, was one of the ten members of that body who voted in favor of Columbia's expansion plan on November 26, 2007. Knuckles was for seven years vice president of Support Services at Columbia University.

183   Columbia students organizing: Allison Abell Schwartz, "Columbia Students Begin Hunger Strike Over Expansion," *Bloomberg News,* November 8, 2007. http://www.bloomberg.com/apps/news?pid=20601103&sid=au5qyI2PRq7o&refer=us (accessed May 18, 2010).

183   Columbia's decision to ignore: Elizabeth Dwoskin, "Columbia Ignores Peril," *Village Voice* (New York), October 1, 2008.

Notes

183   following a Supreme Court decision: Michael White, "Columbia Pulls a Kelo," *New York Sun,* December 20, 2007.

184–185   He'd been brought in a van: Anna Phillips, "Key Committee Rejects Expansion Plan," *Columbia Spectator,* August 16, 2007.

185   "What will Harlem be": James Weldon Johnson, "Harlem: The Culture Capital," in *The New Negro: An Interpretation,* edited by Alain Locke (New York: Albert & Charles Boni, 1925), 308.

186   *the idea of separatism:* A. Philip Randolph, quoted on New York City Parks Department plaque at A. Philip Randolph Square, Seventh Avenue at 116th Street, Harlem.

186   an innovative experiment in slum clearance: See *The House on W. 114th Street* (Washington, DC: U.S. Department of Housing and Urban Development, 1968).

187   *Some members were concerned:* Nina Siegal, "Neighborhood Report: Harlem. A Wary Welcome for a Middle-Class Housing Plan," *New York Times,* September 13, 1998.

189   Reverend Brown's Sunday sermons: Johnson, "Harlem: The Culture Capital," 306.

189   *Revolution is based on land:* Malcolm X, "Message to the Grassroots," in *Malcolm X Speaks: Selected Speeches and Statements,* edited by George Breitman (New York: Grove Weidenfeld, 1990), 3–17.

191–192   *Brothers and sisters:* Lyrics to "Black Star Line," 1924. Recording: Edison Collection, Library of Congress.

192   The Black Star Line: See Marcus Garvey, *Marcus Garvey Life and Lessons: A Centennial Companion to the Marcus Garvey and Universal Negro Improvement Association Papers*, edited by Robert A. Hill (Los Angeles: University of California Press, 1988), 67–91.

193–194   A letter published in the October 1921: *Salvation of the Negro,* letter to the editor published in *The Crusader* (October 1921), 26.

195   the deals between various African governments and various Chinese companies: Sanusha Naidu and Martyn Davies, "China Fuels Its Future with Africa's Riches," in *South African Journal of International Affairs* 13 (Winter/Spring 2006): 69–83.

196   using black foster children for unauthorized experimental drug treatments: Janny Scott and Leslie Kaufman, "Belated Charge Ignites Furor over AIDS Drug Trial," *New York Times,* July 17, 2005.

198   *Hail Lumumba! Man of Africa*: "The Awakening Call," *The Black Challenge,* 1961, 16.

198–199   *"Bring my daughters with you":* Ibid.

199   *one of the greatest:* Carlos A. Cooks, "There Is Going to Be a New Day," *The Black Challenge,* 1961, 9.

Notes

200   *Oh my body:* Frantz Fanon, "By Way of Conclusion," in *Black Skin, White Masks* (New York: Grove Press, 2008), 206.

202   *Well, there can't be a wrong direction for her:* The speaker is New York State Senator Bill Perkins, quoted in Herb Boyd, "Several Plazas Planned for Harlem," *New York Amsterdam News,* October 25, 2007.

203   "Harlem is a victim of cynical": Harold Cruse, "Mass Media and Cultural Democracy," in *The Crisis of the Negro Intellectual: A Historical Analysis of the Failure of Black Leadership* (New York: NYRB Classics, 2005), 86.

205   the New Black Panthers...have been disavowed: The Dr. Huey P. Newton Foundation. "There Is No New Black Panther Party: An Open Letter from the Dr. Huey P. Newton Foundation," www.black panther.org/newsalert.htm (accessed May 18, 2010). See also Dean Murphy, "Black Panthers, Gone Gray, Fight Rival Group," *New York Times,* October 8, 2002, http://www.nytimes.com/2002/10/08/us/ black-panthers-gone-gray-fight-rival-group.html?scp=1&sq=black+ panthers&st=nyt (accessed May 3, 2010).

206   *Look for me in the whirlwind:* Marcus Garvey, "First Message to the Negroes of the World from Atlanta Prison, February 10, 1925," in *Philosophy and Opinions of Marcus Garvey,* 239.

207   *African drumming is wonderful.... Some of these drums are prayed over:* Verena Dobnik, "African Drummers Face 'New Harlemites,'" *USA Today,* August 11, 2007.

209   *the first monuments to be constructed:* UNESCO. "National History Park–Citadel, Sans Souci, Ramiers–UNESCO World Heritage Centre." UNESCO World Heritage Centre, Official Site. http://whc .unesco.org/en/list/180 (accessed May 18, 2010).

209   *corvée:* Nathan J. Brown, "Who Abolished Corvée Labour in Egypt and Why?," *Past and Present* 144 (1994): 116–37.

209   A new building has risen: Josh Barbanel, "Harlem's Newest Beacon," *New York Times,* March 11, 2007.

209   "The vast twenty-eight-story tower": www.5thonthepark.com (accessed August 29, 2010).

210   *Thus, the memory of that building:* Rabbi Sholomo Ben Levy, "The Destruction of Commandment Keepers, Inc." Black Jews, http://www.blackjews.org/Essays/DestructionofCommandm entKeepers.html (accessed May 8, 2010).

210   "It is a shame for the authorities": *New York Times,* "Watch Tower of Harlem: The Old Landmark in Bad Condition, Liable to Succumb to Heavy Storm," September 13, 1896.

Notes

Chapter 7: Back to Carolina

219   the notice of his death: Andy Newman, "Raven Chanticleer, 72, Artist and Self-Made Man of Wax," *New York Times,* April 8, 2002.

219   high fashion from plastic bags: *New York Amsterdam News,* December 12, 1987.

219   Notables who had purchased his work: Hilton Als, "The Talk of the Town: Afrocentricities," *The New Yorker* (June 13, 1994), 39.

219   he enjoyed solo shows: Raven Chanticleer curriculum vitae from Raven Chanticleer File, Schomburg Center, New York.

219   Chanticleer performed: "Wax Museum on New Track," *New York Daily News,* November 24, 1997.

219–220   He made a memorable entrance: Ibid.

220   *immaculately attired:* Mel Tapley, "Visit Raven Chanticleer's Wax Museum," *New York Amsterdam News,* December 4, 1993.

220   *I got into my wax thing:* Als, "The Talk of the Town: Afrocentricities."

220   *wondrous vibrant art form:* "Rebuilding Dreams in Wire and Wax," *New York Times,* November 5, 1993.

220   *I was impressed:* Adam Tanner, "Madame Tussaud Could Learn from Harlem Wax Artist," *Christian Science Monitor,* January 30, 1995.

220   The first figure immortalized: "Wax Museum on New Track," *New York Daily News.*

220   His effigy was soon joined: Als, "The Talk of the Town: Afrocentricities."

220   Local *herons and sherons:* John O'Mahony, "Move Over, Mme. Tussaud: *Artiste* Mixes Wax and Fiction at Black Museum," *New York Post,* December 7, 1993.

220   on loan to an exhibition in Europe: Anthony Ramirez, "At a Wax Museum, Black History Runs in Red," *New York Times,* April 12, 1998.

220   Paul Robeson and Langston Hughes: *New New York Beacon,* "Statues Symbolize the New Harlem Renaissance," September 2, 1999.

221   the singer Madonna, depicted with black skin: O'Mahony, "Move Over, Mme. Tussaud."

221   *Every black home should have:* Nathan Jackson, "Paying Homage to Black History," *New York Newsday,* February 21, 1993.

221   a version of the Last Supper: Ibid.

221   cotton-fields in the South: Ibid.

221   *shanty-life in Haiti:* Tim Cavanaugh, "Waxing Poetic," *New York Spirit,* June 3, 1993.

221   *some skeletal bones:* Jackson, "Paying Homage."

223   the Port Royal experiment: Willie Lee Nichols Rose, *Rehearsal for*

Notes

Reconstruction: The Port Royal Experiment (New York: Oxford University Press, 1976).

223   *And now, kind friends:* Unattributed.

224   *The Harlem rituals of death:* Camille Billops, James Van Der Zee, and Owen Dodson, *Harlem Book of the Dead* (Dobbs Ferry, NY: Morgan & Morgan, 1978), 1.

225   *To make this dead gentleman:* Ibid., 82.

226   *I'll tell you tomorrow:* Ibid., 4.

226   the point of departure for Toni Morrison's novel *Jazz:* Gloria Naylor, "A Conversation: Gloria Naylor and Toni Morrison," *Southern Review* 21 (1985): 567–93.

227   *I didn't know they had stopped:* Billops et al., *Harlem Book of the Dead,* 82.

228   the epic lamentation of Isis: James George Frazer, *The Golden Bough: A Study in Magic and Religion* (London: Macmillian & Co., 1919), 12.

228   The *Tibetan Book of the Dead:* See Karma-Glin-Pa and Walter Yeeling Evans-Wentz, *Tibetan Book of the Dead* (Oxford: Oxford University Press, 2000).

229   *I had to come back:* Jackson, "Paying Homage."

229   *I imagined myself as some kind of pioneer:* "Rebuilding Dreams in Wire and Wax," *New York Times,* November 5, 1993.

229   *crossing West 110th Street:* Als, "The Talk of the Town: Afrocentricities."

229   His father was born in Haiti: "Rebuilding Dreams in Wire and Wax," *New York Times.*

229   *It felt like Harlem was the center of the world:* Ibid.

229   *Harlem is coming back:* Dennis Wepman, "Harlem Waxes Proud," *New York Daily News,* February 7, 1991.

230   *His work is cataloged:* Gloria Smith, "A Profile of Raven Chanticleer," *The New Voice of New York* (Jamaica, NY), September 30, 1999.

233   The reason for the helicopter's flight: Eric Konigsberg and Christine Hauser, "Eight Wounded in Harlem Shootings," *New York Times,* May 27, 2008, sec. The City/NY Region. http://www.nytimes.com/2008/05/27/nyregion/27shoot.html?ref=nyregion (accessed May 11, 2010).

235   *born and raised in Harlem:* Smith, "A Profile of Raven Chanticleer."

235   actually born James Watson: Newman, "Raven Chanticleer, 72, Artist and Self-Made Man of Wax."

236   *old mentors from the University of Timbuktu:* Cavanaugh, "Waxing Poetic."

236   A niece is quoted in the obituary: Newman, "Raven Chanticleer, 72, Artist and Self-Made Man of Wax."

Notes

236   *I could read and write:* O'Mahony, "Move Over, Mme. Tussaud."

236   He appears in 1930: Year: 1930; Census Place: Woodruff, Spartanburg, SC; Roll 2213: Page 5B; Enumeration District 70; Image 263.0. Ancestry.com. 1930 United States Federal Census [database online]. Provo, UT: Ancestry.com Operations, 2002.

238   considered the name: for *chanticleer,* see Geoffrey Chaucer, "The Nun's Priest's Tale," in *Chaucer's Canterbury Tales,* edited by Alfred W. Pollard (New York: MacMillan and Company, 1907), 402–26. For raven mythology in Native American cultures, see Eleazar Meletinsky, *The Poetics of Myth* (New York: Routledge, 2000), 170–72.

238   *I'm an* artiste: O'Mahony, "Move Over, Mme. Tussaud."

240   *I love beautiful things:* Cavanaugh, "Waxing Poetic."

241   *In the midst of ugliness:* Ibid.

242   *I started the museum:* Wepman, "Harlem Waxes Proud."

242   *I created these wax figures:* "Rebuilding Dreams in Wire and Wax," *New York Times.*

242   *The wax museum has been my dream*: Melinda Clare, "Raven Chanticleer's African American Wax Museum," *The Shield* (New York), April 19, 1994.

243   *just in case something should happen to me:* Newman, "Raven Chanticleer, 72, Artist and Self-Made Man of Wax."

243   *Matter of fact:* Angela Briggins, "Raven Chanticleer Takes Wax to the Max," *The City Sun* (New York), May 17, 1993.

Chapter 8: We March Because...

245   "One of the songs played": David Levering Lewis, *When Harlem Was in Vogue* (New York: Random House, 1981), 15.

246   "W. E. B. DuBois summarized": W. E. B. DuBois, "Returning Soldiers," *The Crisis,* Vol. 18 (May 1919): 13.

262   "We march because": Roi Ottley and William J. Weatherby, *The Negro in New York: An Informal Social History* (New York: New York Public Library, 1967), 200.

Index

Note: Italic page numbers refer to photographs.

Affirmation Marches, 204
Africa
  Back to Africa Movement, 61
  and black history, 77, 125, 167, 169
  natural resources of, 195–200
  West Africa, 79–80, 159, 196
African American Day parade, 244, 246–55
African American Wax and History
    Museum, 219–21, 229, 230, 235–36,
    237, 241–43
African Colonization Society, 169
African Communities League, 169, 178
African Freedom Day, 169
African Liberation Day parade, 244
African Nationalist Legion, 169
African Nationalist Pioneer Movement
    (ANPM), 167–70, 180, 194, 197–98
"The African Origins of the Tango"
    (Schomburg), 128
African Pioneering Syndicate, Inc., 169
African Square, 51, 142, 168, 172–73
Africanus, Leo, 59
Afro-American Realty Company, 15
Aldridge, Ira, 55
Alessandro, Florentine duke, 59
Ali, Muhammad, 220
"Alpha" (Tolson), 44
American Negro Academy, 57
Amsterdam News
  apartment listings in, 27, 38
  and Columbia University
    expansion, 184
  and Gumby, 131
  sale of Church of the Master, 189
  and White Rose Home, 47–48

apartments
  evictions from, 30
  furnishing, 29–30
  Lenox Terrace, 9, 10, 65, 83
  renting, 27–28, 29, 38–42, 144
A. Philip Randolph Square, 186
"Autobiographical Notes" (Baldwin), 110

Back to Africa Movement, 61
Bailey's Funeral Home, 231
Baker, Josephine, 19
Baldwin, James
  on Harlem, 107–09
  interpretive role of, 114, 115, 116
  in Paris, 108, 117
  photograph of, *99*
  and white audience, 110
Baldwin, James, works of
  "Autobiographical Notes," 110
  "Fifth Avenue, Uptown," 107, 108, 110, 117
  "The Harlem Ghetto," 107
  "Me and My House," 108–09
  "Notes of a Native Son," 107, 109
  Notes of a Native Son, 108–09
Bamba, Amadou, 80
Baraka, Amiri
  arrival in Harlem, 36–37
  and role of black artist, 115
Barbara, Ms. (neighbor), 65, 70–71,
    213–14, 215, 231, 234
Barker, Melvin, 74
Baxter, Freddie Mae, 231–32
Bearden, Bessye J., 129
Bearden, Romare, 268n
Bessie, Ms. (neighbor), 63, 66, 81–83, 246

Index

The Best of Simple (Hughes), 85
Bilal, 187–88
Bilalian Center, 187–88
Billop, Camille, *The Harlem Book of the Dead,* 224–28
"Bill-Payers' Parade," 173
Bing (neighbor), 83–84
black art
  Black Arts movement, 36
  and European standards, 101
  and Gumby, 126, 131–32, 133
  Locke as spokesman of, 126
  patronage of, 122
black bookstores, 60–62, 161, 164, *165,* 166, 172
The Black Challenge, 168–69
black equality
  and black history, 61, 77
  and cultural and social uplift, 18, 37
  and Harlem in black literature, 24–25
The Blacker the Berry . . . (Thurman),
  and Emma Lou Morgan's arrival in Harlem, 21–22, 23, 26, 46
black history
  and Africa, 77, 125, 167, 169
  and African American Wax and History Museum, 214, 219–21, 229, 230, 235–36, 237, 241–43
  and black bookstores, 60–62
  and Black Nationalists, 168
  and Gumby, 132
  and Schomburg, 58–60, 76–79
  and slavery, 77–78
Black History Month, 86
black literature
  and Gumby, 125
  Harlem in, 21–26, 136–37
  See also specific authors
Black Nationalism, 167–68, 205
Black Organized Crime in Harlem (Schatzberg), 73
Black Panthers, 75–76, 205, 252
Black Power March, 172–73
Black Star Line, 191–93
Blyden, Edwin Wilmot, 61
Bobby's Happy House, 174–75
Bontemps, Arna, 85, 97
Book Exchange, 60–61

Brahma Kumaris, 248
Branch, Willie, 128
Britain, and Israel as homeland for European Jews, 32
Brotherhood of Sleeping Car Porters, 173
Brown, Claude, 95
Brown, W. W., 189
brownstones
  floor-through apartments, 27–28
  one-dollar brownstone legend, 190, 191
  single-room-occupancy, 38–40, 42–43, 209, 222
  Siskind's photographs of, 94
Buy Black campaign, 166–67, 170, 181, 194
Byrd, Frank, 97

Campbell, E. Simms, 19
Cane (Toomer), 25
Caribbean immigrants, 39
Carnegie, Andrew, 60
Carnegie Corporation, 59
Castro, Fidel, 172
Chanticleer, Raven, 219–21, 229–30, 235–38, 240–43
Chaucer, Geoffrey, 238
Chesnutt, Charles, 46
Chicago Defender, 101
Christophe, Henri, 197, 209
churches, 142–44, 154, 155, 189, 218–19, 222
Church of the Master, 189
"The City of Refuge" (Fisher), King Solomon Gillis's arrival in Harlem, 23–24, 26
Clayton, Buck, 19
Clinton, Bill, 7, 253
Coalition for the Future of Manhattanville, 184
Coalition to Preserve Community, 184
Coalition to Save Harlem, 163
Columbia Daily Spectator, 132
Columbia Library World, 132
Columbia-Lippincott Gazetteer of the World, 5–6
Columbia University
  expansion plans of, 183–85, 190, 281–82n
  and Gumby, 119, 122, 132, 133
  and Hughes, 86
  and Hurston, 104

Index

Commandment Keepers, 209–10
Commentary magazine, 108, 114
Consolidated Edison Electric and Gas, 173
The Contributions of Carlos Cooks, 169
Cooks, Carlos A., 167–70, 180–81,
   194–95, 198
Corbett, Thomas, 128
The Crisis, 246
The Crisis of the Negro Intellectual, 203
The Crusader, 193–94
Cruse, Harold, 203
Cullen, Countee, 21–22, 56, 121, 129
cultural uplift, Locke on, 18

Davidson, Bruce, *East 100th Street,* 95–96
December 12th Movement, 172–73
Dessalines, Jean-Jacques, 197
diaspora, 172
Dinkins, David, 185, 281–82n
Dismond, Geraldyn, 129
Douglas, Aaron, 72–73
Douglas, Alta, 19
Douglass School, 64
dreams
   dream Harlem, 35–38, 135–39
   Ellison on, 37–38, 111
   Hughes on, 35–36, 87–88
   Hurston on, 127
DuBois, W. E. B.
   and black history, 61
   and crimes committed against black
     people, 73
   Cullen marrying daughter of, 121
   and Garvey, 206
   on whites' curiosity about black life, 112
   on World War I, 246
DuBois, W. E. B., works of
   The Negro, 61
   The Souls of Black Folk, 112
Dunbar, Paul Laurence, 46, 59

East 100th Street (Davidson), 95–96
Egypt, underground city in, 74, 78
Egyptian winged orb, 78
Ellington, Duke, 36, 91
Ellison, Ralph
   and Federal Writers Project, 97–99,
     101, 110

   on Harlem, 35, 37–38, 99, 110–16
   and inwardness, 116, 117
   photograph of, *99*
Ellison, Ralph, works of
   "Harlem Is Nowhere," 111–17, 160
   Invisible Man, 35, 37–38, 99, 110,
     111–12, 115, 117, 188
   "No Apologies," 114–15
   Shadow and Act, 116
   "The Way It Is," 97–98
Emancipation Proclamation, 169, 171–72
Ethiopia World Federation, 205, 248

Fanon, Frantz, 197, 200
Fauset, Jessie, 25, 36
Federal Writers Project, Works Progress
   Administration, 96–98
Federation of Black Cowboys, 253, 254
Fifth on the Park tower, 209
"Fifth Avenue, Uptown" (Baldwin), 107,
   108, 110, 117
Fisher, Rudolph, "The City of Refuge,"
   23–24, 26
Five Percent Nation of Gods and Earths,
   142, 249
folk art, limitations of, 101
for colored girls who have considered suicide
   when the rainbow is enuf (Shange), 44
Franklin Theatre, 65
Frazier, George, 220
Freedomways magazine, 18–19
Freemasons, 58, 78, 249–51
Friends of Negro Freedom, 179
From Superman to Man (Rogers), 61
funeral parlors, 214, 221–24
funeral portraits, 224–26, 227
funerals, 214–18, 222, 231–35

García Lorca, Federico, *El Poeta en
   Nueva York,* 25–26, 34
Garrison, William Lloyd, 61
Garvey, Marcus
   and Black Star Line, 191–93
   and Cooks, 167, 169–70
   and Harlem, 19, 178
   imperial ambitions of, 179
   marches celebrating, 204–06
   and membership of UNIA, 281n

Index

Garvey, Marcus *(cont.)*
  rhetorical shift from physical
    to metaphysical, 206–07
  See also Universal Negro Improvement
    Association (UNIA)
Georgia Circle, 124
G&G Photo Studio, 227
Giscombe, Eugene, 281n
"Glossary of Harlem Slang" (Hurston),
    105–06
Great Migration
  history of, 54
  peak of, 124
  and political issues, 179
  and warm-bed system, 42
  See also South
Group of 100 Black Men, 247
Group of 100 Black Women, 247
Gumby, L. S. Alexander
  benefit for, 129–30
  and black art, 126, 131–32, 133
  bookplate of, 133–34
  Negroana scrapbooks of, 119–22,
    125, 126–33
  and Southern Utopia Fraternity, 122–25
Gumby Book Studio, 118–19, 122, 125–26,
    127, 128–29, 134–35
Gumby's Book Studio Quarterly, 128

Haile Selassie (emperor of Ethiopia), 205
hairstyles, 181
  See also Natural Standard of Beauty
    Contest
Haiti
  and asylum seekers, 81
  and Hughes, 101
  and Hurston, 104
  and Schomburg, 58
Hamer, Fannie Lou, 220
Hamitic League of the World, 193
The Handbook of Geographical Nicknames, 6
Handy, W. C., 129
Harlem, New York
  black settlement of, 7, 12, 14–17, 20,
    24, 34–35, 46, 56, 185, 245
  and boll weevil, 70
  boundaries of, 6–7, 108
  crowdedness of, 11, 34, 51, 107

defining of, 5–7, 17–19
early buildings of, 8–10, *8*, 12, 14–15
empty lots of, 11–13, 212
gentrification of, 30–32, 112, 146–47,
    187, 201
and horizon, 11, 12
interior life of, 34
neighborhoods of, 19, 79–80
nickname of, 6
as race capital, 17–18, 20, 37, 111, 193
riot of 1943, 109
riot of 1964, 116
tours of, 7–8
and transportation, 14
white flight in, 7, 12, 17
"Harlem [2]" (Hughes), 87–88
The Harlem Book of the Dead (Billop),
    224–28
Harlem Community Coalition, 166
Harlem Document (Siskind)
  Parks's introduction to, 117–18
  subjects of, 90–95, 96
  Untitled [Street Facade 1], *90*
  Untitled [Street Facade 2], *91*
  Untitled [Street Facade 3], *92*
  Untitled [Street Facade 4], *93*
  and Works Progress Administration's
    Federal Writers Project, 96–97
Harlem Fire Watchtower, 210, *211*, 212
"The Harlem Ghetto" (Baldwin), 107
Harlem Hellfighters, 245–46
Harlem Hospital, 196
Harlem Hunches, 137–39
"Harlem Is Nowhere" (Ellison), 111–17,
    160
"Harlem Night Song" (Hughes), 88
"Harlem on My Mind" exhibition,
    Metropolitan Museum of Art, 32,
    268–69n
Harlem Property Owners' Improvement
    Association, 15
Harlem Renaissance
  black literature in, 25
  and boarded-up buildings, 94
  and Gumby, 121, 124–25, 131
  and Hughes, 102
  and Hurston, 103
  and VanDerZee's photo studio, 32

Index

Harlem Square. *See* African Square
Harper's, 108, 116, 117
Haywood, Henry, 73
Henderson, George Wylie, *Jule*, 23, 26
Herero people, 186
Hernandez, Theodore, 128
Holiday, Billie, 29
Holt, Nora, 19
home, meaning of, 3–4
Home to Harlem (McKay), Jake's return
    to Harlem, 22–23
homosexuality, 102–03, 121–22
Horne, Lena, 19
Hotel Theresa, 172
housing
    affordable, 200–01, 209
    boom in, 14
    deficit of, 28, 30
    public housing projects, 185–86
    quality of, 40
Hudson Realty Company, 15
Hughes, Langston
    ashes interred at Schomburg Center, 79
    and benefit for Gumby, 129
    characters of, 102
    Chicago Defender column, 101–02
    on Harlem, 18–19, 35–36, 86–90, 94
    home of, 29
    as homosexual, 102–03, 121
    on Hurston, 104, 106
    and low-down folks, 101–02
    and New York Public Library, 135th
        Street Branch, 56
    photograph of, *99*
    poetry of, 85–90, 94, 96, 101, 102–03
    and Schomburg, 58
Hughes, Langston, works of
    The Best of Simple, 85
    "Harlem [2]," 87–88
    "Harlem Night Song," 88
    Montage of a Dream Deferred, 101
    "The Negro Speaks of Rivers," 79
    "Theme for English B," 85–87
    "The Weary Blues," 89–90
Hunter, Maurice, 128
Hurston, Zora Neale
    and authenticity, 103
    and benefit for Gumby, 129

and cosmic Zora, 103–04
and Federal Writers Project, 97
on Harlem, 103, 104–06, 127
interpretive role of, 114, 115
photograph of, *100*
Hurston, Zora Neale, works of
    "Glossary of Harlem Slang," 105–06
    "Muttsy," 24, 26, 46
    "Story in Harlem Slang," 105
    Their Eyes Were Watching God, 127

immigrants
    assimilation of, 44
    Caribbean immigrants, 39
    West African immigrants, 13
    West Indian immigrants, 19
Invisible Man (Ellison), experience
    of Harlem, 35, 37–38, 99, 110,
    111–12, 115, 117, 188
Is Hayti Decadent? (Schomburg), 58
Islam, 163, 196, 244

Jackman, Harold, 121
Jamaica, 104
Jazz (Morrison), 226–27
Jericho Movement, 252
Johnson, Charles S., 18, 19
Johnson, James Weldon
    on black settlement of Harlem, 15,
        20, 185
    on W. W. Brown, 189
    on Harlem Hellfighters parade, 245
    as resident of Harlem, 36
    and Schomburg, 58
Jones, LeRoi. *See* Baraka, Amiri
"Juke Box Love Song" (Hughes), 88–89
Jule (Henderson), Jule's experience
    of Harlem, 23, 26
Juneteenth, 171–72, 244

Khemet, 74, 78
Ki Egungun Loa Egbe Egungun
    of New York, 247
*Know and Claim Your African
    Name*, 181
Knuckles, Kenneth J., 282n
Koch, Ed, 185
Kongo cosmogram, 159–60

Index

Lafargue Psychiatric Clinic, 113, 116
Larsen, Nella
    as black and Danish, 22
    as librarian, 56
Larsen, Nella, works of, *Quicksand,* 22, 23,
    26, 40–41, 42, 46
Latimer, Catherine, 56
Lawrence, Jacob, 268n
Lenox Terrace apartment complex, 9, 10,
    65, 83
Liberation Bookstore, 61–62, 161
Liberia, 58
Lincoln Theatre, 65
Littlejohn, Doris, 152–56
Little Senegal, 79–80
Locke, Alain
    and black art, 126
    on black migrants to Harlem, 34–35
    on black settlement of Harlem, 17
    on Harlem as race capital, 17–18, 20,
        37, 111, 193
    and Schomburg, 58
    See also The New Negro (Locke)
Louis, Joe, 132
Lumumba, Patrice, 197–200
lynchings
    and Gumby's Negroana scrapbooks, 132
    protests of, 259, 262

Maceo, Antonio, 58–59
Madame Tussaud's Wax Museum, 220
Malcolm X, 36, 172, 189
Malcolm X Commemoration
    Committee, 173
Malcolm X Millennium Committee,
    172–73
Mandela, Winnie, 197
Map to Heaven, 143–44
Marcus Garvey Day celebrations, 169,
    204–08
Marcus Garvey Memorial Building,
    169, 170
Marcus Garvey Park, 205, 207,
    208–09, 244
Mason, Charlotte Osgood, 101, 104
Matthews, Victoria Earle, 44–47, 48
Maxine Lynne Properties, 281n
McClendon, Rose, 129

McKay, Claude, *Home to Harlem,* 22–23
"Me and My House" (Baldwin), 108–09
Melba's restaurant, 200
Messenger, 157–61
The Messenger, 179
Michaux, Lewis, National Memorial
    African Bookstore, 61, 164, *165,*
    166, 172
Mickey Funeral Service, Carolina Chapel,
    221–24, 226
Minnie, Ms. (neighbor), 63, 67–68,
    213–15, 231–35, 238–40
Monroe (Mr. Mississippi), 68–70
Montage of a Dream Deferred (Hughes), 101
Morningside Park, 183
Morrison, Toni, 226–27
Morticians Who Care, 251–52
Mothers Against Guns, 251
Mount Morris, 208–10, 212
Mount Morris Park Community
    Improvement Association, 208
Mount Morris Park Historical District, 208
Mourides (Sufi sect), 80
MPL LLC, 280–81n
Muhammad, Elijah, 172
Mulzac, Una, 61–62
Mussolini, Benito, 205
"Muttsy" (Hurston), Pinkie's arrival
    in Harlem, 24, 26, 46

National Association for the Advancement
    of Colored People (NAACP), 252
National Council of Negro Women, 248
Nationalist Social Club, 169
National Memorial African Bookstore, 61,
    164, *165,* 166, 172
Nation of Islam, 163
Native Americans, 251
Natural Standard of Beauty Contest, 169,
    181, 208
Negro Book Collectors Exchange, 57
"The Negro Digs Up His Past"
    (Schomburg), 76–79
The Negro (DuBois), 61
Negro History Week exhibitions, 126
"The Negro Speaks of Rivers" (Hughes), 79
neighbors
    Barbara, 65, 70–71, 213–14, 215, 231, 234

Index

Bessie, 63, 66, 81–83, 246
Bing, 83–84
Doris Littlejohn, 152–56
and greetings, 3–4, 28, 140, 141
Julius Bobby Nelson, 63–67, 79
Messenger, 157–61
Minnie, 63, 67–68, 213–15, 231–35,
  238–40
Monroe (Mr. Mississippi), 68–70
Shirley, 254
Nelson, Julius Bobby, 63–67, 79
New Black Panther Party, 75, 145, 204,
  205, 207, 252
New Deal, 94
Newman, Charles W., 121, 122
The New Negro (Locke)
and black settlement of Harlem, 17, 20
publishing of, 126
reader annotations, 77–78
Schomburg's contribution to, 76–79
New Negro movement
and Baraka, 36–37
books of, 60
and Gumby, 122
and housing quality, 40
and Locke, 34–35
and Universal Negro Improvement
  Association, 259
New Orleans, Louisiana, 140
Newton, Huey P., 76, 205
New York City Planning Commission,
  188–89
The New Yorker, 30, 32
New York Herald, 15–16
New York Indicator, 16–17
New York News, 128–29
New York Post, 236, 238
New York Public Library, 135th Street
  Branch
Division of Negro History, Literature,
  and Prints, 60
Douglas paintings in, 72–73
exhibition from Schomburg Collection,
  59, 126
purchase of Schomburg Collection,
  59–60, 126
purpose of, 56
reading room, 55, *57*

research in, 54, 72–79, 83–84, 96
as underground city, 78
*Within Thirty Seconds Walk of the 135th
  Street Branch* photograph,
  49–53, *50*, 84
See also Schomburg Center for Research
  in Black Culture
New York Sun, 31
New York Times
and black settlement of Harlem, 15
on Chanticleer, 219, 220, 235–36, 243
and gentrification of Harlem, 30–31
on Gumby, 128, 133
Nkrumah, Kwame, 172
"No Apologies" (Ellison), 114–15
"Notes of a Native Son" (Baldwin),
  107, 109
Notes of a Native Son (Baldwin), 108–09
Nugent, Richard Bruce, 121, 122
numbers game, 73, 83, 98–99, 137–39

Oberia Dempsey Multiservice Center, 176
100 Blacks in Law Enforcement Who
  Care, 248
125th Street Business Improvement
  District, 175
Order of the Eastern Star, 250
Organization of African Unity, 172
Organization of Afro-American Unity, 172
Orthodox African Nationalist Literature, 169
Owen, Chandler, 179

Panamanian drum and bugle corps, 251
parades
African American Day parade, 244,
  246–55
African Liberation Day parade, 244
"Bill Payers' Parade," 173
crowd control following, 255–58
Harlem Hellfighters parade, 245–46
and Marcus Garvey Day, 204–08
Universal Negro Improvement
  Association, 259, *260–61*
VanDerZee's photographs of, 33,
  224, 249
Paris, France
Baker in, 19
Baldwin in, 108, 117

Index

Parks, Gordon, 117–18
Patterson, William, 73
Payton, Philip A., Jr., 14–15, 17
Perkins, Bill, 284n
personal names, 181–82, 197, 240
Petry, Ann, on Harlem, 24–25, 26
Petry, Ann, works of, *The Street*, 24–25, 26, 41–42, 46
Podhoretz, Norman, 114
El Poeta en Nueva York (García Lorca), 25–26, 34
Police Athletic League, 248
political issues
  and African American Day parade, 246–47
  arts-and-culture corridor, 201–02
  and Chanticleer, 230
  and Columbia University's expansion plan, 183–85, 190, 281–82n
  and Cooks, 167–69
  Cruse's assessment of, 203
  and eminent domain, 183
  and flyers, 163, 166–67, 173–76, 184–85, 194
  and funerals, 216–17
  and Garvey, 178
  and Marcus Garvey celebrations, 204–08
  and Memorial Day shooting spree, 232–33
  and platforms, 171, 172
  and Powell, 163–64, 166
  protests and rallies, 163, 166, 172–75, 183, 200–01, 259, 262
  and race, 36
  and rezoning, 163, 176–77, 184, 187, 188–89, 190, 200, 204, 205
  and street names, 162
  and Tubman statue, 202–03
Powell, Adam Clayton, Jr.
  "Don't Buy Where You Can't Work" campaign, 173
  and political issues, 163–64, 166
  speeches of, 172
  State Office Building named for, 166
  statue of, 163, 164, 172, 190, 246, 256
Primrose Patch, 128
Promise Land building, 188

Quicksand (Larsen)
  and Helga Crane's arrival in Harlem, 22, 23, 26, 46
  Helga Crane's search for apartment, 40–41, 42

race
  Baldwin on, 109
  DuBois on, 112
  economic racism, 146–47
  Ellison on, 113–16
  and Gumby, 126, 131
  Harlem as race capital, 17–18, 20, 37, 111, 193
  and political issues, 36
  and real estate, 15–16
  United Nations public hearing on racism, 80–81
  and white supremacy, 37, 116, 117
race consciousness, 56
race empowerment, 15
Randolph, A. Phillip, 19, 173, 179, 186
Rangel, Charles, 166
real estate
  absentee slumlords, 212
  black ownership of, 188–89
  and black settlement of Harlem, 15–17
  and condominiums, 13–14, 31, 186, 187, 189, 191, 207, 209, 212, 258
  deals, 174–75, 280–81n
  and development, 175, 187
  and eviction of black-owned businesses, 174–76
  flyers for, 144, 146
  mixed-income development, 209
  and red-lining practices, 191
  and rents, 27–28, 40, 42, 144, 175, 177
  and rezoning, 176–77
  speculation in, 14
  See also apartments; brownstones; housing
Reid, O. Richard, 128
River-to-River plan, 176
Robeson, Paul, 19, 73, 129
Robinson, Bill, 129
Rockefeller, Nelson, 164, 166, 172
Rogers, Joel Augustus, *From Superman to Man*, 61
Rose, Ernestine, 56

Index

Saint-Georges, Joseph Boulogne, Chevalier de, 58
St. Helena Funeral Home, 222–23
St. Nicholas Park, 86
St. Phillips Apartments, black bookstore in, 60–61
Sans Souci building, 209
Savage, Augusta, 129
Schatzberg, Rufus, 73, 74, 78
Schomburg, Arthur Alfonso
  and benefit for Gumby, 129
  as bibliophile, 57–58, 71, 237
  and black history, 58–60, 76–79
  exhibition at New York Public Library, 135th Street Branch, 59, 126
  in Harlem, 19
  New York Public Library's purchase of collection, 55, 59–60, 126
Schomburg, Arthur Alfonso, works of
  "The African Origins of the Tango," 128
  Is Hayti Decadent?, 58
  "The Negro Digs Up His Past," 76–79
Schomburg Center for Research in Black Culture
  and Chanticleer, 230–31
  development of, 55–56
  enlargement of, 60
  exhibition on Senegalese mystic sect, 81
  and Harlem tours, 7, 8
  Hughes's ashes interred in lobby of, 79
  Langston Hughes Atrium, 79
  oral histories archive, 239
  United Nations public hearing on racism, 80–81
  and White Rose Home archives, 47–48
School of African Culture and Fundamentalism, 169
Schuyler, George S., 128
scorched-earth campaign, of absentee slumlords, 212
segregation
  endurance of, 37
  Hurston on, 106
  and red-lining, 191
Senegal, 79–80
settlement houses, 44
Shadow and Act (Ellison), 116

Shange, Ntozake, 44
Shaw & Company, 15
Shirley, Ms. (neighbor), 254
sidewalk chalk messages, 148–52, 157–61
signs on street, 143–49, 156
"Silent March," 259, 262
Siskind, Aaron
  and neighborhood as laboratory, 111
  photography of, 90–97, 90, 91, 92, 93, 117–18
slavery
  Ellison on, 111
  and Kongo cosmogram, 159
  reparations for, 73, 147
  and role of black history, 77–78
slum-clearance programs, 10, 83, 186
social class, intraracial social caste, 41
Sons and Daughters of North Carolina, 124
Sons of Georgia, 124
The Souls of Black Folk (DuBois), 112
South
  Barbara on, 70–71
  Bessie on, 83
  and black settlement of Harlem, 19, 24, 34–35, 245
  and Ellison, 35, 37–38, 111–13
  and Gumby, 122–24, 125
  home associated with, 4, 141
  and Hurston, 103–04, 105, 106
  and letters written home, 82–83
  and lynchings, 259
  Minnie on, 67
  Julius Bobby Nelson on, 66
  Schomburg on, 58
  See also Great Migration
Southern Beneficial League, 124
Southern Utopia Fraternity (S.U.F.), 122–25
Speaks, Arapha, 189–90
State Office Building
  and political meetings, 156, 216
  and protests, 244
  and Rockefeller, 164, 166, 172
  and Arapha Speaks, 190
"Story in Harlem Slang" (Hurston), 105
street names, referring to, 140–41

Index

The Street (Petry)
 Lutie Johnson's arrival in Harlem,
  24–25, 26, 46
 Lutie Johnson's search for apartment,
  41–42
street scenes
 historical photos, 8–10, *8*, 14–15
 and New York Public Library, 135th
  Street Branch, 49–55, *50*
Street Speaker magazine, 167, 168–69
street speakers, 61, 142, 167–68, 172
Supreme Mathematics philosophy, 142
Survey Graphic magazine, 126
Swahili, 181–82

Texas
 as home, 4, 5, 28, 85, 86, 94, 171,
  180–81, 195, 253
 and Juneteenth, 171–72
 and settlement patterns, 10–11, 12
 slave cabins of, 159
Their Eyes Were Watching God (Hurston), 127
"Theme for English B" (Hughes), 85–87
Thomas, Piri, 95
Thurman, Wallace, 18, 19
Tibetan Book of the Dead, 228
Till, Emmett, 69
Tolson, Melvin, 44
Toomer, Jean, 19, 25
Touba, Senegal, 79–80
Touba Wholesale, 79–80
Touré, Sékou, 169
Toussaint L'Ouverture, François-
 Dominique, 59, 197
Tubman, Harriet, 197, 200, 202–03, 220
Turner, Mrs. Charles, 74

UNESCO World Heritage list, 209
United Nations, 74, 80
Universal African Relief, 169
Universal Negro Improvement Association
 (UNIA), 178, 192, 205, 281n
Universal Nubian Improvement
 Association, 205
Untitled [Street Facade 1], from "Harlem
 Document Series" (Siskind), *90*
Untitled [Street Facade 2], from "Harlem
 Document Series" (Siskind), *91*

Untitled [Street Facade 3], from "Harlem
 Document Series" (Siskind), *92*
Untitled [Street Facade 4], from "Harlem
 Document Series" (Siskind), *93*
U.S. Supreme Court, 183
utopia, 37–38

VanDerZee, James
 funeral portraits of, 224–26
 parade photos of, 33, 224, 249
 photo studio of, 32–34, 227
Virginia Society, 124

Walker, A'Lelia, 121
Walker, Margaret, 97
warm-bed system, 42
Washington, Booker T., 14, 46, 180
Waters, Ethel, 36
Watson, James. *See* Chanticleer, Raven
"The Way It Is" (Ellison), 97–98
"The Weary Blues" (Hughes), 89–90
We Charge Genocide (Civil Rights
 Congress), 73–74
West, Dorothy, 97
West Africa, 79–80, 159, 196
West African immigrants, 13
West 133rd Street, Harlem (ca. 1877),
 8–10, *8*, 14–15
Wheatley, Phillis, 46–47, 59
White, David, 75–76
White, Walter, 36
White Rose Home and Industrial
 Association, 44–48
white supremacy
 Ellison on, 116, 117
 endurance of, 37
Wilkins, Roy, 19
Williams, Bert, 36
Williams, R. Waldo, 199
*Within Thirty Seconds Walk of the 135th Street
 Branch* (photograph), 49–53, *50*, 84
Works Progress Administration, Federal
 Writers Project, 96–98
World War I, 245–46
The WPA Guide to New York City, 6–7
Wright, Richard, 97

Young, George, 60–61